'PASS THE PIG'S BLADDER'

MERCER books

First published in the United Kingdom in 2022 by Mercer Books

www.mercerbooks.co.uk

A CIP catalogue record for this book is available from The British Library

ISBN 978-1-7391224-0-9

Editor – Robin Fletcher
Art direction – Tim Mercer
Design – Reuben Wakeman

Printed in the UK by Interprint, Swindon

RUGBY SCHOOL

Birthplace of the Game

1823-2023

“

WE BREAK BONES AND WE
LOSE TEETH. WE PLAY RUGBY.

”

Martin Johnson

CONTENTS

HRH The Princess Royal enjoying herself at Murrayfield

BUCKINGHAM PALACE

I have been Patron of the Scottish Rugby Union since the 1986/7 season and attend as many of their home matches as I can. My son played for the Scottish U18s while still at school and my daughter is married to a former rugby union player. So there is enthusiasm for the game across the family.

I am pleased that, with this volume, as well as with a large number of events, Rugby School is marking the bicentenary of the year that rugby football was created by one of their former schoolboys, a defiant William Webb Ellis. In 1823, the Rugby School boys played a form of football on The Close, regarded as hallowed ground, and still used, with a great deal of kicking and hacking and not many rules. He caught the ball in his arms, which was allowed; then he ran with it, which was not. It took a while for his action to be accepted and for a mix of kicking and handling to become respectable as a new team game. Since then, the game of rugby has been refined, the rules of play are clear, and it is enjoyed across the world. The winners of the Rugby World Cup are presented with the William Webb Ellis Cup, which acknowledges Webb Ellis' gift to the sporting world.

Team sport is an important part of our national life and culture. We play it, and watch it, with fervour; and rugby is one of our favourites. It is a tough game that demands teamwork, personal courage, skill, speed, peak fitness and a keen eye. It also requires discipline. So it gives one pause for thought, and perhaps a modicum of pleasure, to read that, sometime at the end of the 19th Century, when the Old Rugbeian Committee put up a plaque on a wall at one end of The Close to commemorate young William Webb Ellis, they declared that he had behaved 'with a fine disregard for the rules of the game ....'

I wish Rugby School and the wider Rugby Community every success in their own celebrations for marking the 200th birthday of the game of rugby in 2023.

Anne

FOREWORD

Sir Gareth Edwards

"At around six or seven I got a rugby ball as a Christmas present. There was very little traffic so we would kick it on the road. It would wear out in a couple of months but we thought it was fantastic. I had a younger brother and as we got older we used to play against each other. Of course, he had to be England all the time! We local boys would play in the school yard, or on any bit of land, not necessarily a pitch. You would just put your coats down as goalposts. Someone would get a red Welsh jersey for Christmas and then you would gather and pick your team. We would play until dusk until my father used his piercing whistle when it was bed-time. We would cry: "Just let us score the winning try." And of course, those winning tries took for ever!

"I failed my 11+ exam and went to the local secondary modern in the valley. That's where we started getting some sort of resemblance of prepared sport. There was a rugby pitch on the school ground and on a couple of occasions we would play another village in the valley. We did not have proper coaching, it was very loose, but we did have a PE teacher who took a deep interest in rugby.

"My father came home from work one day with a pair of boots and a helmet and put them on the kitchen table. I thought they were for me, but he told me that as I was not working at school, I would be going underground at the local pit the next week. That frightened the life out of me, so I started working a lot harder. I had a second chance to take my exams after two years and did well enough to go to Ponyclun Secondary School. There I met my teacher and mentor Bill Samuel who taught me all I know about the game. I wanted to be a centre or fullback but he told me to forget it. Because I was a fairly good gymnast and athlete he said if I wanted to get into the Swansea Valley Under 15 team I would need to be scrum-half, so he taught me the skills I needed. Bill was responsible for getting me into Millfield School in Somerset on a scholarship which was a different world, a great platform. I played rugby for the school in the morning and then soccer for the valley team in the afternoon, even being offered professional terms by Swansea City.

"At Millfield I played for the Welsh Schools side and then after two years I went to college in Cardiff to do teacher training. There I played my first senior games and then my first for Wales before joining the Lions tour to South Africa in 1968. It all happened very quickly. I went with Wales to New Zealand, Australia and Wales. Defeat against New Zealand in 1969 made us realise there was a long way to go in terms of achievement and held us in good stead for the Lions tour in 1971 because we learned to play against them. That tour was one of the best I enjoyed in my career. Clive Rowlands was the coach and we went from having a Sunday gathered together to a week and so we came on in leaps and bounds. We had so many good players but we had lacked preparation. Very quickly we all benefited from preparation and the rest is history.

"I am never allowed to forget the try I scored for the Barbarians in 1973 in Cardiff. Even when I am in New Zealand with my wife they put it on the TV! It was the first opportunity the British public had to see the nucleus of the 1971 Lions side, but the game started off as a bit of a mess. There was a bit of pressure on us as the All Blacks wanted to take revenge, but we had no preparation at all, just a quick runout in Penarth. And we had injuries too – Gerald Davies had pulled his hamstring and Mervyn Davies had flu. When Phil Bennett caught the ball, I thought he was going to kick it into touch. I started charging for the ball when John Dawes went past me and I was thinking I had to get there quickly as scrum-half in case it went to ground. The last thing I thought about was scoring a try, but next minute there was a chance, but I had to shift to get there. Cliff Morgan's commentary was fantastic but he was only doing it because Bill McLaren had flu. Cliff was Head of Outside Broadcasting at the BBC and he had to get hold of some notes for the game very quickly!

"Today, I think the game is far too much kicking and static play. It seems easier to teach kids to stop passing than to embrace the game through fluidity and opening up with the ball. Maybe we were just fortunate. In the early days you could kick directly to touch, but when that stopped it really suited our sort of approach. The Lions had Barry John, Phil Bennett, Mike Gibson, David Duckham, fantastic players, and we had the best of it from an enjoyment point of view. Today, when people are paid to play, nobody wants to lose, so it becomes all about coaching and defence. Would I enjoy playing today? Possibly not, who knows? Today rugby is a game of big boys. Myself, Phil Bennett and Barry John loved playing football, so perhaps we would be playing that instead today? The game of rugby and the whole demand of playing it has changed with the evolution of the game. I am not sure William Webb Ellis would recognise the game today."

Sir Gareth Edwards is a former Wales and British and Irish Lions scrum-half. Born in 1947, he appeared 53 consecutive times for Wales during the team's golden era. In 2003, he was voted the greatest player of all time in a *Rugby World* magazine poll of international rugby players. A sculpture of Sir Gareth about to pass a rugby ball stands in St David's Centre, Cardiff, the city where he started to play club rugby.

INTRODUCTION

On rare occasions when life offers a brief opportunity to look up from the computer in my office at Rugby School, I am rewarded with a view of the piece of ground where perhaps the greatest game on earth began.

Not many have that privilege, and it is one I certainly never take for granted.

Growing up in Scotland in the 1970s, rugby was the game I played with friends on frozen pitches or watched when the mighty English, Welsh or Irish visited Murrayfield.

As a young schoolmaster in the 1980s, rugby was the sport I coached, passing on my own love for it to the next generation. As the great Cliff Morgan once said: 'Rugby has allowed me to break bread with the world.'

Today, like many of my advancing age, I mainly watch again, although thankfully often pitch-side watching the XV on Old Big Side, the birthplace of the game, rather than having to occupy a living-room armchair.

That I can do this at all is thanks to the exploits of just one boy who in a moment of sporting madness in 1823 decided to run with the ball in his arms instead of simply kicking it.

In doing so, William Webb Ellis, whose widowed mother moved to Rugby so her son could attend the School free of charge as a local Foundationer, clearly demonstrated 'restlessness', a quality we prize among students today.

Restlessness is not a licence to ignore everything sensible or fail through distraction or laziness. Indeed, Webb Ellis may have been restless on the pitch, but not so much that he could not go on to gain an Oxford degree and enter the church.

Yet thanks to his actions, his decision in the moment to challenge convention, millions of people around the world are fortunate today to have a game they can play, follow, support, coach, watch or read about.

There are those who question the authenticity and veracity of the Webb Ellis legend. Can the origin of one sport really be traced to one boy at one school on one pitch on one day?

It is impossible to be impartial in this debate and I am glad I am not. There is romance in the story and through young William's exploits there is a sport named after an English Midlands town and a World Cup trophy bearing the Webb Ellis name.

When presented with new information on a topic, cynics often cry 'So what?' or 'What does that mean?', which is something they could also say about how rugby started. After all, even if we do believe we know the game's first faltering steps does it really matter one way or another?

I think it does for two important reasons. First, the history of the past is often the best guide we have to the present and future and without it rugby is just another sport without a heritage.

Second, it matters because like all significant historic moments, events at one point in time trigger an evolutionary process, which, in the case of rugby, is simply remarkable.

In Webb Ellis' day football, and later rugby, was simply a game played by rough, able-bodied amateur boys in England. Nobody played it in other countries, or got paid, or started a version with 13 players, or spun off a metal-helmeted variant in the USA. Nobody played it who was female or confined to a chair or who lived on a South Sea island.

The proliferation of rugby in its all its technicoloured forms and varieties is just one of the many reasons why we should mark the 200th anniversary of the game.

We should raise a glass to William Webb Ellis and, when the game is over and we have washed the mud from our knees, maybe settle down in that living-room armchair to read this book in his name.

Peter Green,
Executive Head Master, Rugby School Group,
March 2022

A NAUGHTY
BO
RU

In 1823 William Webb Ellis, who, with a fine disregard for the rules of football as played in his time, first took the ball in his arms and ran with it, thus originating the distinctive feature of the rugby game.

BROKE THE
ULES...

PLAYING THE GAME

JOHNO AND JONNY ENGLAND'S TWIN PEAKS

If anyone had the time or inclination to research letter frequency in the names of rugby union greats, it's possible 'J' might score highly. JJ and JPR Williams, Barry John, Carwyn James, Willie John McBride, John Eales, Jonah Lomu, Nick Farr-Jones, John Smit, John Kirwan, Jamie Burke, Jason Leonard, Nils Jorgensen, Jean-Pierre Rives, Joost van der Westhuizen, Jeremy Guscott, John Dawes and Jim Telfer are not a bad selection of players to illustrate the point.

But however exalted this list, there are two glaring omissions: Martin Johnson and Jonny Wilkinson.

British sport has a rich and enviable history of famous double acts, names like Coe and Ovett, Redgrave and Pinsent, Torvill and Dean, Botham and Brearley conjuring nostalgic images of supreme triumph, often against supreme odds.

In the first quarter of 21st-century rugby, however, it was hard to match the deeds of Johno and Jonny, a pair whose exploits for England in the early years of the new millennium remain legendary.

There is no need for more words to be written listing all their deeds and exploits for club and country. In any event, both players will be remembered, like Bobby Moore and Geoff Hurst in 1966, for just one game.

That England team in that Rugby World Cup final in Sydney was not just skippered by Johnson but utterly commanded. In him Sir Clive Woodward had the right man, a leader who won 34 of his 39 tests as captain.

Johnson's success rate was the equivalent of getting nearly nine out of 10 extremely demanding tasks, in public over several years, perfectly right. Few folk in any job attain that level of consistent excellence.

For all that Johnson can be satisfied with this record, however, he and the world of rugby history know that much of it was down to the contribution of his stalwart fly-half Jonny.

Wilkinson's 1179 test points for England (1246 including Lions appearances) is still a record for an England player and is still second in the all-time rankings behind one D Carter of New Zealand.

Despite their success and stardom, however, it is something of the measure of both men that neither was seduced by their achievements, fame or attention.

Skipper Johnson summed his thoughts up in a manner that would surprise nobody: "As far as the mirror goes, I just see the bloke I always saw. I have always had a level of self-awareness. When you do things and people talk about you, I never took any of that. All the praise and acclaim, I never took it. I always felt I had my feet on the ground."

Being grounded, however, was not enough for Jonny, for whom playing rugby was akin to always being on the hunt for the Holy Grail, and never finding it.

"The problem with me is I always think I should've done better. I felt that after the World Cup final and through my whole career."

If Johno and Jonny did their talking on the pitch rather than babbling into a microphone, others made up for it in their comments on their greatness.
Sir Ian McGeechan, who chose Johnson as skipper on the British and Irish Lions successful tour to South Africa in 1997, believes "he defined an era, both for forward play and for the performances of the teams he represented".

Promoting Johnson as someone still worth listening to, Rugby Speakers describe him as "One of the most world-renowned rugby players, Martin Johnson saw a

glowing career on the pitch. Enjoying a career spanning sixteen seasons, Martin Johnson is regarded as one of England's greatest players of all time."

"His ability to read a game whilst it unfolded, communicating to team-mates the course of action most likely to bring a try two or three phases down the line, was remarkable", wrote *Rugby World* in 2019.

Former Wales captain and commentator Eddie Butler recalled Johnson's somewhat muscular approach to the rugby game.

"Johnson has left a trail of bodies behind him. He has seen so many yellow cards that the colour must dance before his eyes at night… God he was good. What more could you ask for? Big, mean and only too willing to seek revenge and mete out summary justice. I have this image in my mind of him playing at the Stade de France. He has one giant Frenchman in the crook of his left arm, another is being throttled in his right, and he is screaming at the referee."

Rugby writer Brendan Gallagher remembered Johnson's first real test as a rugby leader in the world spotlight on the 1997 Lions tour.

"Johnson wanted to lead from the front at all times, but by displaying self-discipline, by taking the professional approach, he was also leading from the front. That was the approach he would expect and demand from colleagues and he needed to set the example.

"Johnson was immensely focused physically and mentally, that was the essence of his leadership, which is not to discount a computer-like rugby brain."

For all Johnson's no-step-backward leadership, Sir Clive Woodward believes it was Jonny who raised the bar for other players.

"Jonny took the game to a new level. He was legendary for holding up the England team bus because he'd always stick around to practise his kicking. Players today talk about doing their 'extras' and a lot of that goes back to Jonny's approach.

"The thing about Jonny, though, is that he would always push himself to new levels. He proved me wrong on captaincy when he went to Toulon and I saw a video of him in the changing room, bossing these legends around in fluent French. He was giving everything. That summed up Jonny: he wanted to be the best at everything he did… and he usually was."

Dan Carter, Wilkinson's All Blacks opponent, cites him as a formative inspiration.

"Early in my career, probably because I just held him in such high regard and I had a huge amount of respect for him.

"He was an absolute student of the game. It was a wild, windy test match down in Wellington, I was on the bench and I hadn't played a test match for the All Blacks [at that time] and he just took that game.

"As a 10 that wants to control the game, I've never seen anything like it. I got the best seats in the house on the bench and part of me was going, 'Man, do I really want to get on here because he's just completely dominating this game.'

"Thankfully I didn't, I played my test debut the following week, which was a much better game to remember. I remember sitting there going, 'If I ever do play 10 for the All Blacks, this is how you need to control the game.'

"So I had a huge amount of respect for him and loved playing against him."

Rugby writer Owen Slot recalls watching Wilkinson's finest rugby moment, securing England the Webb Ellis trophy in 2003.

"I got to see Jonny kick the winning drop-goal in the most cliffhanging of finals. But, boy, did he make me wait.

"...It was so memorable..., with that knife-edge finish: the game in extra time, the seconds ticking away, Matt Dawson's pass and then Wilkinson drops for World Cup glory" as the iconic commentary has it.

"On top of all of that, having seen up close how fragile the 24-year-old protagonist was, I cannot pretend that I wasn't deeply emotionally invested in the outcome for him. That is why, for me, it still surpasses everything else I have seen."

Whatever their own thoughts on their own talents, or the opinions of observers, there is no questioning the facts.

Through their talent and determination, Johnson and Wilkinson were *the* integral members of the team that drove England, to paraphrase Jim Telfer, to the top of Rugby's Everest. They climbed every step, saw the view from the summit, and descended into sporting folklore.

NEW ZEALAND
ALL BLACKS

SEAN FITZPATRICK

I was four years old when I became the mascot for our local team, College Rifles in Auckland, which my brother played for and which my father coached. I started playing when I was five and wanted to be a No10 but that didn't work out and they put me in the front row. I have quite a few highlights and was very fortunate to play for a number of successful teams including Auckland University where, in 1987, we won the championship with a team that included Gavin Hastings, Grant Fox, David Kirk and John Drake. Of course, winning the Rugby World Cup in 1987 in New Zealand and then captaining the All Blacks to a series win in South Africa in 1996. I also include the 1995 Rugby World Cup (New Zealand lost in the final to South Africa) because it was such a fantastic tournament.

If William Webb Ellis had seen recent matches like Harlequins against Bristol and also the Rugby Championship game between the All Blacks and South Africa (both autumn 2021) he would have said "That's fantastic". I think he would be relatively happy he decided to pick up that ball and run with it!

PLAYING THE GAME

Sean Fitzpatrick was born in 1963. He made his New Zealand debut against France on June 28, 1986 and went on to win 92 caps, captaining New Zealand a record 51 times. His final All Blacks game was on November 29, 1997 against Wales at Wembley. He was awarded the New Zealand Order of Merit in 1997.

PLAYING THE GAME

HEYNEKE MEYER

Had William Webb Ellis not shown such a fine disregard for the rules of football, I would have been deprived of one of the most fulfilling facets of my life:the friendships I have made through rugby.

As a boy, I loved playing rugby but it didn't take me long to realise that I was more drawn to the coaching side of the sport. In my mind, that's where you get to make a difference in someone's life, with team dynamics having the potential to increase that impact exponentially. Understanding people, knowing what makes them tick … well, that ticks all the boxes for me.

In South Africa, rugby is a way of life and never off limits as a topic of discussion, whether at breakfast, school or church. It binds people much more than it divides. I have loved that about our game for as long as I can remember.

In my teens, I stood up in front of my class and declared that I would one day coach my country's national side, the Springboks. Afterwards, a teacher urged me to reconsider my goals: "You won't be able to make a living from rugby," he warned.

He was right. I haven't merely been making a living from rugby, but an entire life. Central to my story is the people I have had the privilege of interacting and

SPRINGBOK
COACH

working with as a coach. Having coached in both the amateur and professional era, I can unequivocally state that certain defining traits of rugby have remained intact, and these separate rugby from any other sport I have been involved with: rugby equals family, camaraderie, suffering followed by triumph, triumph followed by failure and the will to succeed again, and individuals reaching the fullness of their potential as a result of rugby. In this game, getting the human element right is far more critical than merely having the skills to compete.

From my time as a high-schools coach, my fondest memories are those of young players shaping up as adults because of rugby's formative influence. When I coached minor professional sides into contenders for the Currie Cup, I found it immensely fulfilling to see unknown players using their opportunities to grow into some of the game's all-time greats.

Yes, there have been trophies and championships along the way, but pay close attention when those players, coaches and administrators reminisce about the past: they don't talk about the trophies, but about relationships and key events away from the playing field that enabled them to be successful … sharing in someone's pain, celebrating someone's achievements, committing to a seemingly unrealistic goal, and feeling loved when your world is turned upside down, personally or professionally.

I coached the Springboks from 2012 to 2015 and my fondest memories are rooted in relationships with players, fans, members of my management team and even opposing coaches, many of whom are still part of my life today. Stuart Lancaster and I were appointed as the head coach of our respective nations at the same time, and both our first series at the helm were against each other. Our shared journey and aspirations cultivated a friendship between us that I treasure to this day.

Similarly, Steven Hansen and I coached against one another in eight Tests, and today I regard him as a dear friend … not because we were in each other's company that often, but because we shared the belief that we, as head coaches of the Springboks and All Blacks, had a duty to advance the legacy of the game's greatest rivalry. Our love for rugby and what it stands for forged our friendship, and through those commonalities we grew from being acquaintances to becoming friends.

Whether I worked with a player, a member of my management staff, or an opposing coach, my objective has always been to try to impact someone's life positively. Understandably, I sometimes failed at that, but part of rugby's ethos is to pick yourself up after failure and to try again. After nearly three decades as a professional rugby coach – in South Africa, England, France and the USA – I have come to believe that success in rugby, in which ever way you define it, rests on seven principles that are always true. These are also applicable outside of rugby, and to me, the seventh is the most important one:

1. You need a vision.
2. You need to believe in your vision.
3. You need willpower.
4. You need work ethic.
5. You need to be mentally tough.
6. You need to enjoy the journey.
7. You cannot do this alone.

As we celebrate 200 years of this life-altering game, I want to thank Rugby School for being the genesis of the School of Rugby – nothing in this world has taught me more about myself and people than Rugby Union.

Heyneke Meyer was born in 1967 in Transvaal Province, South Africa, and coached the Springboks from 2012 until 2015. As well as coaching at club and national level in his home country, he has also coached the English side Leicester Tigers, the French side Stade Français and the American side Houston SaberCats.

THE
SYDNEY MONITOR.

18/29 The *Sydney Monitor* newspaper made the first mention of a rugby match being played in Australia.

18/43 The world's oldest rugby club was founded at Guy's Hospital in London.

18/62 Richard Linden invented the rubber bladder used inside rugby balls following his wife Rebecca's death from lung disease after blowing up pigs' bladders.

18/64 The first match between Clifton College and Marlborough College took place, the oldest inter-school rugby fixture in England.

200
years of the game

18/64 The great South West rugby club Bath was established, followed by Exeter in 1871 and Gloucester in 1873.

18/72 The first 'Varsity Match' between Oxford and Cambridge was held in Oxford's University Parks.

18/74 The inaugural meeting of the Irish Union to oversee rugby football was held on December 14 at Lawrence's sports shop in Grafton Street, Dublin. The Duke of Abercorn was elected President.

18/74 On December 10, eight Ireland and Ulster rugby clubs (Trinity, Wanderers, Engineers, Bray, Lansdowne, Portora, Dungannon and Monaghan) formed the Irish Football Union. In February 1879 this merged with the Northern Football Union of Ireland to create the Irish Rugby Football Union.

"

ALL WE'RE DOING EFFECTIVELY IS CHASING A PIG'S BLADDER AROUND A FIELD, BUT WE STILL HAVE THE ABILITY TO TOUCH SO MANY PEOPLE.

"

Josh Lewsey

ONE BOY; ONE SCHOOL

By David Ray,
rugby historian and former Master in Charge of Football, Rugby School

The Harwood Scene, the oldest oil painting of a football game on The Close in 1859 by Frederick Whitehead.

Ball games played between young men have a long history. The Romans had *harpastum*: two sides, a large ball thrown into the air, caught and carried forward, support at the maul and thrown into the opponent's goal for a score.

In Georgia there is an ancient sport named *lelo burti* or field ball which is still played today. A priest blesses the ball, the players drink wine from it before it's stuffed with sand and wood shavings until it weighs 16-18 kilograms. Then it's a free-for-all with the other villagers' river the goal. No wonder most males in Tbilisi looks like tight-head props.

Closer to home, historical ball games still being played can be traced back to the 12th century. In Atherstone, Warwickshire, on Shrove Tuesday the main street is cleared, a massive ball roughly oval in shape is thrown from a first-floor window and the annual game begins. Fortunately, the busy A5 now skirts the town, courtesy of a by-pass. Dating back to 1199, the ball was allegedly full of gold. What did it weigh?

Top left: *Harpastum* played by the Romans.
Top right: *Lelo burti* in Georgia.
Above: The Shrove Tuesday football match at Atherstone.

Rugby School from Lawrence Sheriff Street in 1770s.

Matches might be regular, seasonal or annual. Ashbourne's Royal Shrove Tuesday football match is 900 years old, thousands attend, and the playing time is two periods of eight hours stretching into Ash Wednesday. The goals are three miles apart and the four-pound ball is packed with cork chippings so it will float.

The Down'ards take on the Up'ards. One of the earliest rules (and there are precious few), stipulated there should be 'no murder or manslaughter'. A more recent one is that churchyards and cemeteries are out of bounds. Understandably, most shopkeepers board up their windows at the end of trading on the Monday.

The Cornish played hurling and the East Anglians got stuck into camp ball. The Welsh had *cnapan* or *knappen*. This had its origins in Scandinavia and was apparently played in the principality as early as the 16th century. A wooden ball had to be thrown between one player and another. Despite plenty of violence it was 'all in good mirthe, without grudge or hatred'.

THE DOWN'ARDS TAKE ON THE UP'ARDS. ONE OF THE EARLIEST RULES (AND THERE ARE PRECIOUS FEW), STIPULATED THERE SHOULD BE 'NO MURDER OR MANSLAUGHTER'

"Football on The Close" 1888 by Walter Cox

In Derby, the All Saints' party and St. Peter's party played a particularly violent form of football which included ducking in the Derwent. An observer in 1829 witnessed over 1000 players involved in '....a dreadful contest....'. This was the original local derby match. English monarchs, particularly the Tudors, tried to outlaw such games. Further back, Edward II issued an edict forbidding football. Perhaps there were fears it would interrupt archery practice.

In the mid 16th century, 18 miles south-east of Atherstone, lay the small town of Rugby. The local lads played their version of football and from 1567 the boys at Rugby School, founded that year, almost certainly joined in. However, the cramped conditions around the School premises meant there was no space for anything other than activities like carting, conkers, tag and when, they could evade the staff, fishing and poaching.

A highly significant moment came in 1750 when the school moved to a new site on the southern edge of town. Along with an old manor house were 'some enclosures annexed to it, which were capable of offering every accommodation that could be required for the exercise of young gentlemen'. A plot of eight acres, 'within a few perches', became known as The Close. The three fields were known as Pond, Garden and Barn Close. Now the boys had a grass area on site where they could play expansive summer and winter games.

In other public schools, ball games tended to be played on cobbles, paving stones or brick. At Rugby there was grass and, equally important, large numbers involved in playing. These factors had important implications for the development of the style of football played at the school.

Woe betide any boy who tried to avoid playing without a valid reason. There were no written rules for the first 100 years. The code was passed on by word of mouth and observation. Younger boys stood as goalkeepers, wearing top hats, and gradually absorbed the finer points of the game. If play got stuck at one end it was not uncommon for youngsters to start up a smallside game at the other. At the end of an afternoon's activity a small group of seniors would discuss events and any changes that were deemed necessary.

Matthew H. Bloxam left Rugby in 1821 but, being a local man, was a regular visitor at the school and an avid follower of rugby football throughout most of the 19th century. In 1880 he submitted a piece for *The Meteor* (the Rugby School annual magazine) on the game he witnessed during his time at the School.

The construction of the school chapel coupled with the filling in of ditches, removal of fences and ground levelling enabled football to move to the north-east part of The Close. Virtually the whole school would assemble for a match with two of the leading players selecting some 20 others and the rest dividing roughly equally.

"Few and simple were the rules of the game, touch on the sides of ground were marked out and no-one could run with the ball in his grasp towards the opposition line. It was Football, and not handball, plenty of hacking but little struggling," wrote Bloxam.

Progress down the pitch was chiefly by kicking the ball amongst a mass of players or kicking the ball carrier within the melee to release it. There was no school magazine to report on the matches and scores were lost to posterity.

Bloxam continues with a description of the famous event one autumn afternoon in 1823. William Webb Ellis, a town boy and Foundationer, had entered the school in 1816 as a nine year old. His father had died on active service as an officer in the 3rd Dragoon Guards who were serving in the Peninsular War. On July 1, 1812, the French forces were threatening Albuhera, a town close to Badajoz and the Portuguese border. Lieutenant James Ellis and four other ranks were killed in the skirmish. Major-General Slade wrote that "he particularly regretted the loss of Lt. Ellis, who nobly fell at the head of his men".

Moving on to The Close, eleven years later, the young Webb Ellis caught the ball on the bound. This was acceptable and not that uncommon. A misconception, still found today, is that the boys were playing Association Football [soccer] and our pioneer picked it up. Not so. Neither is the more fanciful view that William, Webb and Ellis, were in fact, three different players. William kicked the ball, Webb caught it and passed it to Ellis who promptly knocked it on, thus originating an extremely distinctive feature

ELLIS DECIDED TO RUSH FORWARD WITH THE BALL IN HIS ARMS TO THE SURPRISE AND THEN IRE OF EVERYONE PRESENT.

of the game. What should young Ellis have done? He should have retired keeping hold of the ball while the opposition advanced to the mark where he had caught it. Ellis then had three options: punt it, drop kick for goal or prepare to place it for a team-mate to kick, again, probably at goal. Ellis decided to rush forward with the ball in his arms to the surprise and then ire of everyone present.

Bloxam was considered an honourable man with no hidden agenda. He also clearly had no intention of glorifying Webb Ellis or stating that anything changed overnight. It seems Bloxam had reservations about our young man. He describes Ellis's academic aptitude as 'fair average' and 'he was no swell but didn't lack assurance and was ambitious'.

Thomas Harris, a contemporary of Ellis, wrote: "I am sure that it [catching and running with the ball] was generally regarded as unfair by the leading players of the day." The world had to wait until 1895 before the Old Rugbeians set up a committee to investigate the Webb Ellis incident. There were still a few elderly former pupils from that era who entered into correspondence with the committee. Two years later the report upheld Bloxam's version of events. The act, considered bad form at the time, would obviously have massive implications for the future of the game. Running-in was only gradually and reluctantly accepted in the late 1820s and 1830s before it was formally legalised in 1841. When a player tried it, the cry 'Hack him over' was invariably shouted by more than one person. A player who gave running-in genuine momentum was Jem Mackie, a player of speed, size and charisma and a future Scottish Member of Parliament who was dominating The Close in the late 1830s.

Harris admired Ellis's cricketing ability but wrote: "He was generally regarded as inclined to take unfair advantages at Football. I should not quote him in any way as an authority." So, did the young Ellis have form? With two orphaned sons and a small Army pension Mrs Ellis had moved to Rugby so William would be eligible for a Foundation award. William had entered for the English and Latin prizes in his last year. The top entries received substantial sums of money. Ellis didn't feature even though some staff believed his mother had assisted him with his entries.

The School roll had dropped dramatically at this time and expulsions were alarmingly high. Ellis had fewer contemporaries and with assurance and a good mind he could certainly fight his corner. At Oxford, Ellis played in the 1827 Varsity cricket match, the first sporting competition between Oxford and Cambridge. Ellis batted three and made twelve

IT WAS ONLY IN 1958 THAT ELLIS'S GRAVE WAS DISCOVERED BY ROSS MCWHIRTER IN MENTON. FOR ENTHUSIASTS, HIS DETAILS ARE CAVEAU NUMERO 957 DANS LE CIMETIÈRE DU VIEUX CHATEAU, MENTON, ALPES-MARITIMES, ON THE MEDITERRANEAN COAST.

in an Oxford total of 258. He then took Holy Orders and after a spell at St Clement Danes in central London he moved to the tiny parish of Magdalen Laver in north-west Essex.

It was only in 1958 that Ellis's grave was discovered by Ross McWhirter in Menton. For enthusiasts, his details are *caveau numero 957 dans le cimetière du Vieux Chateau*, Menton, Alpes-Maritimes, on the Mediterranean coast. It's a miracle the plot hasn't collapsed given the number of weighty memorials and plaques lying on top. Ellis died a bachelor on January 24, 1872 leaving a sizeable sum of money, most of which went to charity. He passed away knowing nothing of his legacy. The first rugby football Varsity match took place a month after his funeral.

Ellis's background is widespread south of Hadrian's Wall. He was born in Salford in the north-west. His maternal grandfather hailed from Alton in Hampshire, his paternal grandfather was born in Pontyclun, a village in mid-Glamorgan, just north of the M4, but that side of the family can be traced back to West Yorkshire. His parents were married in Exeter. One could even argue Ellis is close to being a Six Nations man. He was born in England, his father served in Ireland in 1807, Ellis is a Welsh name and his grave almost straddles the border between France and Italy. A couple of lines from Rupert Brooke's poem 'The Soldier' come to mind: "That there's some corner of a foreign field that is for ever England."

In 1900 that Old Rugbeian committee inserted a plaque into the Doctor's Wall at the north end of Bigside. All Rugbeians will recognise the wording (many can recite it from memory):

THIS STONE
COMMEMORATES THE EXPLOIT OF
WILLIAM WEBB ELLIS
WHO WITH A FINE DISREGARD FOR THE RULES OF FOOTBALL
AS PLAYED IN HIS TIME
FIRST TOOK THE BALL IN HIS ARMS AND RAN WITH IT
THUS ORIGINATING THE DISTINCTIVE FEATURE OF
THE RUGBY GAME
A.D 1823

Tom Brown was 'overawed' by the gigantic posts and crossbars at Rugby School.

The wording is upbeat and carefully crafted to avoid saying how he took the ball in his arms. There is no hint of cheating or undermining the spirit of the game. Was he a rebel? Was it a snub to the rule makers' authority and the status quo ? Or was he a visionary and innovator, the founding father? The committee had decided that he was the young man inspired to set in motion a crucial feature of the winter game of football at Rugby School as played in his time.

In the early 1830s, *Tom Brown's Schooldays,* author Thomas Hughes wrote that: "Running with the ball to get a try at goal was not absolutely forbidden but a jury of Rugby boys of that day would almost certainly have found a verdict of 'justifiable homicide' if a boy had been killed running-in." Even then the ball had to be caught on the bound, the player had to be on-side and he must touch down himself. Henry H. Gibbs, later Lord Aldenham, wrote that in 1833-4 running-in was fully recognised and George Benn, writing about 1835, reported that running with the ball was in existence but there was no passing. Players never picked up the ball and drop kicks featured strongly.

The reputation of Dr Thomas Arnold as Head Master along with the arrival of the railway were naturally more important factors in parental decisions than the type of football played on The Close. Arnold arrived in 1828 and numbers steadily rose to over 360 boys from 143 some ten years earlier. More pupils meant more players and more rule changes. The school was academically sound but there was a lot to be done on the behavioural front. Arnold highlighted religious and moral principles, gentlemanly conduct and intellectual ability, in that order, as his essentials of education. It might be argued that physical wellbeing would come under the second target but it was never mentioned specifically. Anyway, that was still a pupil-run part of life at Rugby. Arnold introduced some civility to the fagging system, reduced the incidents of bullying and cleaned up the initiation ceremonies. Regarding sport, even the annual decision about when cricket should give way to football in the autumn remained with the boys. Many issues were decided by a show of hands.

Back on the field, players trying to run-in to secure a try at goal was gradually accepted but they, in turn, had to accept that hacking and collaring would be coming their way. Such attackers were now seen as brave and daring chaps rather than suspect chancers. This attitude intensified as teams started to be House based. The boys were now

TOM BROWN'S SCHOOLDAYS WAS PUBLISHED IN 1858.

playing for their tight-knit communities rather than just themselves. "You play for the School and you die for the House" could be heard well into the 20th century.

Tom Brown's Schooldays was published in 1858 but it's set in the 1830s and dedicated to Mrs Arnold. Chapter V, 'Rugby Football', and chapter VI, 'After the Match', provide further features of the game and it's expressed in a highly readable form. Tom is told by East on arrival that it will take him a month to master all the rules. He was also warned it was not a game for the faint-hearted. "So far this half two collar-bones broken and a dozen fellows lamed. Last year a few had their leg broken."

Tom is overawed by a sort of gigantic gallows, two poles eighteen feet high, some fourteen feet apart with a cross bar 10 feet high. Cross bars were unusual in ball games but due to the number of boys guarding the goal at Rugby the only solution was to kick the ball over it. It was accepted by all that no one ever climbed on to the cross bar to prevent a conversion. The unequal numbers on the pitch intrigued the young man. There's the revealing comment about the new ball: ". .....in the middle, pointing towards the school or island goal". This is the first recorded reference to an oval shape. The 60 or so School House members were taking on well over 100. However, the former seemed far better organised. Much of the terminology has survived from scrimmage [scrummage] and off [your] side to drop kick, punt and place kick. Follow-up remains in usage today as an invitation from the captain of football to play for the School. The try at goal has morphed into a try and a goal or converted try.

Off come the hats and waistcoats. The School House players wear white trousers and know each other well. Tom has got it right. The opposition has divided leadership and no distinct pattern of play or line-up. The playing area boundaries include a gravel walk and a line of elm trees. Three trees form a shorter line near halfway jutting into the playing area making a novel addition to tactics. There are touch judges to decide who touches the ball first to get the right to throw it back into play but there is no sign of a referee. One can pick out the Heavy Brigade, or forwards, and just to the rear the Light Brigade, or backs.

The match is underway and the ball is somewhere in a mass of players struggling to drive it forward. Dr Arnold and his family look on. A goal is scored in the first hour, something that hasn't happened for at least five years. The teams change ends and a local vendor from Hillmorton sells oranges and lemons on the touchline. Some of the seniors reach into their jackets on the touchline and extract ginger beer flasks, although not every bottle contains ginger beer. The age range of the players is staggering by today's standards. Twelve year olds mixing with seventeen year olds. Where was the Health and Safety officer?

Some 10 years later we have an eye-witness account. Grumblings by the football fraternity started in mid September. When will the cricketers give way to the winter

The first rugby 'caps' were given to boys at Rugby School to mark Queen Adelaide's visit in 1839.

game so the whole school can get some genuine sport? The grumbling becomes a growl as the weather starts to change and then delight when a rumour spreads of a Bigside meeting. Both parties are given a hearing; a show of hands is taken and the chair declares: "The Ayes Have It". A count is taken as the boys leave the room and it's confirmed that football is "on". Puntabout balls are dug out of drawers and start flying around the quad. A Littleside2 match is played and new balls are ordered. Soon a Bigside match is arranged with some 200 raring to go. Two Bigside balls have been brought along, the Head of School tosses a coin, the Sixth call correctly and decide to defend the Island goal. The grass is untrodden, the weather ideal and the elms on the Island are starting to change colour. It's a battle of age and weight versus numbers.

The ball is caught, the game proceeds through the three elms. It's a pyramid of human flesh over the ball carrier and his tackler. Eventually the ball is taken in-goal. "Whose ball?" is the cry. "Theirs" is the sullen reply. Chivalry is not quite dead. Now is the chance to score a goal. Perfect timing is needed. The planter carefully places the ball and the kick is made before the defensive chargers get to the ball and it sails between the posts and over the cross bar. The try at goal has succeeded. No-side is declared as the school clock strikes 5 pm. The once pristine whites and jerseys are now soiled and, in some instances, torn. The purposeful and urgent steps to The Close hours earlier have become tired and slovenly shuffles back to the Houses. You must have some sympathy for matron. This match began on September 26, 1846 and was won by School House on the third day of the contest, October 1.

WHY IS A CAP CALLED A

In 1839, to mark the visit of Queen Adelaide, boys wore special caps in her honour. Those boys considered good enough to play for Rugby School's main teams were given 'following up' caps, which later developed into the international cap awarded to the country's top players.

There are sartorial matters to consider and many have had profound influence on how the game looks today. The mixture of caps and jerseys would be both colourful and confusing for outsiders. Various decorations and mottoes were slowly replaced by House emblems. The School House skull and crossbones was one of the earliest. In 1839 Queen Adelaide visited the school. The match she asked to witness was the first recorded where one team was wearing a uniform team cap; this was School House with the royal colours of crimson, velvet, and gold, tassels. Cap wearing helped identify one's team-mates and thus avoid suffering being hacked on the shins by mistake. Boots, nicknamed navvies, often had bevelled soles at the front for greater impact when contact was made between ankle and knee. Caps evolved into a symbol of excellence and allowed a holder to follow-up for his House and later in the century for the school. This was the origin of the International cap.

Trousers tucked into socks were gradually replaced by knee-breeches and then shorts down to at least the knee. Modern shorts would be considered most immodest. Today socks represent 3rd XV colours, the cap 2nd XV colours and the XV badge first team colours. A cap is awarded just once to a player during his time at Rugby while the XV must be earned all over again if a student returns in September.

The first written and codified rules of rugby football were drawn up in late August 1845. They were not comprehensive but served as a tidying up exercise for internal use only. Within three days three senior boys had put together 37 Rules. These young men of 16 and 17 were William Arnold, the Doctor's fourth son, W.W. Shirley and Frederick Hutchins. The draft document was immediately passed by the Sixth Levee and it went off for printing that evening. All but one of the Rules are a mere sentence in length. Rule 1 concerns the fair catch. The 'mark' is still permitted today, albeit only within one's own 22-metre area, and probably remains because of its sentimental value. In the mid 19th century it was a fundamental part of the game. Readers will have noted Rule I is a handling rule. Another vital rule is off-side and references to it can be found in Rules 2, 10, 11, 12, 13 and 14. Rule 4 covers the knock-on, 5 the try at goal, 7 gives permission to run-in and 18 explains what happens when the ball touches a tree. Number 23 states: "All matches are drawn after five days, but after three if no goal has been kicked." Later the booklet states that: "Heads of sides are the sole arbiters of all disputes." There is still no mention of a referee or umpires and Arthur A. Pearson noted ".......and yet [we] got on very well without them!" Rules 26, 27 and 28 cover hacking. The game was obviously

1845 WAS A SPECIAL YEAR FOR THE GAME BECAUSE A PUPIL, ONE C.H. CHAMBERS, DREW FIVE PEN AND INK SKETCHES OF RUGBY PLAYED AT THAT TIME. THEY PRECEDE ANY PAINTING OR OTHER IMAGE AND ARE A WONDERFUL PEEP INTO THE ACTION ON THE CLOSE.

C.H. Chambers' 1845 pen and ink sketches of the game then played at Rugby School.

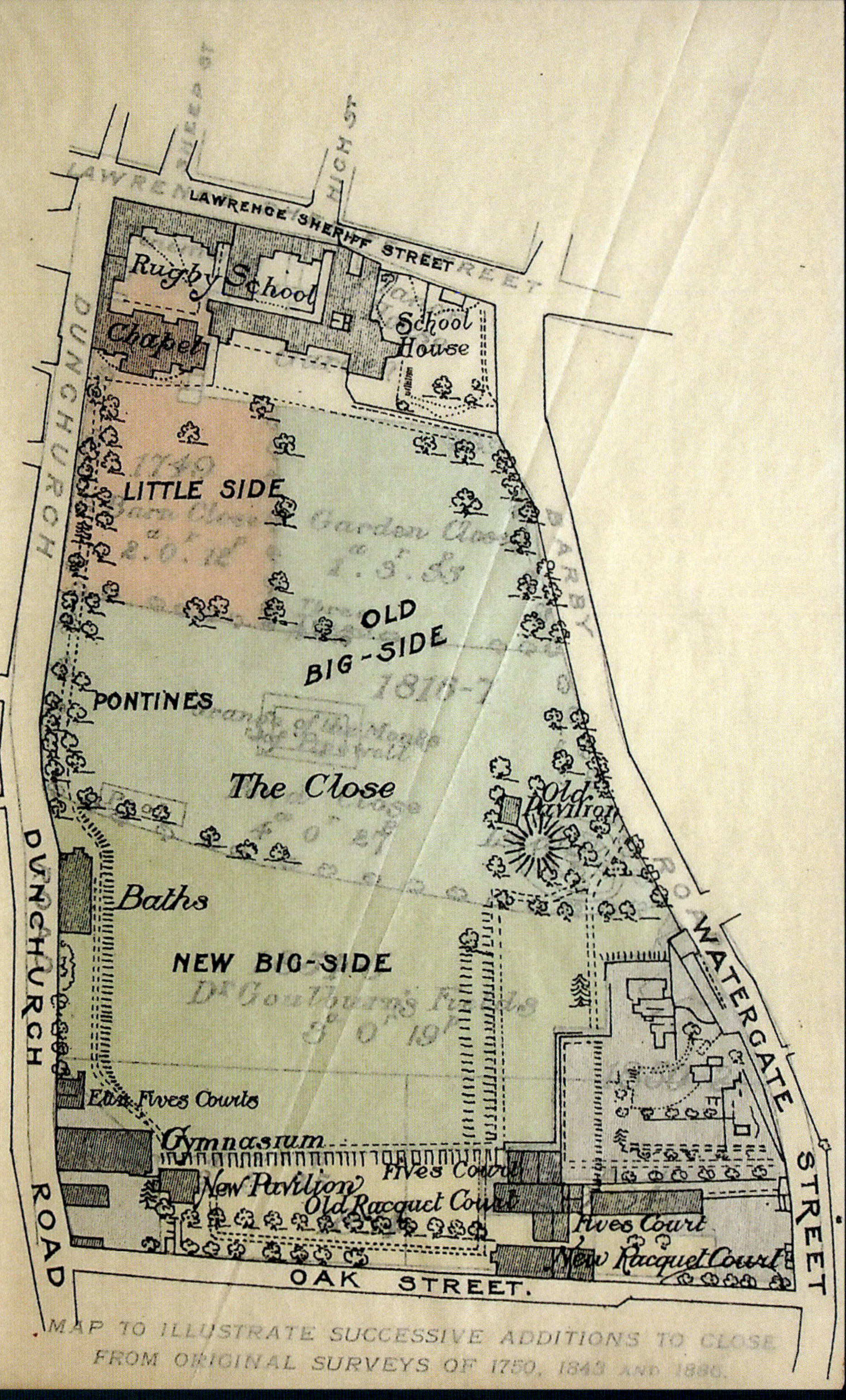

How The Close at Rugby School developed in the 18th and 19th centuries.

going soft as this action was to be restricted to below the knee, could only be done in a scrummage and boots should be free of nails and iron plates.

1845 was a special year for the game because a pupil, one C.H. Chambers, drew five pen and ink sketches of rugby played at that time. They precede any painting or other image and are a wonderful peep into the action on The Close. There's the kick-off and the three elms in the background. The caps are clear to see as are the long trousers, and the ball, not quite round, waits in the middle to be launched to the opposition in the distance. Another page depicts a punt out after a touchdown before the catcher can have a kick at the posts. This ended in 1883 and was replaced with approximately what we have today.

The next drawing shows the build-up to a drop kick attempt. The numbers on the pitch in caps and the numbers guarding the goal in top hats never ceases to impress. No wonder kicks were aimed over the cross bar. There would be little return in trying to score a soccer goal as played today. The fourth sketch depicts the setting up of a line-out with what appears to be some dispute about who has the right to throw the ball in from touch. Finally, there is the moment before the placer puts the ball on the ground for a try at goal before the opposition can start their charge. Some players are taking a break by sitting or lying on the ground, and why not? For the rugby football fan these sketches are priceless even though Chambers was unlikely to win the art prize that year. Rugby School also holds a Harwood painting from 1856 and another by Barnard dated 1859. These are, respectively, the oldest water colour and oil paintings of the game.

The Rules would be re-visited every year and there were a few minor alterations in 1846 and 1847 but the real breakthrough came in 1862. Here was a fully comprehensive set of Rules designed for external as well as internal use. It included a plan of the playing area, a lengthy introduction, four definitions and 45 Rules. This time every one consisted

---

NOTES:

1. Bigside. The premier pitch at Rugby School on the eastern side of The Close. Originally known as Sampson's Quarters. The XV and Cock House matches are played here. Old Bigside [OBS] is the name given to the area originally taken up by the three small enclosures of 1750.
2. Littleside. Pitch originally known as Chapel Piece and used exclusively by the boys of School House in the second half of the 18th century. Today it serves as the second pitch for football at the school where the third, fourth and fifth teams train and play.
3. Smallside. Unofficial pick-up games for junior boys. Sometimes played when the goalkeepers were under-employed.

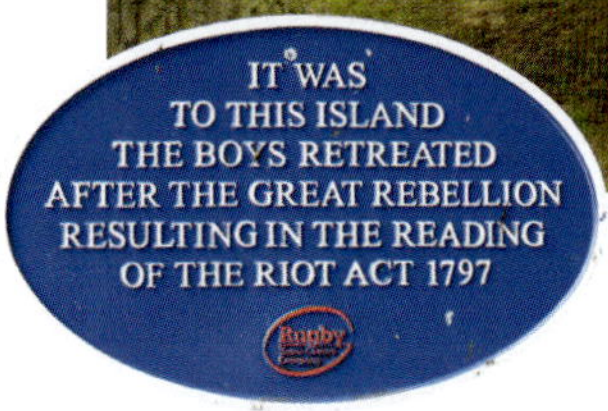

The Mound at Rugby School next to Old Bigside on The Close marks the spot of the Great Rebellion in 1797 when boys who retreated there were read The Riot Act.

of a single sentence. The trigger for this new edition was from outside the walls of Rugby School. Oxford and Cambridge Universities, along with emerging clubs such as Liverpool, Richmond and Manchester, wanted clarification and a degree of uniformity to ease the complexities of different teams with different interpretations and local peculiarities. Nevertheless, even then, there were 10 Rules and two notes specific to the School. The more endearing ones are: "No player may take the ball out of the Close, no player may stop the ball with anything but his own person, Old Rugbeians shall be allowed to play........but no stranger may have a place kick at goal." The Island, an ancient man-made mound, also gets a mention with part of it in touch and part in-goal. It was also the place where early disputes over the Rules were decided. Incidentally, back in 1797 the Island was the site of the final redoubt of the pupils' Great Rebellion when, for the last time in England, the Riot Act was read out. Many of the ringleaders were expelled immediately, including a future Bishop and a future General.

The plan suggested that the pitch shape should be oblong rather than square but offered no dimensions. This was going to have implications at the highest playing level in 1871 and 1872. The object of the game was to kick a goal, either drop or place after a touch-down. No penalties in those days. Aficionados may be interested to read that it took 51 international matches before a penalty was successfully kicked. That was by Wales versus England at Cardiff Arms Park in 1893, the first time England lost on Welsh soil. The introduction also includes, for the first time, some suggestions about the three groups of players in a team. Behind the Heavy Brigade [forwards] would be the clever dodgers [halfbacks] and outside them the swiftest runners and best drop kickers [backs] would wait expectantly.

Now what about the ball? The shape was a case of necessity later superseded by player reference once technology got a grip. Originally the crucial factor was the shape and size of the pig's bladder inside its leather case. Several shoemakers in town made a useful sideline in balls for the school. William Gilbert's shop, for example, was originally based in the High Street but then moved to a small site in St. Matthew's Street in the early 1840s, just over the road from the school. It's still there today. Nephew James used to blow up the balls before a suitable pump was invented. It took considerable lung power and capacity. A clay pipe stem was used to avoid direct contact with the bladder. It didn't save the wife of Richard Linden, one of Gilbert's rivals, from catching a lung disease and passing away.

It was the use of vulcanised rubber and the invention of a suitable adaptor in 1862 that transformed the production process. For the younger boys, balls with reduced dimensions started to be manufactured for smallside games. The earliest balls were rounder and larger than today's ball. So much depended on the size and shape of the pig's bladder. It is believed that players preferred the oval shape for both drop kicking and handling, particularly when passing caught on. Nevertheless, it took until 1892 before the Rugby Football Union stipulated the dimensions of the ball. Player power in 1931 reduced the width of balls further. In Britain four panels was the norm but elsewhere one could come across six panels or even, in South Africa, eight. These balls were not cheap. At Gilbert's

James Gilbert started his trade supplying pigs' bladders to Rugby School. Today the Gilbert name still appears on club and international rugby balls.

only the highest quality leather was used and only expert craftsmanship could stitch the specially selected and treated panels starting, would you believe it, with the ball inside out. William Gilbert didn't lack business acumen. At the Great Exhibition at the Crystal Palace in 1851 he displayed two of his match balls. By the middle of the century he was despatching balls to destinations as far apart as Wellington College, Berkshire and Wellington city, New Zealand.

Back on the pitch running-in was still a rarity. If someone tried it the opposition would do almost anything to stop him. A senior pupil was another who thought the game was losing its vigour. "And there was none of that underhand shuffling play with the ball then that there is now; no passing it along from one to another; all was manly and straightforward. No one thought you worth your salt if you weren't the colour of your mother earth from head to toe ten minutes after the match had begun." "..... young dandies .....mincing across Big Side,....". "Hang the young puppies! we shall have fellows playing in dress boots and lavender-coloured kid gloves before long. My maxim is hack the ball on when you see it near you, and when you don't, why then hack the fellow next you." This reactionary was writing in the *New Rugbeian* in 1859.

The boys started to adjust the scoring system and agreed that if no conversions were successful then the team with the larger number of tries would win. XX-a-side was reduced to XV from 1876 but the larger number was retained for internal matches. After a tackle, if a player hung on to the ball, forcible persuasion might be resorted to compel him to release the ball. Players practised assiduously to improve their drop kicking with either foot. Hacking-over, rather than hacking, ranged from a tap on the leg to a violent lunge. A visitor to the school asked Dr Frederick Temple, the Head Master, whether he ever stopped a match. "Never," Temple replied, "short of manslaughter!" And this from a future Archbishop of Canterbury.

In similar vein, an injured player from a House on the Barby Road tried to enter School House to be met by the aged butler who forbade entry with the words "Let them bury their own dead." In 1858, Dr Temple stopped younger players from standing in goal. He thought they were wasting their time. Old Rugbeians were horrified so a compromise was reached: goalkeepers would be on duty for the three great matches of the year. Anyway, by now, there were seven pitches so the youngsters could have their own matches. This Head's magisterial intervention was very rare. Over 50 years

IN SIMILAR VEIN, AN INJURED PLAYER FROM A HOUSE ON THE BARBY ROAD TRIED TO ENTER SCHOOL HOUSE TO BE MET BY THE AGED BUTLER WHO FORBADE ENTRY WITH THE WORDS "LET THEM BURY THEIR OWN DEAD."

William Charles Macready, the great Shakespearean actor.

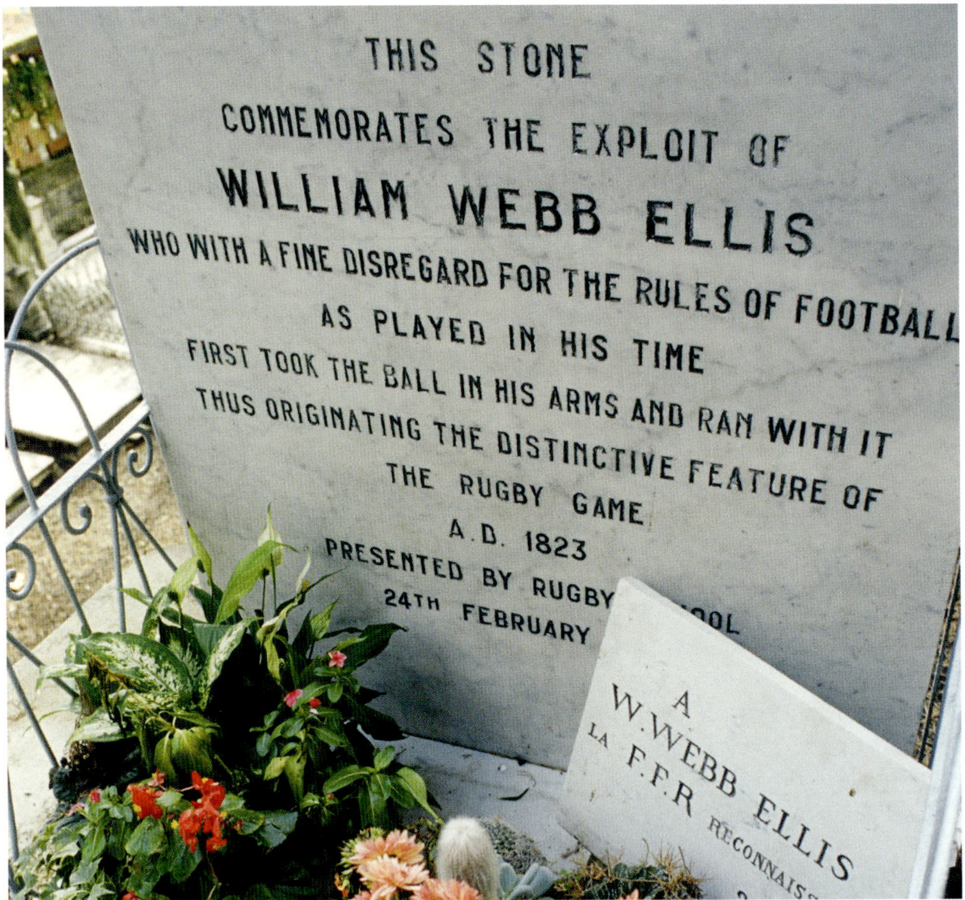

The grave of the founder of rugby, William Webb Ellis, at Cimetière du Vieux Chateau – Menton, France

earlier there was an example reflecting the fluid and casual nature of football at that time. Head Master Henry Ingles called William Charles Macready out of a game. He bid the future famous Shakespearean actor to keep his cap on and walk around The Close to discuss his plans after Rugby. No one seemed to object.

Many footballers outside Rugby were horrified by hacking. We will hear more about this controversial part of the game in the next chapter. Gradually heeling gained ascendancy over driving through the opposition and hacking began to lose its raison d'être. Yet the boys were loath to lose it. It was described as character building, a test of one's mettle and a rite of passage. Hacking-over, the dubious art of tripping the ball carrier, took longer to pass into obscurity. The target could well be startled by this form of attack. The action could be positively brutal, but it might permit a good little 'un to get the better of a good big 'un. Old scores might be settled. Amongst adults the result

OVER 50 YEARS EARLIER THERE WAS AN EXAMPLE REFLECTING THE FLUID AND CASUAL NATURE OF FOOTBALL AT THAT TIME. HEAD MASTER HENRY INGLES CALLED WILLIAM CHARLES MACREADY OUT OF A GAME. HE BID THE FUTURE FAMOUS SHAKESPEAREAN ACTOR TO KEEP HIS CAP ON AND WALK AROUND THE CLOSE TO DISCUSS HIS PLANS AFTER RUGBY. NO ONE SEEMED TO OBJECT.

---

could be worse than brutal. It was not accepted by the Rugby Football Union in 1871 and declared illegal five years later.

To say the Webb Ellis incident has been disputed is putting it mildly. An industry has arisen of myth busters and doubters. The views range from total denial to believing it was natural evolution rather than a big-bang act. It's certainly true that the supporters of the Webb Ellis incident were recording their views long after the event and maybe the Old Rubgbeian committee had a hidden agenda. After all, the game was still recovering from the split between Northern Football and Rugby Football. It would be fascinating to get hold of the minutes of those meetings. The young man in question may not have been without his faults but the School remains proud that his name is on the cup competed for every four years by the International teams that play one of the best team games around. Why and how did this brand of football spread so successfully from this Midland school?

GORDON REID

PLAYING THE GAME

I was from a council estate in Ayrshire and I fell into rugby when I was 12. Rugby clicked for me. It was a proper team sport. Football is more individual but in rugby you have to work as a team. I was not the best player in the world, not the fittest, fastest, strongest. But the thing I had was my mental attitude. If someone got the better of me I would just carry on going until I got them back. I remember my first scrum in a club game against Adam Jones, the Wales and Lions prop, and I just laughed. Me playing against Adam Jones. At the end of the game I asked him for an autographed picture and was not embarrassed to do so. I was so excited when I got my first cap for Scotland playing against the USA in Texas. I was gutted my mum and dad could not come over because of the cost, but secretly my agent flew them and my wife to the game. When I was singing the national anthem I looked up to see my dad in his kilt, and my mum and my wife singing with me. That was so special to me. Playing in the 2015 Rugby World Cup was just phenomenal. Great to get selected for your country and for a world cup in England so my family could see it. It was an unreal experience getting the phone call and email messages. I don't think William Webb Ellis would recognise the game today, it has changed so much. Players are getting bigger, stronger and fitter. But I think rugby is a great game. I have toured the world and gained so many new friends.

Loosehead prop Gordon Reid was born in March 1987 and has appeared 41 times for Scotland, making his debut against the USA in 2014. He was a member of the Scotland World Cup squad in 2015 and scored his first international try against England in the 2017 Six Nations Championship. At club level he has represented London Irish, Northampton Saints, Glasgow Warriors, Ayrshire Bulls and Marr. In November 2019 he rescued his neighbour from a fire after investigating a burning smell.

SCOTLAND
macron
BT
ENGLAND V SCOTLAND
16/03/2019
Gordon Reid
macron

PLAYING THE GAME

DAVID CAMPESE

I started playing rugby in in the small town of Queanbeyan where rugby league was the main sport. I played league from the age of eight until 16 but also enjoyed other sports and won a schoolboy golf tournament when I was 15. I also played Australian Rules Football and cricket and at the age of 16 I went to watch the local fourth grade rugby team at the Queanbeyan Whites and asked the coach after the game if they needed a fullback. I started the next week and it was the best year of rugby I ever experienced. My career highlight was just being able to play this great game and meeting so many people around the world. Rugby gave me the opportunity to travel the world and that is how I met my wife, Lara. I think today William Webb Ellis, like others, would be turning in their graves. It is not about flair, skills and teamwork. It is about winning with big and strong players who are like robots. Coaches are the problem and you end up with structured players.

David Campese AM, also known as Campo, was born in 1962. He was capped by Australia 101 times between 1982 and 1996, playing 85 tests at wing and 16 at fullback. He was a Rugby World Cup winner in 1991 and scored 64 tries for Australia.

18 76

South Africa's first rugby clubs, Villagers and Hamilton, were formed.

18 76

Neath Rugby Club was formed by a consortium of 10 enthusiasts. Founding captain TP Whittington played international rugby for Scotland two years later.

NEATH RFC

18 78

On March 2, Swansea and Newport faced each other in the final of the Welsh Cup, watched by 2000 spectators. The match was won by Newport.

18 78

The oldest rugby club in Germany, DFV Hanover, was founded.

canterbury RUGBY union

78

18 79

In July Canterbury became New Zealand's first established provincial rugby club.

18 84 The first recorded game of rugby was played in Fiji.

18 84 The Canadian Rugby Football Union was founded.

18 86 All forms of payments to players were banned at the annual meeting of the Rugby Football Union.

18 86 A one-armed rugby player kicked 13 successful conversions from 13 attempts in a match between Newton Abbot and Plymouth.

18 87 Emily Valentine became the first known female rugby player when she turned out for Portora Royal School in Enniskillen, Northern Ireland. Her father was headmaster and Emily played in a team formed by her brothers, scoring a try in a match in this year.

"

WHEN I PLAYED WE GOT A PIECE OF ORANGE AT HALF TIME, IF YOU WERE QUICK YOU GOT TWO.

"

Colin Meads

"HOME FIRES"

By David Ray,
rugby historian and former Master in Charge of Football, Rugby School

MATCHES AGAINST PLAYERS NOT AT RUGBY STARTED IN 1867 YET ONLY OLD BOYS AND SELECTED RESIDENTS IN OR NEAR RUGBY WERE ALLOWED TO PLAY. THIS WAS ONE OF THE VERY RARE EDICTS FROM DR ARNOLD.

It's understandable that the boys at Rugby School fiercely defended their brand of football. They had been responsible for all aspects of the game from day one. This was not confined to the main winter sport. Cricket, rugby fives, cross-country and all the other physical pursuits were in the hands of the pupils. For example, during football, deputies on the pitch were the eyes and ears of the captains. Where exactly was the ball? Who was off their side? The Head Master might walk around The Close but very rarely interfere. The occasional Old Rugbeian might turn up for a game and, on rare occasions, a member of staff would chance his arm. He would pretty quickly discover if he was popular or not. The pupils were not reactionary, they were prepared to change rules if something needed altering or tightening up. What they would not stand for was being told what to do by outsiders.

Inevitably, however, as rugby football spread beyond The Close, the boys began to lose their iron grip. Where the Rugby boys dug their heels in were playing against non-Rugbeian teams, limiting the numbers involved and abolishing hacking. Matches against players not at Rugby started in 1867 yet only Old Boys and selected residents in or near Rugby were allowed to play. This was one of the very rare edicts from Dr Arnold.

The initial game pitted the school XX against A.C. Harrison Esq.'s XX. There was a strong wind blowing down The Close. The school captain, after some 50 minutes, gallantly offered his opposite number a change of ends to equal things up a bit. Charming! It is believed this is the origin of half time. Such tussles were dubbed Foreign matches. The School was certainly slow in reducing its numbers from XX to XV. One observer, with tongue in cheek, announced, "We used to win most of our matches in those days.'

The numbers of players for Foreign matches was reduced in 1876. For Internationals the year was 1877, two years after the Varsity match. Internal games at Rugby continued with XX-a-side until 1888.

We will also see that Rugbeians took their game to all corners of the kingdom and beyond. Equally important, in the early days, was the influence of Rugby staff. This may surprise readers but as the Victorian teachers at public schools assumed more responsibility for extra-curricular activities, so the game of rugby football began to spread from the Senior Common Rooms to the playing fields.

The Malborough team of 1864, captained by J.A. Boyle (centre with the tassel of his cap falling forward) who scored the only goal in the Marlborough v Clifton match.

G.E.L. Cotton arrived from Rugby as Head Master at Marlborough College in 1852. Free time for the boys often involved wandering off into the surrounding Wiltshire countryside. Several young staff followed Cotton and a game very similar to that played on The Close took hold. The first Head Master of Clifton College was John Percival who recruited Rugby staff. The first Marlborough versus Clifton clash was as early as 1864. I say 'clash' as the fixture was not repeated until 1891 due to that initial, acrimonious encounter.

A similar development happened at Cheltenham with the arrival of Head Master Henry Highton from Rugby in 1859 followed by T.W. Jex-Blake who had been a boy at Rugby. Other Rugby staff who became Head Masters were A.G. Butler at Haileybury in 1862 and E.W. Benson, Wellington College's first Head in 1858.

Scottish schools were no laggards in adopting the game either. In 1870 the Fettes Head Master had been at Rugby, and Loretto School, a few miles to the east in Musselburgh, began supplying a remarkable number of players for the Varsity matches south of the border from the early 1870s into the 1880s. Merchiston Castle played Edinburgh Royal High School in 1857 and The Edinburgh Academy a year later. There may be earlier inter-school matches in Britain but there can't be many. All this is remarkable when one considers that Rugby School played its first school opposition in 1896.

LET'S CALL IT HALF

Half time originated at Rugby School when the School's rugby captain first stopped a game and announced it was hardly fair as his team was playing with a strong following wind. He offered the opposition the chance to play the rest of the match with the breeze. They changed ends and half time was born. Forty minutes each way was first mentioned in the 1926 rules.

TIME

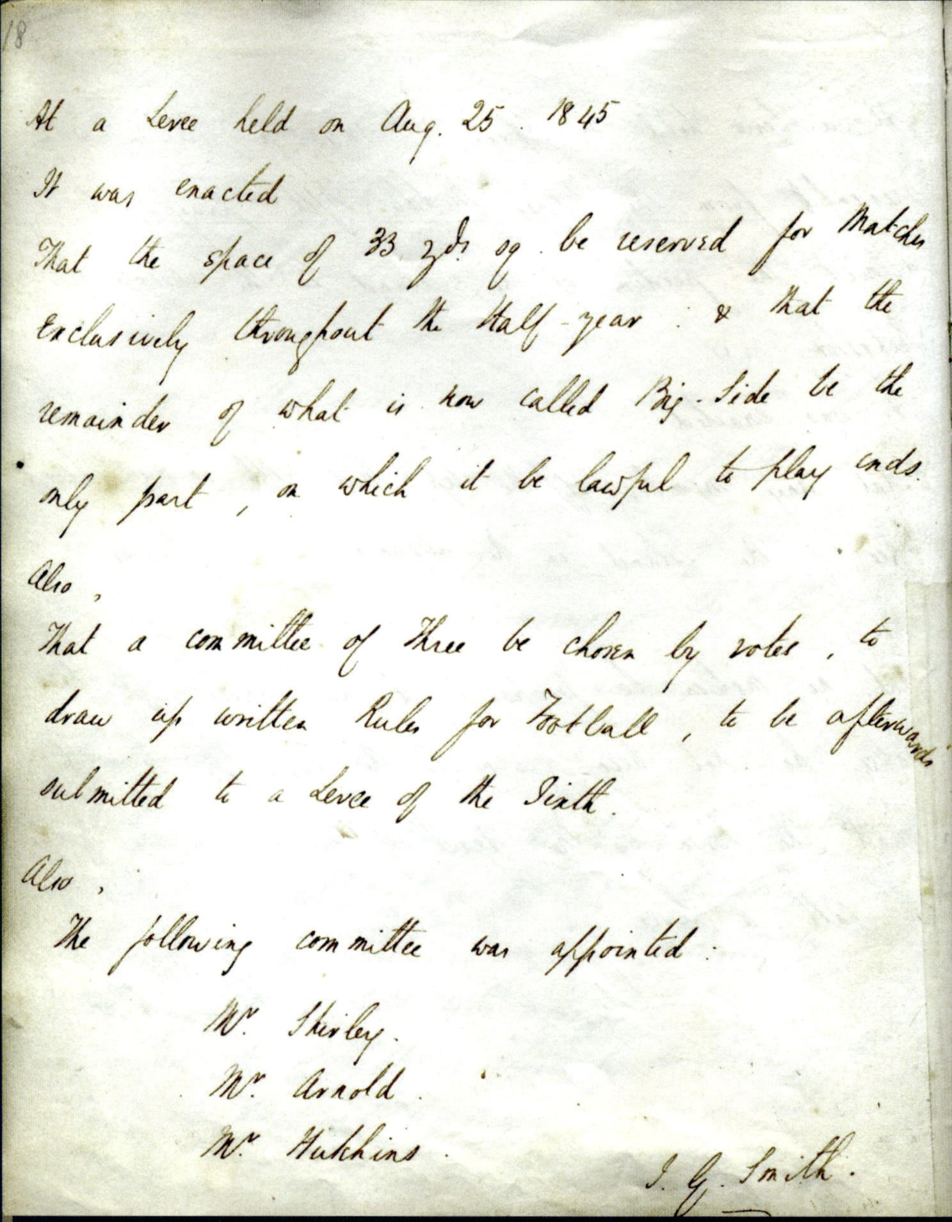
18

At a Levee held on Aug. 25. 1845

It was enacted

That the space of 33 yds sq. be reserved for Matches exclusively throughout the Half-year. & that the remainder of what is now called Big-Side be the only part, on which it be lawful to play ends.

Also,

That a committee of Three be chosen by votes, to draw up written Rules for Football, to be afterwards submitted to a Levee of the Sixth.

Also,

The following committee was appointed:

Mr. Shirley.

Mr. Arnold.

Mr. Hutchins.

I. G. Smith.

Original Rules drawn up by the boys themselves.

IN IRELAND, THE FIRST CLUB PLAYING THE RUGBY CODE WAS TRINITY COLLEGE, DUBLIN IN 1854. THE RULES THEY PLAYED UNDER WERE VERY CLOSE TO THOSE AT RUGBY WITH THE EXTRA REGULATION WHICH READ "ATTEMPTS TO STRANGLE OR THROTTLE ARE FORBIDDEN".

Staff realised that wellbeing and leisure time were important to a boy's overall development but also trespassing could be reduced and surplus energy could be worked off on the pitch. In addition, from the public schools, young men arrived at Oxford, Cambridge and the military academies. Not only did the rugby football playing schools have some of their own rules and peculiarities but many top athletes took part in several of the sporting activities on offer. Specialisation was rare. Blues in more than one sport were not uncommon. Rowing and criocket were seen as the two prestige sporting activities.

Albert Pell must get a mention as the first to organise a football match at Cambridge University on Parker's Piece in 1839. Many were keen to take part but the numerous interpretations of play proved virtually insurmountable. It was not a great success and, to add insult to injury, people walking past invaded the pitch to separate the players, thinking a giant brawl was taking place. Running with the ball was still being disputed and the rules were in a state of flux. A compromise was cobbled together after lengthy discussion amongst a sizeable number of different representatives. No one was really satisfied. Ironically the Cambridge Rules, as they became known, formed the blueprint for the Football Association rules in 1863.

At Oxford, things were more straightforward. Here there were more former pupils and the Old Rugbeian team to take on the school was made up largely of Oxford men. For the 1861 match 38 Old Boys arrived and most had made use of the relatively easy rail journey from the city of spires. The Old Rugbeians against the Old Marlburians became a regular match on the Christ Church cricket ground. That must have pleased the groundsman. 1869 saw a football club established in Oxford with the ruling that the captain, secretary and at least one committee member should be Rugbeians.

In Ireland, the first club playing the Rugby code was Trinity College, Dublin in 1854. The rules they played under were very close to those at Rugby with the extra regulation which read "Attempts to strangle or throttle are forbidden". The Irish Football Union was created in 1874 followed, within two months, by the North Football Union of Ireland. An Irish XX was selected the following February to take on England and to avoid controversy ten were chosen from the north and ten from the south. The match at the Oval was played on a Monday. It had rained the whole of the previous two days and the pitch was a quagmire. Some of the Irish players never materialised, some backs had to play as forwards and many of the participants had never met before. It will come as no surprise that England won. Six of the home team were Rugbeians and there was one in the Irish pack. In fact, between 1874 and 1878, Old Rugbeians were in both International teams on three occasions.

After schools and universities the next step in the development of the game obviously involved establishing clubs. Guy's Hospital, founded in 1843, is almost certainly the first club in England. The earliest open clubs included Blackheath and Richmond in the capital and Manchester and Liverpool in the north-west. The Blackheath Club (1857) proved to be a great defender of the game and Richmond (1861) had played the Harrow Rules in its first season only to switch a year later. The London clubs tended to have a more transient membership but flourished where Rugbeians congregated. The Edinburgh Academicals and the West of Scotland can claim to be the earliest clubs north of the border. The Scottish Rugby Union was founded in 1873, two years after Scotland had entertained England in the world's first International. Clubs needed guidance, rulings and uniformity. Anti-rugby football schools homed in on the strange oval ball, dangerous hacking, passing and even the high cross bar. Many clubs didn't own a ground and had to get to the playing area early on match days to erect the posts and mark out the pitch. They say possession is nine-tenths of the law yet spectators and strollers often strayed on to the playing area. Some ball-carrying players deliberately ran within or behind the crowd to avoid the opposition.

Those Cambridge Rules mentioned earlier were cobbled together by a committee of nine students from six different schools. Much deliberation through correspondence and discussion took place beforehand. One letter, from an unidentified committee member, suggested a set of rules for the rural working-class. The rules, according to this individual, needed to be simple and easy to understand. Another observation to add to this patronising suggestion stressed the importance of country types not wearing their hob-nailed boots for matches. The 1870s witnessed a massive movement to towns, cities and abroad. The problem with rugby football compared with other sports was that it needed more players and Club football was not for youngsters or men of a certain age. One observer on Parker's Piece reported a pitch 150 yards by 100 yards, touchline flags flying at strategic points such as the 25 yards and one goalkeeper per team. Handling was rarely seen, off-side was rigidly enforced and there was a lot of movement. It sounds exactly what it was: a hybrid of today's rugby football and Association football.

Things came to a head in 1863 when *The Times* ran a headline 'The Great Football Question', an attempt to get some uniformity of the rules to enable schools and clubs to play without continuous stoppages and arguments. The gathering, set up by the Football Association, was held on November 1, at the Freemason's Tavern, London.

There were representatives from such bodies as Dingley Dell, the War Office, and Leytonstone. Only Charterhouse of the better-known schools was present. The response from other schools was poor but the lack of publicity was believed to be the main cause. There was no Rugby School representative at any of these meetings. Some of those present seemed reluctant to surrender or compromise any part of their version of the game. Some former pupils stepped in and offered a draft of the Association rules which, surprisingly, retained running with the ball as well as holding or hacking the carrier, but not together. There was noticeable unease in the room.

Within three weeks the Cambridge committee had reconvened and were adamant that rules IX and X, namely running and hacking, should be excluded. A heated debate ensued at the following meeting and the amendments were carried by ten votes to nine. The mood at the following meeting was, if anything, even more ill-tempered. Rugby football champions, particularly Blackheath, believed they had been ambushed and complained that not all representatives were present. It's ironic that if they had accepted the end of hacking the rest might well have been more relaxed on the question of running with the ball. Did the pro-dribbling faction home in on hacking as a diversionary tactic? In other words was hacking a red herring? The Rugby Football group were dubbed the 'hacking men'. After the fourth meeting the two groups were starting to drift apart. Even the signing of the minutes raised further issues.

At the final meeting on December 8, Mr Campbell, the Blackheath representative, stated he approved the broad objectives of the Association but the proposed rule changes would all but destroy the essence of the Rugby game. They would not shift their position. The pro Cambridge camp reminded those present that many of their players "had to go to work in the city on a Monday morning" while the Rugby rules contingent thought the others were going soft. It seems bizarre that the schism came about by such a close decision over a couple of rules. Who knows what would have happened if a compromise had been reached? From here both codes went their separate ways. Yet if one studies the resulting set of rules that went on to become the Association Football rules there are a few surprises. The pitch would be 200 yards long and 100 yards wide. That's massive. There would be no tape or bar between the upright posts and there would be a change of ends if a goal was scored. A player could catch the ball and have a free kick and a player could also throw the ball into play if it went into touch. If the ball ended up behind the goal line a first touch earned a free

WE ALL KNOW THAT BOTH CODES SURVIVED AND DULY FLOURISHED DURING THE SECOND HALF OF THE NINETEENTH CENTURY AND BEYOND. THERE SEEMED ROOM FOR BOTH FORMS OF FOOTBALL.

"The two Cock Houses, 1876".

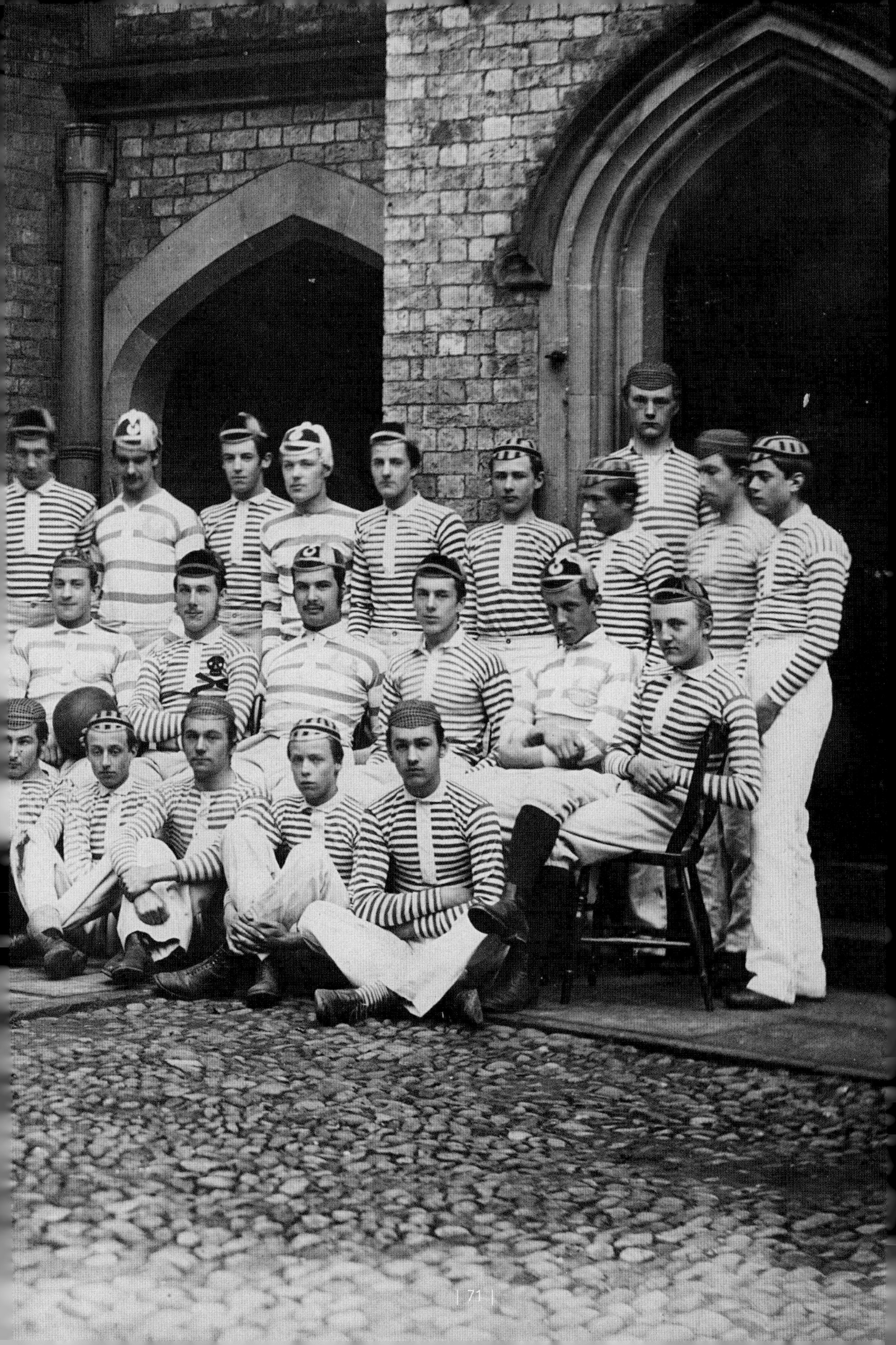

THERE IS A PHOTOGRAPH OF 1855 SHOWING THE PLAYERS IN THE OLD QUAD AT RUGBY BEFORE THE COCK HOUSE MATCH. FORTY PLAYERS POSE FOR THE CAMERA.

kick. So handling was permitted in certain circumstances. We all know that both codes survived and duly flourished during the second half of the 19th century and beyond. There seemed room for both forms of football.

Rugby's reputation was spreading. Businessmen and industrialists living in the north-west liked the Arnold philosophy and the new railway to London now went through the town. Several Rugbeians in Merseyside were keen to continue playing their game and one was planned for December 19, 1857. Liverpool Cricket Club was approached and 50 players assembled for Rugby versus the rest of the world. Some of that team came from as far afield as Yorkshire and Cheshire. The groundsman, understandably, marked out the pitch with chalk rather than cutting the turf. Richard Sykes was asked to bring a ball from school at the start of the Christmas holidays. A Lindon ball was selected that had already seen service on Bigside.

Sykes was one of the players and he helped explain some of the rules. There were no disputes, everyone enjoyed themselves and the Liverpool Club was formed then and there. There is no record of the final score. The Club's first matches were obviously internal but when Sykes left Rugby he founded the Manchester Club in 1860. This pre-dates two other certain clubs in Manchester with the suffixes City and United. Now Liverpool had some genuine opposition.

There is a photograph of 1855 showing the players in the Old Quad at Rugby before the Cock House match. Forty players pose for the camera and sitting in the middle is young Sykes, wearing his cap and holding a ball. He is the only boy wearing school dress rather than playing kit. His left arm appears to be in a sling.

Richard Sykes was adventurous. He sailed to America and got heavily involved in railway track building and acquiring land. He founded several towns in Dakota, including Sykestown, and eventually owned some 92,000 acres. He introduced the Rugby game to California and died in 1923, the same year as the centenary match on The Close.

Rugby football clubs began to spring up all around the country. West Yorkshire soon had a cluster and the Rugby Football Club in Rugby was founded in 1867. Former dayboys at the School were certainly involved as can be seen from the white strip and rampant red lion (crest of the School's Town House) badge on the left breast. Yet the Midlands was hardly a hot spot for clubs. Coventry, founded in 1874, was a rarity. The West Country began to flourish, particularly around the famous quartet of Bath, Bristol, Cheltenham and Gloucester. The South West was not far behind. Redruth, for example, was founded in 1875. In London, Harlequins (1866), Wasps (1867) and Saracens (1867) were formed. Each played variations of football, whether Association, Rugby, Harrow or whatever was the decision of each club. They were now selecting a particular code for the first time. A *Times* article hardly helped with an emphasis on the dangerous nature of the game. Then, on December 8, 1870, a group of Scots challenged England to an International played under Rugby rules. This galvanised the rugby football fraternity and Blackheath and Richmond responded by strongly recommending a common code. Twenty-one club and school representatives met at the Pall Mall Restaurant on January 26, 1871. The Flamingoes, Gipsies and Mohicans attended as well as Wellington College and St. Paul's School. There was still no direct Rugby School involvement. The boys remained suspicious of outside change and, as we know, defending their version of football was ingrained. Nevertheless, the chairman was E.C. Holmes, captain of Richmond and a Rugbeian. Rugbeian Algernon Rutter was elected first president and these two, along with Rugbeian L.J. Maton, were asked to return with a common code of rules. Maton did most of the work having broken his leg. These rules were largely the Rugby School rules but hacking was not included.

The first Rugby Football International took place at Raeburn Place, Edinburgh, on Monday, March 27, 1871. The English XX arrived to find a pitch 120 yards long and 55 yards wide. These 'Scottiish' dimensions were new to the away team and one cynic believed the narrowness of the pitch was due to the canny Scots who, having done their homework, were keen to cramp the free-running England backs. The visitors also agreed to play by one or two unfamiliar rules. There were umpires but still no referee. Both teams weighed in at just over 12 stones average per man. Of the 40 new caps no fewer than ten were Rugbeians. In the team photograph one can pick them out by their Rugby House caps. International caps were awarded after the match in a plum colour with a silver tassel. The players would embroider on the date themselves. 4000 spectators settled down to watch two halves of 50 minutes each way with no hacking or tripping.

England captain, F. Stokes.

Rugbeian F. Stokes was the England captain. Popular, knowledgeable, tactful, good tempered and with the ability to inspire the colleagues around him, he was also a fine all-round player. The first half ended with no score but it was plain to see that the home team had a well-drilled pack, knew each other better and were fitter and sharper. After the break Scotland scored a pushover try which was converted. The English thought this illegal but the umpires over-ruled the protests. Doctor H.H. Almond, one of the umpires, ruled in favour of his fellow countrymen with the aside that, "When an umpire is in doubt, I

WHEN AN UMPIRE IS IN DOUBT, I THINK HE IS JUSTIFIED IN DECIDING AGAINST THE SIDE WHICH MAKES THE MOST NOISE. THEY ARE PROBABLY IN THE WRONG.

think he is justified in deciding against the side which makes the most noise. They are probably in the wrong." England replied with an unconverted try but, with a few minutes remaining, Scotland got their second touchdown. On one occasion the Scottish forward J.F. Finlay of Edinburgh Academicals was running towards the English line when R.R. Osborne of Manchester folded his arms across his chest and hit Finlay very hard. Both players recoiled several yards before hitting the ground. A try-saving act then, but a red card today. A points system was still several years away.

The following year was pay-back time. The return match was scheduled for February 5,1872, the venue was the Oval and the pitch was considerably wider than at Raeburn Place ten months earlier. Call it home advantage. This time seven Old Rugbeians were in the England XX and F. Stokes was again captain. After ten minutes Scotland succeeded with a drop-goal and that was it as far as they were concerned. The English backs showed their skills and the forwards steadily gained ascendancy. Their scores were a goal, two tries and a drop-goal. What a difference a year makes. It's not surprising drop-goals feature so strongly until after World War II as, once a scoring system was agreed, they were worth four points.

Stokes was still captain in 1873. The year after that the match against Scotland witnessed five Rugbeians on the England side and an Old Rugbeian in the Scottish pack. This was a first. In the England versus Ireland fixture in 1875 there were six Old Rugbeian Englishmen and a lone Irish former pupil. This was Ireland's International debut and was also played at the Oval. In 1878 Rugby had the unusual distinction of seeing Old Boys G.L. Fagan and T.G. Gordon turn out as halfbacks for Ireland.

Wales were to make their International debut on February 19, 1881. They had held their own against Somerset and Gloucestershire in preliminary matches but the game at Blackheath was a disaster. The score by today's system would have been 82-0. It could have been worse. Referee Rugbeian A.G. Guillemard made a decision that seemed to go back almost to the Webb Ellis era. England scored yet another try with L.Stokes passing a long distance to put R. Hunt in under the posts. Mr. Guillemard declared such a tactic as 'not football' and disallowed it. However, Wales were quick learners. In 1884 they defeated Ireland and a year later they drew with Scotland. Wales had to wait until1890 before England lost. This match took place at Crown Flatt, Dewsbury, in bitter mid February. The sturdy Welsh forwards outplayed the somewhat statuesque English and the visiting backs combined cleverly. Two minutes into the second half at a line-out Bill Staddon of Dewsbury dummied to throw long. The home forwards moved infield, Staddon threw the ball into the field of play, recovered it and ran to score in the corner. The conversion failed and Wales had won 1-0. Staddon was working in Dewsbury at the time and was the only 'local' player on the pitch. The try over the years has therefore increased from naught, if unconverted, through one, two, three and four to today's five points. To be fair, all the Welsh players came from top clubs in the principality and one from London Welsh.

Back at Rugby, the boys remained content to play matches amongst themselves. That didn't stop the Old Boys playing for their college, club and country. Up to the time of the split over broken time in 1895 the school's representation at the top of the game was remarkable. Admittedly the pool of players was relatively small by 21st-century standards but figures don't lie. There had been 40 Oxford and 20 Cambridge Blues including 10 Oxford and two Cambridge captains. The Oxford captaincy number needs clarifying. At a meeting of Rugbeians held at Balliol College on November 2, 1869 the first rule they came up with was that the captain, secretary and one of the three members of the committee must always be Rugbeians. We have heard that before. This neat arrangement held good for seven years. One formidable player was J.D. Boswell. He was one of 13 boys who went on to play for his country but never made the school team. That doesn't say much for the football selection policy at Rugby in the early days. J.D. Boswell played for Oxford in three University encounters and then went on to represent Scotland in 15 matches. He was captain in his last four appearances. He also scored four tries and kicked four conversions as well as two drop-goals. Boswell was an all-round player in more ways than one and was President of the Scottish Rugby Union in 1898-1899.

What would today's players, pundits, officials and spectators make of the game towards the end of the Victorian era? A surprising amount of it would be familiar. Different interpretations of the Rules began to fade away, there were rumours of players getting financial reward for playing, known as boot money, and there was the inevitable example of sharp practice. Yet there were no replacements, scores remained relatively scarce and some of the kicking was at least as prodigious as it is today. After sterling work by Cheltenham College, a points system was adopted by the Rugby Football Union in 1886. Worth four points, those drop-goal attempts kept coming and, mercifully, there were no penalty goals at International level until 1890. Dribbling by forwards, particularly in Scotland, was a common tactic. Furthermore no one wore numbers and the forwards packed down in scrums in the order in which they arrived.

THE TRY OVER THE YEARS HAS THEREFORE INCREASED FROM NAUGHT, IF UNCONVERTED, THROUGH ONE, TWO, THREE AND FOUR TO TODAY'S FIVE POINTS.

WHAT F
IGNITED
LY

RST THE MPIC FLAME?

Inspired by what he had read about Dr Arnold in *Tom Brown's Schooldays*, Pierre de Coubertin visited Rugby School several times during the 1880s and concluded that organised sport could be used to raise the aspirations and improve the behaviour of young people. This idea fuelled his vision for universal amateur athletics which culminated in the first modern Olympic Games in Athens, 1896.

Today's players would be appalled at having to play on some of the pitches of that time. Quite often they were either rock-hard or a mud bath after a few minutes. Eighteen tons of coal were used overnight to ensure a harsh frost didn't cancel the Wales versus England match in Cardiff in 1893. A few examples from Internationals may help to give an insight into the attitudes and mores of the time.

Positions in the team remained relatively fluid. Specialisation was growing but it was still possible to play at the top level as a back in one match and in the forwards in the next. However, things were obviously getting serious because in 1876 Mr. A. Rutter was asked to referee an International match for the first time. Ireland played England at Lansdowne Road in 1880. After a particularly rough crossing R. Woodhead of Dublin University played for the visitors after one of them was too ill with sea sickness to take the field. Three years later, after an equally appalling boat trip, R.W. Hughes was forced to retire soon after the start of the match. Ireland played the rest of the game one short. The next year S.A.M. Bruce of Ireland broke his leg against England and they were down to 14 men once again. Replacements are a relatively new phenomenon. Ireland eventually defeated England in 1887. J. Macawley (Limerick) got married that weekend. It was the only way he could get leave of absence to play. England beat Ireland by three tries to nil in 1890 which translated into a 3-0 win. That same year England got the better of Wales 7-3 at Rodney Parade, Newport, in what was described in the media as a "decisive victory".

The game soon spread beyond Britain and Ireland. In France British residents started playing. In 1872 Le Havre Athletique were playing a cross between rugby football and soccer. In Paris the English Taylors put out a team and in 1892 Racing Club played Stade Français, refereed by Baron Pierre de Coubertin. He was the founder of the modern Olympic Games and much of his philosophy about amateurism and sportsmanship emanated from his visit to Rugby School coupled with the influence of Dr. Arnold and his reading of *Tom Brown's Schooldays*. Incidentally, the USA are the current holders of the Olympic Games XV-a-side gold medal having won the last time it was played in 1908.

The British took rugby football to New Zealand and teams travelling there have normally regretted it ever since. A game approximating to rugby football was being played there in the late 1850s. In Cranmer Square, Christchurch, there is a stone plaque commemorating a game of 20-a-side football in 1863 between Christ College and the

THE BRITISH TOOK RUGBY FOOTBALL TO NEW ZEALAND AND TEAMS TRAVELLING THERE HAVE NORMALLY REGRETTED IT EVER SINCE.

England v Cape Colony, Cape Town 1891.

town. However, most interested parties believe the first recognised rugby football match was in Nelson, South Island, in the Botanics Reserve. At 2pm on May 14, 1870 a match between Nelson Football Club and Nelson College kicked off. It was 18-a-side. The Club won by two goals to no reply, Nelson had the new suffix rugby Football Club and there is a stone cairn to that effect in the Reserve. There is evidence of rugby football being played in New South Wales, Australia, as early as 1829. The Australian Rules game was created by, of all people, an Old Rugbeian by the name of Thomas Wentworth Wills who believed the grounds in that country were too hard for rugby football. He had been sent to England for his education and played cricket for Oxford University. Today, given rugby football in Australia has to compete for players and money with Rules, League and Association Football, the Wallabies punch well above their weight.

Clashes between New Zealand and South Africa only began in 1921. In fact the first 10 matches played by the Springboks were against Great Britain sides (today's British and Irish Lions). Back in 1891 a squad of 20 players set sail for Cape Town and reached it in a then record 16 days. The RFU were adamant all the home players and tourists were amateurs. Cecil Rhodes agreed to underwrite the tour. Many of the journeys between venues were by horse-drawn carriage as the trains lacked dining facilities. Herbert Hayton Castens captained South Africa in the first of the three Tests. One report said he was dropped for the second Test and refereed the third. This is rather misleading as each province selected their own team to play in Port Elizabeth, Kimberley and Cape Town. Castens was an Old Rugbeian. He played for the XI, captaining them in his second year

BACK HOME CRACKS WERE APPEARING IN THE RUGBY UNION EDIFICE. IT WAS ABOUT MONEY AND, SOME WOULD ARGUE, CLASS.

and was in the XV in 1881 and 1882. He won two Rugby Football Blues at Oxford and then emigrated to Rhodesia via South Africa. Incidentally, Great Britain won all 19 of their matches on that tour and the only score they conceded was a single point in their opening match versus the Cape Town club. By comparison, consider the British Lions' tour to South Africa in 1997. They played 13 matches and used, with replacements, a total of 40 players. Furthermore, the visitors found themselves much the bigger team, particularly in comparison with the home team three-quarters. How times change.

The first recorded game in Argentina was in 1873 and it was an exclusively ex-pat British affair. In a match in 1890 in Buenos Aires both teams and all 2500 spectators were arrested. The police believed it was cover for a political meeting. Today, the Pumas can give any country a run for their money. The earliest rugby football matches in Japan were between teams of long-term foreign students and visiting ships. In the previous chapter the Roman game of *harpastum* was mentioned. There are several ball games played in Italy today that can trace their origins back many centuries. It is believed the rugby game was brought to the Genoa region in the early 1890s, possibly reinforced by locals returning from work in southern France.

Back home cracks were appearing in the Rugby Union edifice. It was about money and, some would argue, class. In 1893 the Rugby Union had more than 480 clubs, many of the strongest being in Yorkshire and Lancashire. Northern clubs were taking substantial gate money as the viewing of the game became as popular as playing it. The Rugby Union began paying expenses, excluding hotel costs, for International players. What of manual workers in the industrialised north? Broken time payments and professionalism did not sit comfortably with southern clubs and the Rugby Football Union establishment. The Yorkshire Committee proposed that players 'be allowed compensation for bona fide loss of time'. The RFU President put in a counter-measure. This was ably supported by the evangelical H.E. Steed who worked hard on amateur-loving clubs and the colleges of Oxford and Cambridge, all of whom had a vote. It's alleged several new clubs in the south sprang up overnight. The northern support was not helped when one group from Yorkshire got lost in London on the way to the Westminster Palace Hotel and thus missed the vote.The result was that 20 northern clubs met at the George Hotel, Huddersfield, on August 29 and all resigned from the Rugby Football Union to form the Northern Rugby Football Union. Twenty-two teams contested the first league in 1895-96. In 1906 the number of players was reduced to 13 and in 1922 it changed its name to the Northern Rugby Football League.

A few years later the word Northern was dropped. So almost overnight some of the finest clubs seceded and others followed suit over the next 10 years so that by 1903 the Rugby Union Football list of clubs had halved. What became the cream of these players from such clubs as Wakefield Trinity, Rochdale Hornets and St. Helens was lost. England's record in Union Internationals up to the separation was played 54, won 35, drawn 8 and lost 11. Taking the next 54 matches after the break-away the corresponding figures read 17-6-31. England didn't win the championship from 1893 to 1909. Financial inducements were offered to Union players in Great Britain and League scouts were often seen at club matches in South Wales right up to the time that Union turned professional.

Meanwhile at Rugby some things seemed destined never to change. On the field dribbling and drop kicking remained popular. Foreign matches became the norm even if the opposition were nearly always Old Rugbeians and Oxford Colleges. However in the mid-1890s the desire to play another school grew. On another rare occasion of staff intervention it seems Head Master Dr. James had arranged a match with Cheltenham College. This was scheduled for early December 1895. It was put back a couple of weeks only for scarlet fever to break out at Rugby. Cheltenham sensibly decided not to travel. Earlier in that year there had been an outbreak of eczema and the school was under orders to play Association Football instead for a week.

At last the day arrived. It was February 22, 1896 and the school was in for a shock. Cheltenham were superior in almost all elements of the game, particularly in passing by their backs. The match kicked off early to allow the visitors to catch a convenient train home. Cheltenham had scored two goals, a try and a drop-goal by half time. Rugby began to pull themselves together after the break but the score remained at 0-13. It took five attempts before Rugby chalked up a victory against their oldest opponents. That year Uppingham joined the fixture list and it stayed like that until Haileybury (1915), Oundle (1918) and Wellington (1919) swelled the ranks. It was a late entry into playing football against other schools and about time too.

MIKE BROWN

PLAYING THE GAME

I first got involved playing rugby at the age of five at my local rugby club. My parents took me down. Rugby was in the family on both sides so it was always going to be something I was going to try. I remember turning up and they were all playing Bulldog for the warm up and I just sat on the side not wanting to get involved. But with a little encouragement I did, loved it and never looked back.

Stand-out moments of my club career are winning Amlin Cup with Harlequins in 2011 as it was my first major trophy in rugby. Winning the premiership with Quins in 2012 because it's obviously our bread and butter which we all work so hard all season to achieve. Plus it was with a great group of players and staff, many of the players I'd grown up with through the academy.

Stand-out moments of my international career are winning my first cap even though it ended up a terrible game to be involved in. We got smashed v South Africa. Winning 2014 Six Nations player of the championship. Winning the Grand Slam with England in 2016 was amazing to achieve, coming off the back of an incredibly low point for the team after being dumped out of the home World Cup in 2015 and also for me growing up since the age of five watching other England teams win grand slams it was something I'd always wanted to be part of.

A game that's become very strategic and a battle of attrition. It now requires more physical and mental detail and preparation to play by individuals and teams than Webb Ellis could ever have imagined.

Mike Brown was born in 1985 and played 72 times for England, scoring 65 points and winning three Six Nations Championships. After playing youth rugby for Salisbury and Melksham, he joined Harlequins in in 2005, appearing 351 times before moving to Newcastle Falcons in 2021.

canterbury

18/88 The New Zealand Natives toured Great Britain, winning 49 of their 74 matches.

18/89 The South African Rugby Board (SARB) was established and the country's first provincial championship. Eight years later the South African Coloured Rugby Football Board was also formed.

18/90 Percy Carpmael founded the Barbarians Rugby Club in Bradford.

18/90 The Barbarians made their first tour, beating Hartlepool Rovers and Bradford.

1891 Cecil Rhodes guaranteed to underwrite a tour by a British side of English and Scottish players which set off from Southampton in June.

NEW ZEALAND ALL BLACKS

1892 The New Zealand Rugby Football Union was established.

1892 The first French Club Championship final was held in Paris with Racing Club de France beating Stade Français.

1893 On April 28 the first rugby sevens match took place in Scotland as part of the Melrose Sports carnival.

1895 416 adult clubs were members of the Rugby Football Union.

"THE WHOLE POINT OF RUGBY IS THAT IT IS, FIRST AND FOREMOST, A STATE OF MIND, A SPIRIT."

Jean-Pierre Rives

COMMEMORATING WEBB ELLIS

FROM MEMORY TO MYTH TO INCARNATION

By Dr Jonathan Smith,
former Archivist Rugby School

Matthew Bloxam

> ...THAT CHANGE IN ONE OF THE RULES, WHICH MORE THAN ANY OTHER HAS SINCE DISTINGUISHED THE RUGBY SCHOOL GAME FROM THE ASSOCIATION RULES...

It is opportune to look back upon old times and let nothing remarkable escape us. (Matthew Bloxam in *The Meteor*, 9 October 1879)

William Webb Ellis is rightly revered for accidentally 'creating' the rugby game. But praise must also go to the prodigious memory of 19th-century antiquarian Matthew Bloxam, a fellow Rugby School pupil. Writing in the School's *Meteor* magazine Bloxam recalled Webb Ellis's football antics:

In the latter half year of 1823, some 57 years ago, originated, though without premeditation, that change in one of the rules, which more than any other has since distinguished the Rugby School game from the Association Rules. A boy of the name of Ellis, William Webb Ellis ... (December 22, 1880)

In a speech the year before on his 80th birthday, Bloxam stresses the importance of memory to preserve the past: 'I consider myself in some respect as one connecting the past with the present.' For nothing then was written down. In 1823, 'After the games of the day were concluded, however vigorously they may have been contended, all further remembrance of the game was consigned to the limbo of oblivion, our tasks to be learned at night were sufficiently onerous to allow leisure for discussion, and there was no Meteor in which the incidents of each game could be recorded.' How fortunate we are then that Bloxam found it 'opportune to look back upon old times and let nothing remarkable escape us.'

FROM PERSONAL MEMORY TO POPULAR MYTH

Given the lack of written evidence, it was naturally felt after the chief witness had died that his 'remembrance of the game' should be enshrined in some more permanent memorial. And so it was that only after Bloxam's death the *Meteor* received a letter quoting Bloxam's account of 1823 at length and lamenting:

...that the memory of the epoch-making heretic is not as green as it ought to be at Rugby. I was at the School myself when Mr. Bloxam contributed the letter from which the above words are taken to the Meteor (No. 104, Od. 10, 1876), and I know that the story was at that time a complete revelation to everybody. Would it not be possible for you to set on foot a collection, from Rugbeians in the first Instance, and secondly from Rugby football players outside, to put up some lasting memorial at the School, in honour of William Webb Ellis? If everyone who had taken part in a game of Rugby Football would subscribe even a modest penny, the sum required for a statue or a picture would be collected ten times over. Or if such a mode of commemoration were deemed too extravagant, an inscription recording the achievement in suitable terms might be affixed to the "Doctor's wall", overlooking the Close, for which a very small sum would suffice. I make this suggestion in all seriousness, for I believe that the binding together of the present and the past by means of recorded traditions

is both good and useful, and the daring of the ambitious town-boy of 1823 has had such far-reaching effects upon one of England's most important pastimes – and who knows but upon the national character as well? — that it deserves, I think, to be handed down to future generations. I may add, for the information of your readers, that Mr. Ellis is still well remembered at St. Clement Danes, where I made enquiry of the churchwardens a few weeks ago. It would not be difficult, I imagine, to procure some likeness of him from his surviving relatives, if it were decided to commemorate him by a picture or a statue. … (*Meteor*, October 31, 1891)

In short, Bloxam's 'revelation' should be preserved for posterity because it concerns 'the national character' and should benefit 'future generations'. The conditions of a religious cult are already present, so no wonder the writer thinks a 'likeness' of Webb Ellis would be suitable. In the event, however, it seems there was insufficient enthusiasm for a picture or a statue, because a mere inscription was preferred and duly written into the fabric of the School:

The tablet commemorating the exploit of William Webb Ellis, whom we claim to have been the inventor of what is now known as the Rugby Game of Football, was placed in position in January last, by John Parnell and Sons (O.Rs.) who carried out the work in the most satisfactory manner, and free of all cost to the Society. The tablet, which is of red Peterhead granite, with lettering in gold, is fixed in

Former Rugby School student
Ed Anthony as William Webb Ellis.

SUDDENLY WEBB ELLIS BECAME, IN THE POPULAR IMAGINATION, A REBEL IN A GOOD CAUSE.

the Headmaster's garden wall, immediately behind the centre of the School Goal. (*Meteor*, November 15, 1900)

The choice of lettering over a likeness proved fateful, however, as it raised the question of which words to use. As Jenny Macrory writes in her book on *The Birth of Rugby Football*:

The big mistake made by the Old Rugbeian Society was in the wording of the plaque which they decided to erect on the Close in 1900 to pronounce their understandable pride in the game which had developed there. They intended to celebrate the game, but instead created a myth. As soon as they decided to mention Webb Ellis they were in trouble. He was more anti-hero than hero, and the only adjective they had to describe him was 'unfair'. In a piece of inspired rhetoric he was instead recorded as having shown 'a fine disregard for the rules of the game as played in his day', and his obstinate refusal to comply with custom was translated into a spirited and imaginative defiance of regulation. Suddenly Webb Ellis became, in the popular imagination, a rebel in a good cause. (Macrory, p.35)

Mistake or not, individual and event were now literally set in stone, 1823 fixed as the defining year in this sporting origin myth. And a commemoration was already being contemplated a year ahead of the centenary when, on October 21, 1922, the School Debating Society met in Old Big School to debate the founding event.

The motion, significantly, did not question whether it had happened but whether it should have: 'That this House regrets the action of William Webb Ellis, who first picked up the ball and ran' (*Meteor,* November 22, 1922). It is clear from the false premise (Webb Ellis caught the ball in his arms) that memories needed to be refreshed. And it is worth quoting the *Meteor* report at length because it shows the power of a founding event to generate passionate debate with a flagrant disregard for historical truth. The founder's originality is challenged by citing games in ancient times similar to the one he invented and, contradictorily, by claiming that the game he changed continued after him. The audience is offered specious political analogies (between a rebellious Webb Ellis and an aggressive Germany) and spurious written evidence (Webb Ellis's purported diary). The debate is precisely that mix of fact and fiction, of mock denunciation and affected partisanship, theatrical posturing and deliberate obtuseness, that characterises a cult.

Mr. A.G. Ellinger (F.J.K.) "kicked off" — we feel the metaphor is justified in consideration of the nature of the debate — by drawing a parallel between the deed

under discussion and the German entry into the late War. The only conceivable justification of the act was to found Rugby football, and even so the dangers incurred should have outweighed the intention, but this, as was proved conclusively, he did not. All he did was to introduce the spirit of antagonism between players and referee and thus ruin the game. In fact, the speaker seemed to display doubts as to whether "internationals" would be forthcoming next year to celebrate the centenary of this much abused "exploit." The speech, which was otherwise good, seemed rather to lack logical arrangement. It was answered by Mr. A. MacLehose (S.H.). This was his first appearance in debate and he is undoubtedly a worthy successor to those whose talent forsook us last term. He considered the last speech beside the point. The real issue, he said, was: "Are we or are we not going to uphold Rugby football?" He urged us to beware of his opponent's double-dealing and quoted "true" data concerning Ellis' sentiments from a fictitious diary. He ended with the wise assertion that, were the motion passed, the centenary celebrations would not occur at all. This Ciceronian declamation was undoubtedly the speech of the evening, especially in the ears of a somewhat prejudiced audience. Mr. R. M. A. Hankey (F.W.O.), anxious to bring home that fact of which his partner had already convinced us — that the performance which we were discussing did not found Rugby football – sought evidence from the classics of a variety of football in which the ball was handled. "Soccer" continued for quite ten years after 1823 and, therefore, Ellis had no connection with the game we play today. Altogether the speech was rather an echo of Ellinger's and, like most echoes, rather feeble. Mr. A. Ker (S.H.) started us off on the eternal question of the end justifying the means; he seemed to think it did. He appeared entirely to ignore his opponents' proofs and thanked William Webb Ellis for the fact that we were not still playing "Soccer" on the Close. The speech was good on the whole, though the speaker showed signs, probably fallacious, of waning confidence in the middle.
(*Meteor*, November 22, 1922)

If some debaters had 'doubts as to whether internationals would be forthcoming to celebrate the centenary', few others did. The teams invited to play represented all the home nations and the spectators reflected the international spread of the game. *The Times* of October 30, 1923 looked forward to 'the rugby football centenary: a historic match' without any 'regret', indeed the invited guests were no less fortunate than the players themselves as all would be part of 'a memorable and historic scene' that owed its power partly to a work of fiction:

The Centenary of Rugby Football will be celebrated officially on Thursday, November 1, taking the form of a match at Rugby School – the most appropriate of all places. One team has been selected from the players of England and Wales – a notable and intriguing combination. The other team, quite as interesting and formidable in its own way, is composed of the Rugby men of Scotland and Ireland. As for the spectators they will be as fortunate and highly honoured as the thirty players, for they will be

England-Wales Team, Centenary Match 1923.

Scotland-Ireland Team, Centenary Match 1923.

invited as guests of the Headmaster of Rugby and of the Rugby Union. There will be representatives of the Dominions and of foreign countries in which the game is played, survivors of the first international match, representatives of clubs who have been members of the Rugby Union for fifty years, and representatives of the Public School. Here, surely, are the makings of a memorable and historic scene, and who can doubt that among all those privileged individuals will be scattered the unseen representatives of **Tom Brown's Schooldays?** (*Meteor*, October 30, 1923)

The imagined presence of fictional characters shows that the game has now gone beyond Bloxam's historical aim of 'connecting the past with the present' and become embedded in the timeless present of myth. The exact antiquarian would surely not have compared Webb Ellis to Admiral Nelson, despite their common fondness for unconventional tactics, but *The Times* clearly felt that both were now part of the national legend:

The whole atmosphere, in fact, is certain to be one of the Past rather than the Present. To start with, the honouring of the greatest of all Real Man's games will involve a visit to the spot in Rugby Close where a tablet was erected some years ago in memory of the legendary founder of the splendid idea of Rugby football. Here one will be able to read that William Webb Ellis, 'with a fine disregard for the rules of football... first took the ball in his arms and ran with it'. The singularly apt wording lends something of 'The Nelson touch' to young Ellis's exploit and, fortunately, there is documentary evidence to prove that Rugby School really was the home of the game to which it has given a name; and, further, that it was indeed in 1823 that the game more or less suddenly reached a decisive stage in its evolution. (*Meteor*, October 30, 1923)

In its report, *The Meteor* surpasses *The Times* in its play with analogies aimed at celebrating this 'birthday of historical forces'. This match, it claims, marks the first birthday of a baby whose birth is comparable to that of Christianity. After all, both founders were unorthodox, both annoyed their contemporaries, both would be rejected if they returned. Webb Ellis here becomes the hero of a religious myth:

Twenty-three years ago, Christianity was celebrating her nineteenth birthday, but few remembered to send their presents. Let us hope they will not forget her twenty first. On All Saints' Day, we celebrated the Centenary of Rugby Football. It was the first centenary and had all the charm and triumph of a baby's first birthday. That first dangerous year is over; the proud parents and godparents cluster round; what a fine baby he is, to be sure! (...) We do not know much of the effect which Ellis' action had upon his contemporaries, and, to judge by the little that we do know, it must have had a remarkably small effect. Perhaps they thought it a good idea, or perhaps amusing; more probably they were extremely annoyed. Tom Hughes was certainly

THE CENTENARY C

ENGLAND AND WALES :—S. Baker (Newport) full back ; T. Johnson (Cardiff), H. M. Locke (Birkenhead Park), R. A. Cornish (Cardiff), Rowe Harding (Swansea), three-quarter backs W. J. A. Davies (United Services), C. A. Kershaw (United Services), half backs ; W. W. Wakefield (Leicester), T. Voyce (Gloucester), G. S. Conway (Rugby), W. E. G. Luddington (Devonport Services), T. Roberts (Newport), A. Baker (Neath), S. Morris (Cross Keys), G. Michael (Swansea). forwards.

An interested spectator, the Headmaster.

England and Wales attacking.

The Headmaster's Guest

A powerful kick up the field.

A stoppage for repairs.

A Composite

RUGBY FOOTBALL.

Special "Rugby Advertiser" Photographs.

The two Touch Judges, Mr. C. F. Rutherford (France) and Mr. R. J. Warren (Ireland).

SCOTLAND AND IRELAND:—W. E. Crawford (Lansdowne), full back; D. J. Cussen (Dublin University), A. L. Gracie (Harlequins), G. V. Stevenson (Queen's University, Belfast), H. W. Stevenson (United Services, Portsmouth), three-quarter backs; W. E. Bryce (Selkirk), J. B. Dykes (West of Scotland), half backs; J. H. Bannerman (Glasgow High School), J. C. E. Buchanan (Stewartonians), L. R. Stuart (Glasgow High School), D. S. Davies (Hawick), J. R. Lawrie (Melrose), W. P. Collopy (Bective Rangers), T. A. McClelland (Queen's University, Belfast), R. T. Crichton (Dublin University), forwards.

hool House Garden.

An exciting incident.

of the Playe

A "scrum" near the touch-line.

A race for the ball.

distressed by its results. Ellis himself cannot have realised the magnitude of his deed. (...) We hope that in the future, if another William Webb Ellis comes to bless the world of football, his enterprise, too, will be rewarded and turned to account; although we have a slinking fear that the tradition of the first innovator would oppose rather than encourage one who followed his spirit rather than his action. (*Meteor*, 9 November 1923)

The editor's wistful tone, regretting the perennial triumph of tradition over renewal, puts the centenary match into a long historical perspective equating Webb Ellis with the founder of Christianity. Balancing this, we find in the same edition a detailed account of the game itself, written by a sports commentator expert in the emotions of a crowd as well as the merits of the players, the importance of every position, the dynamics of a match, its high points and surprises. This writer, in other words, is not a mythmaker but a storyteller, and his story would be worth quoting in full if space allowed. Suffice it here to quote his conclusion:

When all is said and done, there was next to nothing to choose between the two sides, and not much more between the individuals. We are more than grateful to them for giving us a match so ideally suited to the circumstances, although it would have filled the cup of my own enjoyment to see a goal kick taken as a result of that last rush, with a chance of equalising. (*Meteor*, 9 November 1923)

This official account of the match is clearly written by someone competent to assess the men on the field of play. The student magazine, by contrast, putting the match in the context of the whole day's celebrations, strikes a reverential note with the accent less on the deeds of men than on the presence of gods. The writer recalls 'a never-to-be-missed opportunity of discussing matters of interest with an avowed hero', of feeling 'flattered by being asked polite questions by men, whose positions on Select Committees make them the ruling Gods of a little world'. Nor did he merely walk with Gods that day, it seemed the day was made by them: 'The occasion was ideal. There is nothing that increases the atmosphere of shaded antiquity as does a bright sun and a gentle breeze, which the fates of the Gods decreed to us.' Here surely speaks a classical scholar. And having recognised the Gods, he is quick to draw the implication for Man: 'The whole occasion interested our self-respect, our traditions, and our expectations. It was a tribute which set us thinking and made us realise that we are become a name. And to me it brought this thought – that we owe a duty both to and beyond those, who have won us this honour.' ('The Centenary Match', in *The Rugbeian*, 23 November 1923, pp.76-7) Participation in a myth brings moral obligations as well as metaphysical glamour. The centenary match clearly had divine blessing, but it was also a salutary reminder of Rugby's debt to the past and responsibility to the future.

World Cup Relay launch on The Close in 1991.

FROM RELIGIOUS MYTH TO HISTORICAL RE-ENACTMENT

It is therefore striking that the year 1823 is scarcely mentioned in the School record for the next 69 years, and on the 150th anniversary in 1973 not at all. For the next celebration of note we have to wait for the Rugby World Cup in 1991. Again it was written up by a Classicist (this time a member of staff) and again 'miraculous' fine weather 'answering all our prayers' proved that the Gods were smiling on the day. This time, however, it is not a competitive match played by professionals according to modern rules, but an imagined re-enactment of the founding event performed by young Rugbeians. The game is framed, moreover, by an imaginative recreation of school life at the time, complete with fags and carriages and characters in contemporary dress. In the late 20th century, the accent is not so much on playing a real match to commemorate a legendary event as on staging what that legendary event might really have looked like.

World Cup Relay Launch (on the Close) Speech Day, June 29th 1991.
Planning for this had been going on for over a year. It was originally Ray Williams, the Tournament Director, who conceived the idea of a message relay, like the Olympic torch, from Rugby to Twickenham. His ideas married with those of the school's own World Cup committee who had been toying with the possibility of some kind of pageant. Thus was born a fruitful partnership, which continued with the appointment of Tony Ball Associates as the production company. The script-writer they selected,

Jack Crawshaw, is by a happy coincidence a childhood friend of Elizabeth Mavor [wife of the then Head Master, Michael Mavor]. One of the most rewarding aspects of the whole operation was the high degree of harmony established between the school and the production team: rarely can a project of this kind have produced so little aggravation. Similarly the co-operation within the School from all quarters was remarkable: all seemed to recognize that this was a unique opportunity for the School to show its best face. And so it was proved.

Speech Day dawned bright and warm, answering all our prayers. After the previous ten days when we had had to cancel several rehearsals because of monsoon conditions this was little short of miraculous. That afternoon something over 3000 people crammed the three sides of the pitch set in front of School House at right angles to Bigside. The grandstand and the covered standing area behind the Dunchurch Road goal were gaily decked in green and white, and the stunted goalposts, familiar from old pictures, gave an authentically ancient touch. Meanwhile the cast (110 members of the school, 4 masters, 1 GAP student and 1 O.R.) were garbing themselves in period costume specially made for the occasion. The scene of 1823 was set by a number of small boys emerging from the school to play – cricket, bat-fives, wrestling, conkers, glove football – all authentic pastimes of the period. Then through the Queen's gates an open landau bringing a new boy and his mother drove up to School House. While they were dismounting another carriage appeared, this time drawn by three fags pulling their whip-toting fagmaster on his afternoon drive (again an authentic touch of the period, but one now consigned, as the Head Master said in his speech of welcome, to the new Museum).

The Full Cast – Players and Guests First Steps of the Relay. This was the sign for the arrival of the players who engaged in a puntabout, as the commentary, spoken with humour and passion by Cliff Morgan, described the rules, such as they were, of the time. Teams were picked by the Head of Side, the fags dispatched to keep the goals, and the game began. At that period it was very much kick and rush with the ball only being caught in order to kick it. Before long though, "Webb Ellis" resplendent in yellow waistcoat, had caught the ball and run with it, finally dropping a goal before being mobbed by his protesting fellows. An interesting sidelight here is that Alex Crombie, who played Webb Ellis, has since discovered that his great-great-grand father of the same name was responsible for the introduction of Rugby Football to Scotland in the early 1850s. In organising this scene and the subsequent one of 1845 we were seeking to make the point that the game of Rugby Football is a creation of boys, doing their own thing for fun. Initially the game was governed solely by convention, and rules only became necessary when the game began to spread. Even then they only sought to clarify disputed points. So in creating a re-enactment we were forced to proceed very much by trial and error (as the Lawmakers do even now) seeing what worked in practice, and using analogies from soccer, American football and Australian rules. We

can make no claim to have been precisely accurate, since no one knows precisely how the game was played. IMMB (*Meteor* 1992)

If the re-enactment was created 'very much by trial and error', the script, once written, was strictly adhered to with a fine disregard for actual events. 'Andrew Blyth (Michell, 1989-94), perhaps the best player the School had produced in the last fifteen years, was required by the script to drop a goal, but on the day itself the ball narrowly passed outside the post. "A great goal," shouted Cliff Morgan without hesitation! Ian Barlow, Staff 1959-97' (*with a fine disregard…*, p.107).

Despite worries about historical accuracy, or perhaps because myth removes the need for it, re-enactments then became increasingly popular and on diverse pretexts. Admittedly, there was no re-enactment for the Rugby World Cup in 2003, but there was much mention of the founding event, often with a fine disregard for the central facts. 'R is for Rugby School', enthused the *Guardian*, 'which is where it all began in 1823, when William Webb Ellis, a precocious schoolboy bored with the antics of the overpaid professionals … first picked up the ball and made a dash for the goal-line.' Where the *Guardian* saw the revenge of a boy on the rich and powerful, the *Daily Mail* already sensed a quasi-military triumph: the appearance on The Close of Martin Johnson 'and his all-conquering team… with the Webb Ellis trophy glittering in the sun within kicking distance of the plaque… would do nicely.' On the day of the final between England and Australia, *The Australian* caught the English mood, observing that 'England winning tonight's final will be tantamount to a religious experience. Or a miracle, depending on where you stand.' The School newsletter hoped fervently for the making of history, 'if, as we hope, William Webb Ellis revisits Rugby in January in the golden form of the trophy named after him' (News from Rugby School, Advent 2003). In short, whatever their national or political agenda, the myth could be turned to account by everyone.

As it turned out, NFRS was a little impatient, but England's victorious World Cup squad did visit Rugby to receive the Freedom of the Borough in the following May. Clive Woodward unveiled a plaque at the Webb Ellis statue and gave a speech in the Temple Speech Room invoking the shade of 'William Webb Ellis, wherever you are.' His spirit could clearly now be everywhere and anywhere.

The very next day, as if on cue, ITV cameras arrived to film *Tom Brown's Schooldays* and the *Times Educational Supplement* put the legendary headmaster Dr Arnold, played

ENGLAND WINNING TONIGHT'S FINAL WILL BE TANTAMOUNT TO A RELIGIOUS EXPERIENCE. OR A MIRACLE, DEPENDING ON WHERE YOU STAND.

Stephen Fry as Dr Arnold.

by Stephen Fry, on its front page: 'A stern schoolmaster in mortar board and gown strolls leisurely through school grounds, peering at gambolling boys over half-moon spectacles.' Sternly strolling, he nevertheless 'stood on the touch line and looked pleased when the rugby match of 1837 was recreated on the Close and top hats were thrown into the air as a boy touched down between the rough-hewn posts by the Green Pavilion'. Here the Arnold legend and the Webb Ellis legend fuse in a way that must have gripped the imagination of the 200 pupils (mostly boys) who volunteered as extras and, we are told, 'looked unusually smart in waistcoat and tails'. The School News remarks on the potentially confusing realities in play, echoing the *TES*: 'Press photographers snapped actors between takes with earphones in their ears and iPads in their laps. Media Studies groups filmed the filming. The *TES* relished the irony of a boarding school, an artificial world to some, letting the real world of television in to produce high artifice. But the extras' experience was real enough. Some admitted to emoting in the funeral scene. Others had wearied of singing *Jerusalem* "over and over again – in tight trousers". All now knew how much rehearsing – and even more waiting – goes into one minute of film.' (NFRS Summer 2004). Bloxam could not have imagined 'connecting the past with the present' in this way, but there could surely be no better education in the complex relations between reality and myth than this first-hand experience of the waiting and repetition required by art.

While the film of *Tom Brown's Schooldays* required a historical match looking like one played during Arnold's time, the bicentenary of Webb Ellis's birth (November 24, 2006) was celebrated by a real match played by boys roughly the age Webb Ellis would have been in 1823. Shortly after his birthday, Webb Ellis and Rugby School were the inaugural inductees into the International Rugby Board Hall of Fame, whose purpose, IRB Chairman Dr Syd Millar said at the awards ceremony in Glasgow, was 'to recognise the proud history and traditions of the game, including its origins'. Accepting the award on behalf of the School and its most famous pupil, the Head Master recalled Webb Ellis's feat in 1823. He said it was the system at Rugby…

'…maintained by visionary Headmasters such as Dr Arnold who gave ownership of the game to the boys without interference from masters, a revolutionary boarding house structure promoting competition and identity, two half-days a week encouraging physical activity, and large playing fields – the Close – enabling up to 300 boys to take part, that had combined to make this possible. Ultimately it was the boys who created the game. It was thus fitting for the new inductees to be capped with a blue and gold velvet tasselled cap modelled on those still worn by members of the XV today.'

The founding hero was thus identified with his countless anonymous heirs and the XV consecrated the bond on the last day of term with a celebration match against the Cadets from Menton, the Mediterranean French town where Webb Ellis died and was buried. 'The match was supported enthusiastically by the School chanting from the touchline, filmed by Channel Four Wales and Total Rugby for Sky, and attended by ex-internationals Gareth Davies and Micky Steele-Bodger, who unveiled a new commemorative plaque at half-time.' (NFRS Advent 2006). The man may have died in Menton, but his spirit was very much alive at his bicentenary, both on The Close and on television.

As recent commemorations had alternated between re-enactments and real matches, it was perhaps predictable that the next celebration would combine them both. Just three years later, in 2009, ***'As a preview to the Six Nations Championship, Blue Peter cameras came to the Close to film some 40 E Block boys playing Rugby Football. The point of the film was to show how the game has changed over the past 150 years by dividing the game into two halves: The two presenters Andy and Helen each coached a team playing the first half in modern dress and by the rules of today, the second half in period costume and according to the somewhat looser laws of the time, which the boys seemed particularly to enjoy. Both games were officiated by RFU professional referee Greg Garner. The BBC crew, commenting on the boys' enthusiasm, politeness and good manners, said they were "a delight to work with". For the boys, who had narrowly missed out on a place in the quarter finals of the Daily Mail Cup the week before, it was a tonic, especially as Blue Peter badges were awarded to all involved.'*** (NFRS Spring 2009)

“DON'T WORRY JONNY, IT WILL NEVER CATCH ON.”

Prince Harry and Jonny Wilkinson during filming at Rugby School, 2015.

The Olympic flame comes to Rugby School, 2012.

Another three years later, in July 2012, the Olympic Torch visited The Close on its nationwide tour and was welcomed by a crowd of over 2000 pupils, parents, staff, local schoolchildren and Olympic gold medallist, Edwin Moses. Not an obvious cue for Webb Ellis, we might think. It is therefore striking that ***'The event began with the re-enactment of a nineteenth-century game of rugby football, with 35 boys kitted out in old style rugby kit battling out a match against the backdrop of School House and some old-style wooden rugby posts – much to the delight of the watching crowds! The game was halted on the arrival of the torch, which made its way onto the Close and through a tunnel of rugby players who waved their velvet caps in the air as it passed. After a brief pause for a photo with Edwin Moses and other dignitaries, the torch made its way along the touchline to exit the Close by Queen's Gates. AH' (Meteor 2012). The Olympics were a mere interlude, it seems, in the ongoing commemoration of Rugby football. And this re-enactment was clearly at pains to be as realistic as possible: 'Even a "death cart" (the original is in the School Museum) was wheeled out to collect the token "injured" player.'*** (NFRS Advent 2012)

FROM HISTORICAL RE-ENACTMENT TO LIVING INCARNATION

The most recent opportunity to re-enact 1823 was when the Rugby World Cup came to England in 2015. This time, thanks to modern technology, it was part of a multi-media multi-location spectacular which achieved the ultimate translation of the Webb Ellis myth into telereality. As *The Meteor* reported of 'the school behind the game':

450 MILLION VIEWERS WATCH RUGBY SCHOOL STAR IN WORLD CUP OPENING CEREMONY. Rugby School reached across the globe when it featured

The "Death Cart".

in the Rugby World Cup Opening Ceremony at Twickenham on Friday night (18 September) watched by 450 million people across the globe. The top independent school and birthplace of the game soared into the spotlight with film footage capturing its historic buildings and the School's main playing field – The Close – where William Webb Ellis, a schoolboy in 1823, famously broke the rules of football when he caught the ball and ran with it. Rugby School pupil, Ed Anthony, 14, played a starring role in the ceremony as Webb Ellis, both in the film and live at the stadium – scaling a tower of rugby players to seize the ultimate prize of the Rugby World Cup, the Webb Ellis Trophy.

The secret days of filming in June saw a state-of-the art drone, equipped with a camera, flying through the School's ancient cloisters and quads to capture a re-enactment of the moment when the game of rugby as we now know it began. Historic school buildings were converted into wardrobe and make-up studios, while classrooms were commandeered for costume racks and catering. Old Big School, the very first classroom, became an atmospheric base for the hi-tech drone and latest filming equipment. Pupils from the School's youngest rugby team were selected for the re-enactment game alongside the Head Boy role, which was played by professional actor, Asa Butterfield, star of Hugo and The Boy in the Striped Pyjamas. Rugby School teachers and pupils, including the Head Boy, Rory Farquharson, were among the 140 extras involved in the filming. They were joined by a stellar cast of rugby greats including Sir Clive Woodward, Jason Leonard, Sir Ian McGeeghan, Maggie Alphonsi, Serge Betsen and Gonzalo Camacho. Stephen Brown, England Rugby 2015 Managing Director, said: "The School's history and

England hero Jonny Wilkinson and Prince Harry watch Rugby School student Ed Anthony in character as William Webb Ellis in 2015, the year England hosted the Rugby World Cup.

heritage with the game meant it was the perfect location to bring the story of Rugby alive for fans across the world."

Ed, who auditioned for the role of Webb Ellis along with some of his rugby-playing peers, said he could never have envisaged he would be offered such an amazing opportunity. "It's been an incredible time being at Rugby School during the World Cup year, but to get this role as well was quite something," he said. "Being selected to play the role of William Webb Ellis has just been fantastic – a real dream come true. I auditioned for the part, never believing I'd get it. But I do love playing rugby!" (*Meteor* 2015, p.7)

Thus, the founding event was again re-enacted on The Close and again a current Rugbeian selected to play Webb Ellis. But this time the performance on The Close was not live theatre but part of a pre-recorded film which led into the real-time ceremony

THIS TIME THE PERFORMANCE ON THE CLOSE WAS NOT LIVE THEATRE BUT PART OF A PRE-RECORDED FILM WHICH LED INTO THE REAL-TIME CEREMONY AT TWICKENHAM WHERE THE BOY IN THE FILM REALLY APPEARED.

at Twickenham where the boy in the film really appeared. This was not only a way of 'connecting the past with the present' Bloxam could not have imagined, but of connecting Rugby with the world, legend with reality, on a global scale. 1823 was no longer merely set in a tablet of stone, or merely talked about by the Debating Society, or merely re-enacted for a 3000-strong local audience: it was now planted in the imagination of television viewers all around the world. Who could doubt the Rugby story now that the boy running with the ball had been seen leaving The Close one moment and entering the stadium at Twickenham the next, there to seize the trophy bearing his name? The identification of founding hero and ultimate prize was complete. And in case anyone doubted, not one but two doubters were wittily incorporated into the story, duly to be refuted by events:

But the best part of Ed's experience was yet to come with the arrival, a week later, of HRH Prince Harry and Jonny Wilkinson, who had agreed to play the part of 19th century school gardeners watching while 'Webb Ellis' made rugby history. He spent a morning with Prince Harry and Jonny Wilkinson who, in period dress, were instructed to look on sceptically while 'Webb Ellis', with a fine disregard for the rules of the game, charged past with the ball under his arm. 'It'll never catch on,' they agree. (*Meteor* 2015, p.7)

Just as the school gardeners fail to recognise Webb Ellis, he runs past them – real royalty and Rugby royalty – without recognising them. Who will recognise the truth then, we ask? What does true royalty look like? We are answered seconds later when the boy appears to the multitudes at Twickenham and ascends the human pyramid in an apotheosis of lone rebellion made good.

Yet again, we may say, such divinising spectacle is all very impressive, but it loses sight of the man. What was it like to be Webb Ellis? Fortunately, we have Ed Anthony's first-hand account in 'My experience as William Webb Ellis'. And his account breathes precisely that mixture of pride and humility we would expect of one chosen above all others to reincarnate the founder and to represent so many:

Playing the part of William Webb Ellis feels as though it has been the single greatest experience of my life so far, and it truly has. As a pupil of Rugby School, William Webb Ellis is a prestigious person to play as he pioneered the game which was named after the School. It was a great honour to stand up in front of the world and lift up the Cup that bears the famous name of Webb Ellis, representing my School, the country, rugby (the sport) but most of all my friends and family eagerly watching at home and fully supporting me. Standing on top of the huge pyramid of people with the eyes of the world gazing upon me, it brought new meaning to the phrase, "standing on top of the world". (*Meteor* 2015, p.8)

Then, as Ed tells the story, it is remarkable how many elements of his experience match the tropes of religious myth or the archetypal 'hero's journey', as described by mythologists like Joseph Campbell, from departure and separation through initiation to return.

The call to adventure comes on an ordinary day and is both promising and troubling, as double-edged as the adventure to come: 'My journey first began on a sunny April afternoon in the Lent term. I and eleven others were ushered up to the Sports Centre Café, where we were met by a beaming Mr Brown and two other intimidating strangers.' The meaning of the encounter is obscure, but its importance is clear: 'Obviously, at the time I had absolutely no idea what the role would entail, but nevertheless I felt the scary suspicion that it was going to be something big.' Not long after, following auditions and a 'sunny cricket tour to Dubai', his father tells him he is the chosen one: 'Two nights after the tour my dad asked me for a word in my room and sat me down on my bed. I was eager to know what he had to say. It was rare and out of the ordinary to have a serious chat on my bed. The first thing he said was that I had been chosen but that there was no pressure on me to do it.' Once chosen, however, the hero does not hesitate and promptly crosses the threshold: 'My answer danced on the tip of my tongue before I could finally force the words out from behind the surprise. I spluttered out a yes.'

Despite being chosen above all others, or perhaps because of this, the hero is beset by fears of inadequacy and rejection: 'I felt that [my first day of filming] had gone fine, but I was scared that I hadn't quite been what they wanted. This fear was what haunted me most of the time, the fear of being rejected and replaced.' A mentor is at hand in the form of 'the film company's rep', but it seems initiation requires separation from the familiar world just when he needs it most: 'She explained to me that my next bout of filming was to happen two days from now but without the comfort of my friends nearby.' Not only must he go on without his friends, he must enter the company of superior beings: 'This time, she said, I would be in "higher company". I immediately pressed her for more information and she finally gave in and told me that I would be having a shot with not only Jonny Wilkinson but also Prince Harry!'

The hero is naturally thrilled to meet royalty, just as the student writer of 1923 was to meet the 'ruling Gods of a little world'. But Ed's reaction to them is ambivalent: 'Meeting Jonny was scary but he is a really nice guy. The one thing I struggled to get over was that he was smaller than me. I never formally met Prince Harry but he had small chats with me between takes. He was surprisingly normal and a really nice fellow but at the time I was too overwhelmed to enjoy it as much as I could. After all, it's not every day you get to meet him.' The hero's meeting with these human gods is ironically as disabling as it was desired, perhaps because he has not yet grasped their dual nature. For he is also struggling with his own dual status, as he must reconcile

BEFORE I COULD BLINK THE NEW SCHOOL YEAR HAD STARTED AND I WAS JUST ANOTHER SCHOOLBOY AGAIN.

knowledge of his special calling with the return to everyday life: *'For the next six months or so I had to just forget about the world cup and focus on getting on with normal life, which wasn't easy.' He must go to London during the summer holidays 'to learn how to climb the huge human pyramid and grab the Cup', but 'Before I could blink the new school year had started and I was just another schoolboy again.' The hero must somehow square his divine calling with mundane obligations, and this is the more difficult as he must keep his mission secret until his time is come: 'One of my toughest challenges was keeping quiet about what the ceremony consisted of and my role in it.'*

These challenges pale, however, before the final ordeal and the ultimate reward:

On the day of the performance I was nervous, scared yet excited. As the coach approached London and the striking stadium loomed into view, my nerves worsened dramatically. For the entirety of the morning I couldn't sit still, my twitchiness was only broken when I got to lift the real Cup without gloves for the first time above my head prior to the ceremony. Lifting the Cup for the real thing would mark me as only the second Englishman to lift it officially, after Martin Johnson. As the day progressed and the fans started to enter the stadium and fill up the seats, my excitement rose a level and my nervous nausea quickly quelled the excited feeling. Evening descended and I was led into the tunnel. I could feel the waves of noise centred around the pitch and to my astonishment my nerves started to subside and I felt more at ease. Suddenly my cue was being blared through my earpiece and I was steadily jogging onto the pitch. The next five minutes felt like twenty seconds and the noise of the crowd was swept up with adrenaline. All I could focus on was the gleaming Cup and the pounding of my heartbeat between my ears. I started to climb. I grasped the two golden handles of the Cup and lifted the most valuable object ever placed in my hands above my head to the roar of the crowd.

Previously the hero was afflicted by a double life; now he has only to obey the voice inside his head to exist entirely in the present moment. Time is compressed: 'The next five minutes felt like twenty seconds.' Space is concentrated in a single object: 'All I could focus on was the gleaming Cup', 'the most valuable object ever placed in my hands'. Far from being disabled by the gods, the hero is now (briefly) a god himself, clutching the Holy Grail, the centre of a universe whose circumference is the roaring crowd and, beyond them, 450 million television viewers.

After his triumph the hero must return to everyday life, which is both a relief and an anti-climax: ***'Returning to school was accompanied by the greatest feeling of relief I think I've ever felt. Of course I was going to miss being in the limelight and I was bound to get used to the Webb Ellis jokes, along with catching up all the work I'd missed, but being Webb Ellis made me feel the proudest I'd ever felt. Can life get any better than that?' Edward Anthony (SH)*** (*Meteor* 2015, p.8)

Life cannot get any better, of course, because the distance between man and god, earlier so disabling, has been abolished by apotheosis. At the start, Ed proudly admitted that 'William Webb Ellis is a prestigious person to *play*'; by the end he feels proudest when '*being* Webb Ellis' (my italics). For a moment at least, a player of the game has become one with the founder of the game. As the mythologist puts it: 'the man or woman who can honestly say that he or she has lived the role … *is* something in the full sense of the verb *to be*.' (Campbell, p.383-4). In a sort of mystic union, the hero has overcome the dualities that once afflicted him and found his true self.

Thus, while the historian of 1885 thought of himself 'as one connecting the past with the present', the hero of 2015 actually embodied the past in the present. The remembered rebel of 1823, who became the 'legendary founder' of 1923, was now a living incarnation of the archetypal hero. In him, distant memory was translated into present reality, sporting myth into an iconic young man recognisable to a global audience. The world of Rugby was now ready for 2023, when William Webb Ellis will surely come again in glory.

World Cup opening ceremony 2015.

GILBERT

PLAYING THE GAME

LAWRENCE DALLAGLIO

PICKING UP A BALL AND FINDING THE RUGBY FAMILY

As a young boy I loved playing sport, but it was really soccer. But the dad of the boy next door one day took me to Staines RFC when I was seven or eight. I walked in, started playing, and something felt very right. After prep school I attended Ampleforth College where they seemed to only play rugby. They had 27 pitches and despite being a Catholic school the real religion appeared to be rugby.

After I arrived there, I remember phoning my dad and he asked what sport I was playing. I told him rugby and because he is Italian he asked what that was! Later when I came home I went into his study and saw he had bought a book on the laws of rugby union. I told him there weren't really any laws.

For me rugby has been a journey and a metaphor for my life. After I lost my sister in the *Marchioness* disaster in 1989 I was wandering around. Then I joined Wasps and the minute I walked in it felt like a family. I needed a support system at the time. Wasps is not a place or a city like other places, it's all about the people. Wasps became my family. I needed something. Rugby was therapy for all of our family having had our world blown apart shortly before that. I played rugby to honour the memory of my sister so I was driven by a slightly higher purpose. I just loved it, the ultimate team sport.

WORLD CUP GLORY

Later, playing for my country was such an honour. When you pull on that shirt you represent the hopes, dreams and aspirations of millions of people and with that comes huge responsibility.

The path to the 2003 RWC final was again a journey for me. My first cap was against South Africa in 1995 and my last was against them again in 2007. In the period 2000 and 2003 we had Clive Woodward as our coach and an amazing group of players. Looking back on that, it was pretty special.

During this period we played and won against Southern Hemisphere teams 14 times and won 14. We were the number one side in the world, and we felt we were going to win – it was an inner belief, destiny.

I have vivid memories of the final. It was a long journey to the stadium, over an hour, so there was plenty of time for reflection. We were playing the ultimate final, the hosts in their own back yard, our great rival, Australia. We knew we were better than them and they knew that too, but we still had to go out and do it. We conceded first try, but produced a pretty decent first half and should have been out of sight by then.

However, we came out and played the second half and lost it 9-0 which was a disaster really. We were on the wrong side of the ref, but by the time we reached extra time, we had used our subs pretty strategically – Jason Leonard, Lewis Moody and Mike Catt came on, but Australia had already emptied their bench.

During extra time there was still a lot of clarity in everyone's thinking. We were under the posts. They kicked a penalty. We chatted as a group about what next. We kicked long, set up a line-out and then all the lessons we had learned built up to that moment. Getting ourselves into that position. Jonny Wilkinson had already missed three drop-goals in that match, but that was the one to get.

Then we had to deal with kick off. Trevor Woodman, our prop, caught it and then passed it to Mike Catt who put it out. It was a great feeling, a great moment. To be with all those fans.

The best moment was getting back into the changing room afterwards, shutting the door and looking around the room, some people laughing, some crying, a very special place to be. Success on your own is one thing, but there is nothing greater than sharing that success as a group.

We liked to celebrate as well. Marking that moment was special. We eventually got back to the city and being reunited with our families, staff, friends, inner circle, was pretty special. Lots of relief, a big sense. Immense satisfaction.

WEBB ELLIS AND THE GAME

I have always reflected on history and heritage coming from an Italian family – it's all about where you come from. I knew about the Webb Ellis story, how rugby was created and I knew the Rugby World Cup was his trophy.

England did not win the Cup until 2003. In 1997 Clive Woodward got us together in a room and asked us what we wanted to achieve. We said to be the number one side in the world and to bring the cup home, which we were able to do.

I think Webb Ellis today would recognise the fundamentals of the game, although today maybe it's a bit more scientific than artistic. We all owe him a debt. The image of him running with the ball and scoring a try. That's what it's all about.

WHAT I WOULD SAY TO MY YOUNGER SELF IF HE WAS TAKING UP RUGBY TODAY

My mum used to say: "Shoot for the moon and you will be among the stars." I was fortunate in my childhood to have unconditional love and a belief system that you could conquer the world. You don't need much else.

Former England forward 'Lawrence' Lorenzo Bruno Nero Dallaglio OBE was born in August 1972 and was inducted into the World Rugby Hall of Fame in 2016. He appeared 326 times for Wasps, 85 times for England and won three caps with the British and Irish Lions. He is one of a very small number of players to have won both the Rugby World Cup (2003) and Sevens World Cup (1993).

B·S·R·U

18/98 The Bristol Schools Rugby Union was formed.

18/99 Sydney Cricket Ground hosted Australia's first rugby international with the home team beating a British side 13-3.

18/99 Rugby was introduced to Keio University in Japan by Edward Clarke, a graduate from Cambridge.

19/00 France, captained by Frantz Reichel, were crowned the first Olympic Champions at Rugby by beating Frankfurt FC 27-17 and Moseley Wanderers 27-8. Moseley Wanderers, the UK representatives, featured players from Midland clubs.

19/03 Australia and New Zealand competed against each other for the first time, the All Blacks winning 22 points to 3.

19 06
The All Blacks tour of Europe made a profit of 6,000, but the players only received three shillings a day expenses.

19 06
Naval supervisor Jack Davenport became the first black player to play for England.

19 06
South Africa made their first tour of Britain, landing at Southampton.

19 07
Wales beat the touring Springboks 17-0 at Cardiff Arms Park.

19 07
A world-record 52,000 people watched the All Blacks play in Sydney.

“

AMERICAN FOOTBALL IS
RUGBY AFTER A VISIT FROM THE
HEALTH AND SAFETY INSPECTOR.

”

Anon.

THE GLOBAL SPREAD OF RUGBY FOOTBALL

By Guy Steele-Bodger,
former pupil and Admissions Registrar, Rugby School

NORTH POLAR OR ARCTIC OCEAN
ARCTIC OCE
Sea of Okhotsk
KAMTCHATKA SEA
MONGOLIA
MANTCHOORIA
TURKESTAN
INDEPENDENT TARTARY
CHINESE TARTARY
PERSIA
AFGHANISTAN
BELOOCHISTAN
HINDOOSTAN
INDIA
Bay of Bengal
ARABIAN SEA
Sea of Japan
JAPAN ISLANDS
Yellow Sea
PHILIPPINE ISLANDS
Tropic of Cancer
North Equatorial Drift Current
Equatorial Counter Current
South Equatorial Drift Current
Equator
PACIFIC OCEAN
INDIAN OCEAN
North Pacific Drift Current
Sandwich Islands
Marquesas Is.
Arafura Sea
NORTH AUSTRALIA
WESTERN AUSTRALIA
SOUTH AUSTRALIA
Tropic of Capricorn
South Australian Current
TASMANIA
NEW ZEALAND
Antarctic Polar Drift Current
ANTARCTIC OCEAN SOUTH
Line of Barrier Ice
Antarctic Circle
South Victoria Land
Hours after Noon when it is Noon at Greenwich

THE WORLD
The British Possessions throughout the World are coloured Red.
Ocean Currents indicated by the Blue Shading.
NORTH POLAR
POLAR OR ANTARCTIC
GREENLAND
BAFFIN BAY
HUDSON BAY
BRITISH ISLES
ATLANTIC OCEAN
INDIAN OCEAN
HINDOOSTAN
Sahara or Great Desert
Gulf of Guinea
Equator
Tropic of Capricorn
Arctic Circle
Bay of Bengal
SOUTH SHETLAND
Hours after Noon when it is Noon at Greenwich

THE LEAP FROM WARWICKSHIRE TO WORLD PARTICIPATION DID NOT HAPPEN OVERNIGHT. RATHER, THE SPREAD OF THE RUGBY GAME BEGAN IN THE 1820S WHEN VARIOUS 'OLD RUGBEIANS (ORS) TOOK THEIR VERSION OF FOOTBALL WITH THEM AROUND GREAT BRITAIN AND ACROSS THE GLOBE.

Charreada, the national sport of Mexico, comprises nine events for men, one for women, and many horses and cattle. This 16th-century, rodeo-style event is older than the oval ball game but is known to just one nation.

Rugby, a sport for seven, 10, 13 or 15 men or women (but no animals), started with one boy on a field in an English town in the 19th century. It is known today, to paraphrase Churchill, from Port Stanley in the South Atlantic to Nunavut in the Arctic Ocean.

The leap from Warwickshire to world participation did not happen overnight. Rather, the spread of the Rugby game began in the 1820s when various Old Rugbeians (ORs) took their version of football with them around Great Britain and across the globe.

The first overseas country where the game of rugby football was transplanted was Australia and the most quoted first reference to football in Australia is from the *Sydney Monitor* of July 25, 1829 stating that "privates in the barracks are in the habit of amusing themselves with the game of football".

Thomas Wills, an Australian-born OR

While there was no mention of what sort of football game it was or any rules or laws, we should expect that it was pretty rough and a test of bravery. A key figure in the development of football in Australia was Thomas Wills, an Australian-born OR. His idea was for football to be the game played during the winter by cricketers to keep fit, though in his view the ground was too hard in Melbourne to allow the rugby tackle so leading to the evolution of Victorian Football and later Australian Rules football.

In 1865 the Sydney Football Club was formed as the first rugby football club in Sydney, quickly followed by the Sydney University Rugby Union Club which still exists. In 1870 the first inter-school rugby game was played between Newington and King's School. In 1899 players from New South Wales and Queensland combined to form a national team to play a touring team from the British Isles which had been arranged by two English cricketers, Alfred Shaw and Arthur Shrewsbury, in an attempt to recoup losses sustained by an earlier cricket tour to Australia. Four 'test matches' were played in Sydney and Brisbane with the British team winning 3-1. Without an agreed national jersey, the Australian team played in sky blue in Sydney and maroon in Brisbane.

The first test match between Australia and New Zealand was played in 1903 at the Sydney Cricket Ground and won 22-3 by New Zealand. The first Australian representative team to tour overseas went to the UK, Ireland and North America in 1908. The Australian jersey was effectively the NSWRU jersey – blue with the waratah, but with 'Australia' embroidered beneath. NSWRU was the senior Union which would explain why their jersey was used as the national jersey. The disrespectful British press branded them 'the Rabbits' but the players insisted they should be 'Wallabies' and the nickname stuck. They took part in in that year's London Olympic Games and won the gold medal by defeating the only other competing team – Cornwall representing GB. On this tour the Wallabies won 32 of their 38 matches including a 9-3 win over England. The Australian jersey was sky blue with the waratah emblem, then from 1929 they chose a dark green jersey, except when playing South Africa, before adopting the familiar gold jersey from 1962.

In 1947 the Australian Rugby Union was founded and in 1984 the eighth Wallabies completed a Grand Slam tour of GB and Ireland under Andrew Slack's captaincy. In 1991 the Australian team won the second Rugby World Cup held in England and won the Webb Ellis trophy again in the fourth Rugby World Cup in Wales in 1999. Australia hosted the fifth Rugby World Cup in 2003.

Until recently it had been accepted that rugby football in Japan started in 1899 when Edward Bramwell Clarke introduced it to Keio University. However, research by long-time Rugby resident, parent of Rugbeians and general Japanophile, Mike Galbraith led to a different story. He found evidence in the *Japan Times* in 1866 of rugby being played and of a meeting being held to found the Yokohama Football Club. Officials were elected and a committee set to work to determine the rules for the football to be played by the soldiers of the 20th Regiment's 2nd battalion stationed at Yokohama in 1864 to protect the foreign community following assaults on British citizens in 1862. Many of the young officers had been educated at rugby football playing public schools in Britain. In 1868 Rugbeian George Hamilton arrived in Yokohama and was described as captain of the Yokohama rugby team. From 1870 he was joined by James Fraser, another Rugbeian.

British sailors staging a game in Yokohama, 1874

Later, from 1899 students at Keio University were introduced to the game by Professor Edward Bramwell Clarke and Ginnosuke Tanaka, but Japanese rugby really started to grow from the 1920s. Clarke taught English and coached rugby union at Keio from 1899 to 1910 after which a leg injury forced him to give up playing. Clarke said that he wanted to give his students something constructive to do. In 1901, Keio University played Yokohama Foreigners losing 35-5. Professor Clarke played in this game, taking the conversion after a student called Shiyoda scored a try. From Keio, Japanese rugby spread to the other universities of Japan, and to this day the private universities remain a stronghold of the Japanese game. Doshisha and Waseda played their first inter-university game in 1923. The match between Keio and Waseda, a long-running rivalry between two of Tokyo's most prominent universities, has been played annually since 1924.

The Japanese Rugby Football Union was founded in 1926. Oxford University toured Japan in 1952 and 1956 and Cambridge University in 1953. In 1959, a combined Oxbridge side toured the country. In 1971 England toured Japan. The Japanese national team play in a red and white hooped jersey with a sakura, or cherry blossom emblem. They are known as the Cherry Blossoms, Sakura, or recently, the Brave Blossoms. The Japanese lost by just 3-6 to England in Tokyo on September 29, 1971 in the RFU's centenary year. The first tour by Japan of Great Britain was in 1973.

At the 2015 Rugby World Cup, Japan beat South Africa 34–32 in their opening Pool B match, one of the biggest shocks in international rugby history. In the 2019 World Cup, hosted by Japan, the Cherry Blossoms beat Russia 30-10, Ireland 19-12, Samoa 38-19 and Scotland 28-21 in their pool matches to become the first Asian nation to top their group at a Rugby World Cup and to progress to the knockout stages. Japan played South Africa, the eventual tournament winners, in the quarter finals, losing 26-3.

The first recorded football match in South Africa took place in 1862 between the Army and the Civil Service. It was organised by George Ogilvie, headmaster of Bishop's College, and played to Winchester College rules. By about 1875 rugby football was being played in the Cape colony and was made more popular by the

AT THE 2015 RUGBY WORLD CUP, JAPAN BEAT SOUTH AFRICA 34–32 IN THEIR OPENING POOL B MATCH, ONE OF THE BIGGEST SHOCKS IN INTERNATIONAL RUGBY HISTORY. IN THE 2019 WORLD CUP, HOSTED BY JAPAN, THE CHERRY BLOSSOMS BEAT RUSSIA 30-10, IRELAND 19-12, SAMOA 38-19 AND SCOTLAND 28-21 IN THEIR POOL MATCHES.

Japan beat South Africa 34–32 in their opening Pool B match in the 2015 Rugby World Cup, one of the biggest shocks in international rugby history.

arrival in Cape Town of William Milton in 1878. Milton had played rugby football for England in 1874-5 and was an important promoter of the Rugby code, also representing South Africa at cricket.

In 1891 the first British touring team arrived in the Cape winning all 19 matches. A second British party toured in 1903, this time winning 11 and losing 8 matches. Until the last match of this series the South African team played in white jerseys or the colours of the host club and had no badge. For the third test, however, it was suggested that they should adopt a permanent jersey and, given that all that was to hand was a supply of dark green jerseys, the colours of the Old Diocesans' club, they played in these and since then have stuck with this colour.

In 1906 the first South African tour to Great Britain and Ireland was organised. The team's colours were myrtle green with a gold collar and the emblem on the jersey was a springbok, a small African antelope. Led by captain Paul Roos, they told the press that they wished to be known as the Springboks. This team played 28 matches and won 25, defeating Ireland and Wales, drawing with England and losing only to Scotland in the four test matches played.

Although the springbok was adopted briefly by the first coloured national rugby team in 1939, and by their first black counterparts in 1950, it came to be regarded as associated with segregation and even apartheid itself. The first rugby Springboks refused to play against a Devon side that included Jimmy Peters, the first black player to play for England.

Post-apartheid the springbok continues to represent all of rugby in South Africa.

As a result of political pressure, from 1992 the national rugby jersey featured a king protea alongside the springbok. Pressure to replace the springbok as the emblem of the national rugby team came to a head in 1994, but because of Nelson Mandela's direct intervention (Mandela himself was a devoted fan of the Springbok rugby team), it was decided not to do away with the springbok emblem but to re-appropriate it. After the national team won the 1995 Rugby World Cup it was said that 'The Springboks play for all of us'.

South African national teams were consistently strong throughout the 20th century, regularly defeating the Home Nations and competing strongly with New Zealand. South Africa's return from the exile imposed in response to apartheid came in the 1990s and they hosted and won the 1995 RWC, winning again in France in 2007 and Japan in 2019.

Rugby football was introduced to New Zealand by Charles Monro, son of Edinburgh-born Sir David Monro, Speaker of the New Zealand House of Representatives. Charles had played rugby while studying at Christ's College Finchley in London. On his return to New Zealand he suggested a game be played between Nelson College, his old school, and Nelson Football Club, of which he was a member. Coincidentally, the Rev FC Simmons, an alumnus of Rugby School, was the headmaster of Nelson College at the time (as were his two predecessors) so one imagines he was intrigued.

RUGBY FOOTBALL WAS INTRODUCED TO NEW ZEALAND BY CHARLES MONRO, SON OF EDINBURGH-BORN SIR DAVID MONRO, SPEAKER OF THE NEW ZEALAND HOUSE OF REPRESENTATIVES.

Following the 1868 rules, and playing with the new Gilbert oval ball, the match took place on May 14, 1870. The two captains agreed to have 18 players, made up of three half-backs, two fullbacks, three three-quarters and ten forwards. A crowd of 200 (including 'a fair sprinkling of women') gathered at the Botanics ground to watch.

The College team ('the Gown') wore tight striped shirts and blue caps, while the Football Club men ('the Town') – inexplicably wore their own street clothes. However, they won the game with a 2-0 score.

Both local newspapers (*The Colonist* and the Nelson *Examiner*) excitedly reported the game:

'Almost as soon as the ball is amongst the Town players, the College have followed up, when a kick sends it over their heads again, and then it is seen in one place, and then another, the whole field in pursuit. Now some player runs with it, and a general scrimmage ensues; it is all shove, pull, rush and roll in a confused mass till "Down!" is cried and away the ball goes again ...'

Nelson Botanical Gardens where the first rugby match in New Zealand was played, 1870.

The first recorded and known game of Rugby played in the land of the long white cloud happened on a clear day on May 14th, 1870. Nelson Football Club and Nelson College played the first game.

The College vs Town by Paul Wilding. Collection Nelson College, New Zealand.

By the mid-1870s rugby union was being played across the two islands of New Zealand (with Charles Monro, now recognised as 'the father of New Zealand rugby', refereeing the first game played on North Island). The first NZ touring team travelled to New South Wales in 1884 and won every one of their eight matches. Four years later, the first visit of a NZ team to Britain took place. They were called the Natives as all of them, many of them Maori, had been born in New Zealand. They adopted the silver fern as their national symbol in recognition of the Maori saying- 'When one warrior dies, another arises; when one fern dies, another emerges' representing the replacement of a player being tackled in order to maintain forward momentum – as one goes down another rises.

The first test match was in 1903 when NZ beat Australia and in 1904 they beat a touring British team in Wellington. Although the 1884 team had played in dark blue jerseys with a gold fern leaf, when the NZRFU was formed in 1892 it resolved that the representative colours should be a black jersey with a silver fern and these were worn with black shorts by the 1905 Originals touring team under the captaincy of Dave Gallagher. The British press referred to them as All Blacks because of 'their sable and unrelieved costume', though it was also reported that the term All Blacks was a misprint for All Backs in reference to their preferred playing style. Whichever, the name quickly caught on in Britain and then New Zealand. The team defeated England, Ireland and Scotland and only lost to Wales (3-0) at Cardiff Arms Park, thereby achieving legendary status in New Zealand and setting the standards to which future All Black teams aspired.

New Zealand teams had performed pre-match haka challenges since 1888 but the common performance of the haka really began on the 1905 tour and has captured the imagination of the British and worldwide public ever since. New Zealand hosted the first RWC competition in 1987 and then again in 2011. NZ have won the Webb Ellis trophy three times in 1987, 2011 and 2015.

As major Southern Hemisphere teams emerged, so too did an appetite from the Northern Hemisphere's rugby players to tour and compete with players on the other side of the world.. From 1888 onwards combined teams from Great Britain and Ireland toured the Southern Hemisphere. As mentioned above the first tour was a commercial venture run by Shaw and Shrewsbury – two cricketer entrepreneurs.

The 1888 team played in a jersey with wide red, blue and white hoops with white shorts. For the 1910 tour they wore dark blue jerseys with white shorts and red socks with a single lion rampant as the crest. The 1924 tour retained the blue jerseys but now with blue shorts and the single lion was replaced by the four quartered badge with the symbols of the four Home Unions. On the 1930 tour the Irish players complained that there was no Irish green, so a green turnover was added to the

The mercurial Barry John, nicknamed 'The King' by the New Zealanders.

socks. The red jersey was adopted for the 1950 tour with white shorts and blue socks with a green turnover

The 1910 tour was the first official tour selected by and representing the four Home Unions. The South African team won the test matches 2-1. In 1924 in South Africa again, three tests were lost and one drawn. In 1930 the British Isles toured New Zealand losing the test series 3-1. In 1938 in South Africa the test series was lost 3-1 with the team being named the Lions by players and the South African public.

The first post-war tour was in 1950 to New Zealand and Australia; New Zealand won 3 and drew one test while Australia lost both tests. In 1955 in South Africa a thrilling test series was drawn 2-2. In 1959, touring Australia and New Zealand, the Australian tests were again both won while the New Zealand series was lost 3-1. During the 1960s there were tours in 1962 to South Africa with the Lions losing 3-1, in 1966 to New Zealand and Australia with Australia being beaten twice but all four tests against New Zealand being lost; the team also played Canada on the way home. In 1968 in South Africa three tests were lost and one drawn.

The 1970s was a resurgent decade for the Lions with victory over New Zealand in the test series of 1971. The team was coached by Carwyn James, captained by John Dawes and with the mercurial Barry John pulling the strings for the outstanding backs. Victory was achieved too in South Africa in 1974 where the team was unbeaten over the tour and led by the legendary Irish forward, Willie John McBride. The 1977 tourists lost 3-1 to New Zealand and also played Fiji on the way home. The 1980 tour was to South Africa where the test series was lost 3-1; this was to prove the last to tour to that country until 1997, post-apartheid. In 1983 the tourists lost the test series 4-0 in New Zealand. In 1989 the Lions toured Australia and won the test series 2-1. The 1993 tour to New Zealand was the last of the pre-professional era with the test series lost 2-1.

Post-1995 Lions tours, though still regarded by players and the rugby public as the very pinnacle of the game, have often struggled to keep their place in the congested global international calendar which has been increasingly dominated by the commercial interests of national tours and professional league commitments.

Rugby football was introduced to France by British students in the 1870s. In 1872 a group formed Le Havre Athletique, in 1877 the English Taylors RFC was formed and in 1878 Paris FC, Racing Club de France in 1882 and Stade Français in 1883. In 1892 the first French rugby union championship match was played between Racing and Stade Français, refereed by Pierre de Coubertin of Olympic Games renown; Racing won 4-3. Rugby football was played at the 1900 Paris Olympics and France won the gold medal, but the first official test match was in 1906 against New Zealand which

RUGBY FOOTBALL WAS INTRODUCED TO FRANCE BY BRITISH STUDENTS IN THE 1870S. IN 1872 A GROUP FORMED LE HAVRE ATHLETIQUE, IN 1877 THE ENGLISH TAYLORS RFC WAS FORMED AND IN 1878 PARIS FC, RACING CLUB DE FRANCE IN 1882 AND STADE FRANCAIS IN 1883.

was lost 8-38. France joined the Five Nations tournament in 1910 and played South Africa for the first time in 1913.

Accusations of professionalism led to France being expelled from the Five Nations in 1932, re-joining again in 1947. In 1911 the national team adopted the rooster as their emblem and traditionally play in blue with white shorts and red socks representing their tricolour. Led by the legendary Jean Prat of Lourdes they shared the championship in 1954 when they also recorded their first win over New Zealand in Paris. The first victory over South Africa came on tour in 1958 with the team still led by Prat. The first grand slam was won in 1968, followed by a second in 1977 and a third in 1981.

France hosted the RWC in 2007 and have reached the final three times in 1987, 1999 and 2011 without yet winning the competition. They will again be host nation in 2023.

Rugby union began to be played in Argentina in 1873 at Buenos Aires Cricket Club. The first inter-club match between Buenos Aires FC and Rosario AC was played in 1886. The national team are nicknamed Los Pumas and wear blue and white hooped jerseys. The first international match was played in 1910 against a British Isles touring team. The British Lions toured again in 1927 and 1936. Argentina first toured South Africa in 1965. Argentina have qualified for all nine RWC competitions and took third place in the RWC 2007. In 2009 they joined the three Southern Hemisphere giants to create the Rugby Championship. Argentina have now beaten all of the Home Nations, France, South Africa and New Zealand; they also drew with a British Lions XV in 2005. In Agustín Pichot they have a leading World Rugby administrator who was Vice Chairman from 2016-2020

British workers brought rugby football to Italy in the early 1890s. The national team, known as the Azurri, played their first game in Barcelona in 1929 where they lost 9-0 to Spain. Italy were invited to take part in the first RWC in 1987. In 1997 they beat France for the first time and then Scotland in 1998. In 2000 they were finally invited to join the Five Nations to make the Six Nations competition, and beat Scotland again that year. Sergio Parisse is widely considered to have been Italy's outstanding rugby player, winning 142 caps between 2002 and 2019 and playing in five RWC competitions. Of the so called Tier 1 nations Italy have beaten Scotland eight times,

Legendary Italian forward Sergio Parisse.

Ireland four times, France three times, Wales twice and South Africa once, but not yet beaten England, Australia or New Zealand.

Rugby football was introduced to Fiji in 1884. In 1924 the national team played their first test against Western Samoa. This team wore black jerseys rather than the white jerseys now worn. In 1964 Fiji toured Europe and in 1970 beat a very strong Barbarian XV. In 1974 they lost 14-13 to New Zealand and in 1977 defeated the British Lions. Fiji qualified for the quarter-finals of the 1987 RWC and again in 1991.

Catholic educators the Marist Brothers brought rugby football to Samoa in 1920. The national team known as Manu Samoa, have competed in the RWC since 1991. Their first international was against Fiji in 1924. In 1986 they toured Wales. In 1991 they beat Wales in Cardiff.

By 2021 rugby football had never been a more global sport. Although the Four Home Nations, together with France and Australia, South Africa and New Zealand in the Southern Hemisphere, dominated international rugby on the field during the 20th century, Argentina, Japan, Italy, Fiji and Samoa have all shown that they can compete with these countries on their day.

The rugby football culture in Georgia, Romania, Uruguay and Tonga has also been bright – though for shorter periods. In 1987 the 16 countries which competed in the first

IN 1987 THE 16 COUNTRIES WHICH COMPETED IN THE FIRST RUGBY WORLD CUP DID SO BY INVITATION. FROM 1991 THERE WAS A QUALIFYING PROCESS WITH 33 COUNTRIES TAKING PART. BY 2011 THIS NUMBER HAD GROWN TO OVER 100 COUNTRIES.

Rugby World Cup did so by invitation. From 1991 there was a qualifying process with 33 countries taking part. By 2011 this number had grown to more than 100 countries.

Despite this growth, the dominance of the Big Eight nations has remained, both on the field and, perhaps more importantly in leading the committees which determine the direction of travel for World Rugby in the 21st century. The Webb Ellis trophy has been won by only four countries in the nine RWC competitions to date and the chairman of the IRB and its successor, World Rugby, has always come from one of the Big Eight nations.

There are many challenges facing the game today, not least player safety and welfare and allowing a fairer distribution of income, but also much that looks rosy.

RUGGER ON THE RO

Trinity College, Dublin, cradle of Irish football, adopted Rugby School's rules in 1854.

The first rugby international match was played between England and Scotland at Raeburn Place in Edinburgh, on 27 March 1871. Half of the England team were Rugbeians.

The Welsh Rugby Union (WRU), was established in 1881, the same year that Wales played their first international against England.

OAD

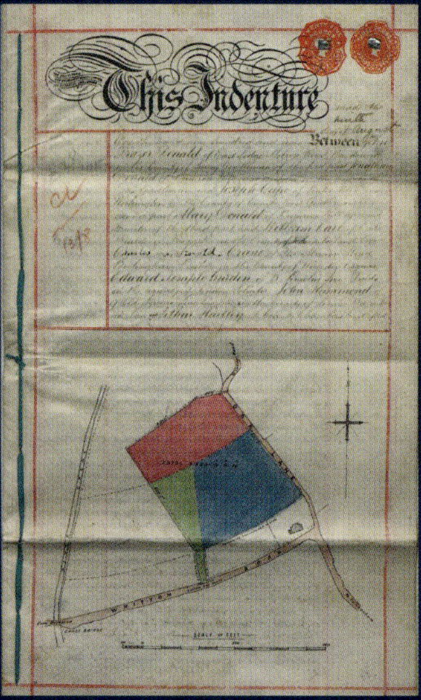

19 / 07 The RFU purchased land north of Twickenham for £5,572 to build a stadium.

19 / 10 France played all four home nations for the first time and Twickenham was first used for international matches.

19 / 12 New Zealand or South Africa held top place in the international rugby rankings for 77 of the next 79 years.

RUGBY ROMÂNIA

19 / 13 The first rugby match was played in Romania.

19 / 14 The First World War claimed the lives of nearly 100 international players from the countries playing in the then Five Nations – 30 from Scotland, 27 from England, 24 from France and 13 from Wales.

19
20

France won an away international match for the first time, beating Ireland 15-7 at Lansdowne Road.

19
20

A total of five players in the New Year's Day test between Scotland and France had each lost an eye during the First World War.

19
22

The England against Wales match in Cardiff was the first time both sides wore numbered shirts in the Five Nations match.

19
22

Edinburgh Polo Club sold the Scottish Rugby Union land at Murrayfield to build a new 70,000-capacity stadium.

19
23

Scotland achieved their first victory over Wales in Cardiff for 33 years. The encounter included a try by Scottish winger Eric Liddell, the sprinter and missionary later immortalised in the film *Chariots of Fire*.

"I SHALL NEVER PLAY AT TWICKENHAM AGAIN"

The reputed last words of England captain Ronnie Poulton Palmer

FROM FRIENDSHIP TO FLANDERS

By Simon Penniston,
former Captain of the XV and former Governor, Rugby School

How the Great War took the lives of Oxford University friends who were two of the best players of their era.

Ronald William Poulton was born on September 12, 1889 at Wykeham House, 56 Banbury Road, Oxford. He was the fourth child of Edward Bagnall Poulton, a renowned lecturer in zoology at Oxford University. His mother Emily (formerly Palmer) was the daughter of George Palmer of the giant Huntley Palmers food company. Emily's brother George William eventually became the senior director in the firm.

Poulton had one elder brother, Edward, and two elder sisters, Hilda and Margaret. Another sister, Janet, was subsequently born in 1892. By all accounts they lived a happy Victorian family life with a father who extended his considerable academic work to sport, amateur dramatics, music, walking, carpentry, landscaping and travel. At a time when it was fashionable for families to develop their collective activities, the Poultons became enthusiastically involved with the rather grander Palmers and their own academic social circle. Ronnie was an energetic, occasionally shy child who had several successive family nurses. Despite their different personalities and interests, the Poulton children occupied themselves with mixed hockey games and hide and seek in their garden, the latter game considered by Professor Poulton as a source of Ronnie's dodging abilities and unusual and graceful running style.

In September 1897, aged eight, Ronnie entered the Oxford Preparatory School known as 'the Dragon'. He did not come to athletic attention until 1899 when on the school sports day he came first equal in the under-10 high jump and second in the 100 yards. It would seem that Ronnie's athletic ability took time to develop but in spring 1901, still only 10, he won a couple of open events in the long jump and swimming events against boys two years older. He made his debut in the school 1st XV that year and it was immediately apparent he possessed a level of skill denied to others. His ability to evade opponents caught the attention of those knowledgeable spectators who could see that he had an extraordinary talent to swerve and accelerate. While devastating in attack, Ronnie's one weakness seemed to be in defence where he 'fell off' tackles, although this was not through lack of effort or courage. Ronnie also starred on the hockey field and was also installed as captain of cricket in the summer of 1903 when he topped the school batting averages. He also won the Athletics Cup by coming first in four events and afterwards the Head Master informed Ronnie's father that he was the best all-round athlete to have attended the school.

In the autumn of 1903 Ronnie Poulton arrived as a boarder at Rugby School and entered School House. Ronnie soon learned that there were three compulsory roll

A Poulton family group photographed at Ryde on the Isle of Wight in 1895. Back row Edward Bagnall Poulton (father); sisters Janet, Margaret, Hilda; mother Emily; front row Edward ('Teddie'); Ronald ('Ronnie').

George Palmer (1818-1897). The original Palmer in the partnership. Ronnie's grandfather on his mother's side was the driving force behind the world's largest biscuit manufacturer from 1841.

A 1901 Poulton family picnic on the beach at the Isle of Wight with relations. Nearest the camera a nanny and a cousin's governess. To the extreme right, to liven things up, the eleven-year-old Ronnie has decided to stuff what seems to be an apple in his mouth.

The Sedbergh School 1st XV of 1905. Freddie Turner is fifth from left in the back row. He went on to captain the team in 1906 before going up to Oxford University.

The Rugby School XV of 1905. Two of this team came to be regarded as the most celebrated Rugbeians of their era and were the subject of a joint memorial service at the school in May 1915. The last man to receive his colours was Rupert Brooke standing in the back row, fourth from right. In the same row on the extreme right is sixteen-year-old Ronnie Poulton, the star of the team that season.

In Ronnie Poulton's last football season at Rugby (1907) his house, School House, won the final of the inter-house rugby football competition (Cock House). Ronnie, as captain, sits on the right of the trophy and his chum Robert 'Dum' Cunningham (later a fellow member of the great 1913/1914 Liverpool team) sits on the left.

calls a day, a fagging system and several meal and activity periods to combine with up to eight hours' academic work. In addition to Ronnie's talent as an alto tenor, it did not take the School long to realise his ability as a rugby footballer. His first mention in *The Meteor* school magazine noted his excellent performance in a junior School House 39-3 victory over Collins' House. In 1904 he swept the board in the Under-16 Junior Sports where he won eight individual victories including the 100 yards. Ronnie's lack of conceit in victory and his natural charm impressed his fellow pupils and masters. In the school holidays Ronnie enjoyed the company of his family at St Helens and expeditions to excavate Palaeolithic remains. In 1905 in the Lent Term Ronnie made his debut in the school 1st XV. This was a term when the School played against 'adult' sides and had three consecutive victories inside 10 days including one against Blackheath 'A' in which Ronnie scored two tries.

It was also in this year that Ronnie made his first visit to the Rugby School Home Mission Camp at New Romney in Kent. The Mission was set up to foster relationships between pupils and disadvantaged working-class boys. Rugby's mission was based in Notting Dale (subsequently called The Rugby Clubs – now the Rugby Portobello Trust) and, after acquiring some land on the Kent coast, started a series of summer camps. Ronnie was to dedicate much of his time to helping with the Mission.

In the Advent term of 1905 Ronnie was awarded his 1st XV colours at just 16 and two months old. In the previous summer term Ronnie duly took the Athletics Cup, again winning four events outright. In the 1906 Advent term Ronnie played well in a team that, while better than the previous team, was still less than strong. In the summer of 1907 Ronnie again dominated various events and won the Athletics Cup, while on the cricket field he finished third in the batting averages. His hard work in the classroom paid off when he won the Senior School prize for practical chemistry.

At the end of term he expressed a desire to go to the Rugby Mission Camp at New Romney rather the traditional family holiday, but his parents prevailed with the argument that family time together was limited and the usual holiday to St Helens duly took precedence. But Ronnie still went to New Romney instead of heading with the family to the Isle of Wight. In September 1907 Ronnie was made joint captain of the XV and the team enjoyed a wonderful season with his attacking skills to the fore. *The Meteor* described him as: 'A brilliant centre three-quarter. Holding the ball in both hands, at arm's length, he relied on his great pace and a most deceptive swerve to get through and seldom without success….' Ronnie was invited to join the Harlequins club by Old Rugbeian Adrian Stoop, but rejected the invitation at the time. Stoop's 'breaking the mould' concept of creating broken play by using well-drilled three-quarters to win games by scoring more points than the opposition was new and innovative. This moved the sport into an era when the spectators derived much more pleasure than from the previously forward-dominated game.

In December 1907 Ronnie went home to Oxford for the week of the combined scholarship examinations for University entrance. Following this he was awarded an Exhibition (Natural Science) which delighted his father. Following the award later that month Head Master Dr James wrote to his father:

'...I do most warmly congratulate you and Mrs Poulton on Ronald's signal success. I do not know when anything of the kind has given me half the pleasure that this has: for when a boy who is a supremely good athlete is also a conscientious worker, sets the highest possible example of character and conduct, and is utterly unspoilt by all the homage he receives in a school and a world which crowns and enthrones the athlete above all others – one can only thank God for his presence in our midst.'

Ronnie left Rugby in summer 1908 after he had had considerable success with the bat and, in the Cock House match against Collins', scored 148 of their first innings total of 339 to help take his School House team to victory. Straight after the end of term Ronnie once again joined the Rugby Mission camp at New Romney where he described his stay as *'....really a splendid time'.* Indeed, Ronnie's time at Rugby School had been a splendid time, but now a bigger stage awaited him at Balliol College, Oxford.

In the County of Lancaster, Frederick Harding Turner was born a year before Ronnie Poulton, on May 29, 1888 at 39 Ullet Road, Toxteth Park. The son of William Neil Turner, a business printer, and his wife Jessie Stuart (formerly Holder), Freddie had an elder brother William Stewart and a sister Alice. Two younger siblings would follow in John D. and Katharine Mary.

Little is known about Freddie's early family life, but we know he was educated first at Green Bank School, Liverpool, like his elder brother, and that in 1902 he entered Sedgwick House at Sedbergh School. Located in the West Riding of Yorkshire (now officially Cumbria), Sedbergh was established in 1525 (42 years before Rugby) by Roger Lupton, a former Provost of Eton. Sedbergh's beautiful and rugged location lends itself to outdoor pursuits and sport. It was in this environment Freddie found that he could thrive as an all-round sportsman. Turner's brand of hard, straight and rugged forward play in rugby was nurtured during his time at Sedbergh. He was especially admired for the excellence of his tackling and for the length and accuracy of his goal kicking, particularly from the touchline. Freddie first appeared for the Sedbergh 1st XV in 1905-06 in a team

The Sedbergh School 1st XV in 1906 which was captained by Freddie Turner.

Rugby School School House team 1907, winners of Cock House with Ronnie Poulton as captain.

Trinity College Oxford team 1908. Freddie Turner is in the back row in the doorway on the right.

Oxford University XV 1911 with Ronnie Poulton seated middle as captain.

Balliol College XV 1909 with Ronnie Poulton
seated extreme left in his slippers.

captained by future Scottish international J.M.B. Scott. He also had another future Scottish international alongside him as well as a future English international, J.A. Scholfield. They had a mixed start to the season, but then put in an unbeaten run with Freddie starring against Liverpool 'A' where two strong breaks led to tries and an 18-8 score in Sedbergh's favour. The key features of this campaign were the ability to combine forwards and backs playing at pace to ensure that most teams were 'run off their legs by half-time'.

In the following 1906-07 season Freddie captained the side containing eight Old Colours and they started well with four consecutive victories. Things, however, did not continue well with a narrow defeat to Mr Todd's XV followed by a crushing defeat by Scottish rivals Loretto 5-21. The remainder of the season was more successful and Freddie excelled in the match against Barnard Castle where a conversion by him from near the touchline ensured a win by the narrow margin of 8-6.

Freddie was also captain of cricket opening the bowling and batting at number three. With formidable strike power, his smiting the ball into what is now known as Evans House garden was well known and much celebrated. He was also President of the Debating Society during the term that he captained the Sedbergh 1st XV and seconded the motion that 'Killing for the sake of sport is unjustifiable', vigorously deploring bullfighting and pigeon shooting. Despite his eloquence the motion was lost.

Freddie Turner's all-round talents led him to winning a place at Trinity College, Oxford, to study law. He entered the University one year earlier than Ronnie Poulton in 1907.

At Oxford, Freddie won three consecutive Blues from 1908 to 1910. Although Ronnie was available in 1908, he was overlooked for the Blues team by the Club Captain, H.A. Hodges (Old Sedberghian) who considered him to be too individualistic. 'Hanged if I ever knew where he was going,' one team-mate recalled. This, of course, was countered by opponents, one of whom asked 'How can one stop him when his head goes one way, his arms another and his legs keep straight on?'

Although Ronnie had missed selection for the Varsity match in 1908, he was called up to win his first cap at centre for England against France on January 30, 1909 with England coming away with a 22-0 victory. Ronnie was kept on to play the remaining Championship games against Ireland and Scotland. Whilst at Oxford, Poulton played infrequently for Harlequins under the leadership of Adrian Stoop, but enjoyed the freedom of the attacking Stoop system which gave him licence to show his natural instinctive running game.

During his time at Balliol, and much as he had done at Rugby with the School's Home Mission in Notting Dale, Ronnie was a supporter of the Balliol Boys' Club, exhibiting a strong sense of social responsibility and support of social justice in helping young people without the advantages and privileges he enjoyed. He also stood up against an Etonian elite at Balliol (18 of 53 1906 freshers came from Eton) who belonged to the Bullingdon Club and the even more Etonian-only Annandale Society. This Society exhibited bad behaviour in the form of over indulgence with alcohol and outright vandalism. They would also abuse other non-Etonian students by calling them 'plebs' and generally insulted and treated them as socially inferior. Ronnie Poulton stood up to the boorish behaviour of the 'Eton Rowdies' and strongly supported those less fortunate than himself. Later, as captain of England, Ronnie risked his position by writing to the *Sportsman* in support of 'broken time payments' to players who suffered financially by playing for their country, with some being unable to make trips to play the likes of France because they simply could not afford to do so. Ronnie's sense of social justice is the subject of *Into Battle,* a play by Hugh Salmon which opened to considerable critical acclaim.

Meanwhile, Freddie Turner could not be overlooked for long on the rugby field and he made his place a certainty being selected for the clash with the first Australian tourists aged 20. He duly made his Varsity match debut in 1908 which was played in front of a record gate of 16,000 at the Queen's Club ground. The game failed to live up to its billing and it ended in a rather dull 5-5 draw. It was during this time that the deep friendship between two kindred spirits in Turner and Poulton started to blossom and Freddie and Ronnie enjoyed playing and socialising together. In the Varsity match the following year Poulton took centre stage inspiring a record 35-3 rout of Cambridge by scoring five of the nine tries which remains a record to this day. During the match Freddie was forced off the field for a while, following another team-mate to the sidelines to reduce Oxford to 13 men for precisely 13 minutes. In an act of sporting heroism and selflessness he returned to the field of play in great pain just before the break to see his team home.

In their final year together at Oxford, Turner was Captain of Rugby with Poulton as Club Secretary. While Freddie had been in a team that boasted 10 current or future internationals in 1909, he was only one of five Blues who returned in 1910. Turner's side won by more than 50 points on three occasions and ended the season with 22 wins and only five defeats, scoring a record 597 points and 172 against. They loved to attack, but relied heavily on the brilliance of Poulton to take them to victory over the light blues at Queen's Club by 23-18.

Three weeks later Freddie won the first of his 15 Scottish caps coming into the side at the start of the 1911 Five Nations Championship. The Scottish selectors capped 17 new players in the four-match campaign as the team slipped from one disaster

Oxford University team 1910 with Freddie Turner as captain. Seated next to him on his right is the Club secretary Ronnie Poulton.

Balliol College XV 1910 with Ronnie Poulton seated second from left.

The Scotland team of 1913 captained by Freddie Turner.

The Scotland team of 1914. Freddie Turner is third from the left in the middle row.

to another. Turner was one of six new caps selected for the first capped match against the French at Stade Colombes on January 2, 1911. Turner and Fraser were the only two forwards who played in all four matches and it says a lot about the selectors' view of Freddie that he only missed one of the 16 internationals played between his debut and the outbreak of WWI. His debut could not have been worse as it was France's 13th international and their first victory. Next, they played one of the greatest ever Welsh sides and were thrashed 32-10 conceding eight tries. They then lost to the Irish and three weeks later faced England in the Calcutta Cup – the first to be played in the new Twickenham stadium. Although the Scots struck first, they went down to a 13-8 defeat with Turner facing his friend Poulton and two other former Oxford team-mates.

The 1912 season started well for Freddie as Scotland avenged their defeat against the French with a 31-3 seven-try victory. Freddie scored one try and kicked five conversions, a record which stood for 60 years. Despite this start the team suffered away defeats to Wales and Ireland, but had the satisfaction of gaining an 8-3 Calcutta Cup triumph over the auld enemy whose team included Freddie's old friend Ronnie Poulton. In the following season Turner kicked seven conversions in four games, the most by a Scottish player in one Championship season and a record which stood for over 70 years. Turner had been turning out at club level for London Scottish (where he seems to have picked up his nickname 'Tank' or 'Tanky') since he left Oxford, but by the 1912/13 season was playing for Liverpool, where he was working as an apprentice in his father's print business, and was asked by the Scottish selectors to captain his country. Meanwhile, Ronnie Poulton had been working for the Huntley Palmers family business in Reading where he found time to attend the Reading Boys' Club evenings while continuing to play for Harlequins.

Ronnie and Freddie Turner had formed a bond at Oxford where both exhibited an interest in helping others less fortunate and were undoubtedly believers in what we would call today social responsibility. This bond was further strengthened when Ronnie arrived in Manchester in September 1913 to spend 10 months at the Mather Platt works in Manchester under the supervision of Sir William Mather, a magnate in his mid-70s, work experience arranged by his uncle G.W. Palmer. In continuing his work with boys' clubs he visited a large number of the Manchester clubs, most of whose activities were built around regular assemblies, prayer meetings, sports such as boxing, gymnastics and fives, draughts and chess.

In the Manchester area lived several of Ronnie's personal friends and acquaintances including a number from his Rugby School and university days. Amongst these was Robert Cunningham, an old School House contemporary, who was in Liverpool working for his family's cotton-broking business; Cunningham and Hinshaw, alongside Ireland's fly-half and captain Dickie Lloyd. Lloyd had joined

Cunningham at Liverpool FC who were captained by Freddie Turner and to Ronnie it must have seemed a small world.

With other friends also working in the vicinity and with Ronnie about to be appointed captain of England, and needing to keep fit and in form, it was impossible to play for Harlequins while based in Manchester. So it took little persuasion from his great friend Freddie Turner to see him turn out for such a prestigious club which had the distinction of fielding three national rugby captains of the same era in the 1913-14 season. Liverpool FC had a remarkable season, winning 27 of their 31 matches (in three of the four matches they lost they were below full strength). In the match against Sedbergh (where the future great Sedberghian footballer and England captain, Wavell Wakefield, ran the touchline) their victory was largely due to the almost flawless kicking ability of Freddie Turner. They had a rather easier victory in another school match against Rugby. In the match against local rivals Liverpool scored an almost unheard of 78 points such was the quality of their three-quarters fed amply by their forwards.

Shortly after the start of the 1913-14 season G.W. Palmer suffered a stroke and died aged 62 on October 8. In Palmer's will Ronnie was left a significant fortune by his uncle on condition that he changed his surname to Palmer. As a result, he is often referred to as Poulton Palmer or Poulton-Palmer but, in strict legal terms, this is inaccurate – in fact, in 1914 he simply changed his name from Poulton to Palmer.

At the start of the 1912/1913 season the Scots gained a victory over France 21-3 in Paris with Freddie making three conversions. A narrow loss to Wales 8-0 followed with a subsequent victory over Ireland 29-14. This left just the Calcutta Cup game against England chasing a first grand slam at Twickenham where the Prince of Wales turned up to watch a real tussle which England edged 3-0 with one try scored. Turner missed out on the Scottish trials in the 1913/14 season and Scotland lost their first match against Wales 24-3. This was followed by defeat away against Ireland 6-0, but at least Freddie was back in harness. In the final match of that season at Inverleith, the Scots met the auld enemy who were chasing a second grand slam, this time under skipper Poulton. In a rousing match where no quarter was given by either team and Ronnie scored a try, his men edged to victory over his friend Freddie 16-15. This was the Championship's last match for six years as the Great War took hold. After the match both men travelled down to Sedbergh to see the famous 10-mile Wilson run and to run round the course on the afternoon of their arrival.

Ronnie Poulton gained 17 caps in total for England over the five seasons following his debut in 1909. He was involved in the so-called golden age between 1910 and 1914 when England won 16 of their 21 matches, drew one and lost just four. In 1912 Harlequins supplied the entire three-quarter line except the then defensive

The England rugby team in 1913/14 which won the modern equivalent of a Grand Slam under Ronnie Poulton's captaincy.

The great Liverpool side of 1913/14 captained by Freddie Turner - seated middle row three from the left with Ronnie Poulton next to him, two from right with Dicky Lloyd on the other side next to Turner. Turner, Poulton and Lloyd captained Scotland, England and Ireland respectively.

fullback position. Whilst Ronnie performed sensational things for England in the Five Nations, possibly his most memorable match was against the unbeaten touring South African team of 1913. In the opening minutes, England were driven back by the huge Springbok pack and were defending desperately deep in their 25. Suddenly the capacity crowd erupted and cried 'Poulton's through' – he was and ran the length of the pitch to score a sensational try. Several similar breaks were made by Ronnie and afterwards the South African press were fulsome in their praise for Europe's 'finest centre'.

When the Great War broke out Freddie Turner and his brother William joined the King's (Liverpool Regiment). After 10 weeks in France, Freddie was killed by a shot from a German sniper on January 10, 1915 aged 26. He was buried in Kemmel churchyardin Belgium, but his grave, along with others, was consumed later by the conflict, and his remains have never been found. There is now a memorial to him in Kemmel cemetery. Later that year his brother was killed, on June 16, 1915 aged 32. He is commemorated on the Ypres (Menin Gate) memorial.

Ronnie Poulton (by then Palmer) was a Lieutenant in the 1/4th Royal Berkshires when his regiment left for the Front in April 1915. He was shot and killed, aged 25, by a German sniper near Ploegsteert Wood on May 5, 1915. He is buried in Hyde Park Corner (Royal Berks) Cemetery near Ploegsteert, Belgium.

Tributes poured in mourning the deaths of these great men:

Of Freddie Turner *The Sedberghian* recorded 'in such a short sketch as this it is quite impossible to do justice to the character of the man'...'His love for Sedbergh was remarkable, and never a term went by without at least one visit, either for cricket or football or merely for a walk over the hills he loved so well, with a game of Five fitted-in when there was an hour to spare. Most delightful and loyal of friends, he embodied all that is best in Sedbergh life and tradition. Freddie Turner will be sorely missed, but if future generations of Sedberghians take him as a model of all we would wish them to be, he will not have lived in vain.'

News of Ronnie Poulton's death reached Rugby when the School was still reeling from that of poet Rupert Brooke on the Western Front. The Head Master, the Reverend A.A. David, delivered a sermon entitled 'Counting the Cost'. 'We have indeed given of our best. If we were asked to describe what kind of manhood Rugby helps to make, I think we should have Ronnie in mind as we spoke of it. God had endowed him with a rare combination of graces...what we hoped would come of it...strong and tender and true, he lived for others and died for others.' *The Meteor* stated 'He did, in a quite peculiar way, sum up a generation and realise an ideal.'

Ronnie Poulton's grave in Hyde Park (Royal Berks) Cemetery near Ploegsteert in Belgium.

In 2015 a dinner in memory of these two great men was held at Rugby with a football match played the following day between the Sedbergh and Rugby School XVs. A commemorative bench was also unveiled on the Mound next to the Bigside 1 pitch on The Close where it will remain as a reminder of their great friendship prior to their untimely deaths in the service of their country. The inscription on the bench reads:

RONALD POULTON PALMER (RUGBY 1903-08)
FREDERICK TURNER (SEDBERGH 1902-07)
TWO OUTSTANDING PLAYERS, NATIONAL CAPTAINS,
AND FRIENDS, KILLED IN WW1, 1915
PRESENTED IN THE CENTENARY YEAR OF THEIR
SACRIFICE ON THE WESTERN FRONT

PAUL THORBURN

Rugby has been in the family blood, my father was a member of Cardiff Rugby Club back in the 1950s, but also represented the Royal Air Force and played for Saracens and, with two older brothers who both played, rugby became a key part of family life from a very early age. With the three of us going to Hereford Cathedral School as boarders, given my parents' travels and commitment to a Forces life, a life in sport was very much part of the daily school routine and this continued beyond school to university and then into the senior game at club level.

To play first-class rugby and then be awarded your first cap has to rank as one of the highlights, especially when it comes out of the blue. Although during a period of relative decline in Welsh fortunes, in no small part due to the mass exodus of some of our leading players to rugby league, there were some highlights, including winning the Triple Crown and championship in 1988, the year after we had secured third place in the inaugural Rugby World Cup.

I was also very fortunate to be part of the Neath team, which was unquestionably one of the best club sides in the Northern Hemisphere during the mid-80s/ early 90s, when we took many scalps and took all three Southern Hemisphere international teams to the wire. Winning two Welsh Cup Finals in front of then, two world-record crowds for domestic cup finals, were also highlights.

Off the field, my role as tournament director of the Rugby World Cup 1999 is also a highlight, especially as it was the first Rugby World Cup event staged during the professional era of the game.

I think today William Webb Ellis would probably be glad there were no television match officials involved when he first picked up the ball and ran with it at Rugby School – there were many 'off the ball' incidents back then!! But on a more serious note he would be delighted with the overall growth of the game, not just amongst other rugby-playing nations but also in the development of women's and girls' rugby.

PLAYING THE GAME

Paul Thorburn played for Neath and 37 times for Wales. In the 1986 Five Nations he successfully completed a penalty kick against Scotland in Cardiff measuring 70 yards, eight and a half inches (64.2m), the longest in an international test match.

19
25

On January 3, England faced the All Blacks at Twickenham watched by the Prince of Wales (later Edward VIII) and Prime Minister Stanley Baldwin. In a fierce exchange, referee Albert Freethy sent off New Zealand forward Cyril Brownlie after just seven minutes of play. However, England still managed to lose the match 17-11.

AN UNFORTUNATE INCIDENT: THE REFEREE, MR. A. E. FREETHY (WITH EXTENDED ARM) HAS TO ORDER AN "ALL BLACK" FORWARD OFF THE FIELD AFTER WARNING BOTH SIDES.

19
26

The standard length of rugby matches was set at 80 minutes.

19
26

The Japan Rugby Union was formed with Crown Prince Hirohito, who later became Emperor, as its patron.

19
28

South Africa hosted the first visit by the touring All Blacks.

1928 The introduction to the Italian fascist regime's guide to rugby, Il Gioco del Rugby, was written by Lando Ferretti, Mussolini's press secretary.

1929 New York RFC was founded, gaining registration with the RFU three years later.

1929 133 public and rugby schools in England were affiliated with the RFU, a rise of 106 in a decade.

1929 On February 13, Ireland first beat England at Twickenham by six points to five.

1934 Moscow Dynamo won the Soviet Union's first national rugby championship.

"

ONE THING THAT RUGBY IS GENERALLY IS INCREDIBLY FAIR, AND WITH IT BEING A TEAM SPORT, NO INDIVIDUAL IS BIGGER THAN THE GAME ITSELF.

"

Jeremy Guscott

WHEELCHAIR WONDERS

By David Pond,
former CEO Great Britain Wheelchair Rugby

adidas
USAWR
10
WHEELER

AS ALL MEDIA OUTLETS SEEK EXCITING, CREATIVE AND DIFFERENT CONTENT, WHEELCHAIR RUGBY WITH ITS CRUNCH OF METAL, SCREECH OF TYRES, AND COLLISIONS SENDING CHAIRS AND THEIR DISABLED OCCUPANTS SPRAWLING ACROSS THE COURT, IS THE ULTIMATE ADRENALINE EXPERIENCE!

Photo courtesy: Megumi Masuda

IN THE BEGINNING

February 1976, Winnipeg, Manitoba, Canada. As the winter sun fades, the temperature falls to minus 11 degrees. Duncan Campbell manoeuvres from the car passenger seat into his wheelchair. He has arrived at his local gym for weekly rehabilitation and to meet with Jerry Terwin, Randy Dueck, Paul LeJeune and Chris Sargent. All are quadriplegic and enjoy getting together to lift a few weights with the help of a volunteer. Duncan is 19 and just two years before had broken his neck diving into shallow water, paralysing him from the chest down. Before his accident he had been a pretty reasonable ice hockey and baseball player. Like many young Canadians he is a sports fanatic and had thrived playing team sports. Since his injury he has tried to get back into sport and has participated in the Canadian Games for the Physically Disabled. But these are individual sports, like swimming and wheelchair racing, not the same buzz as being part of the a team.

The five men pushed around the gym in their wheelchairs not particularly noticing the cold, not uncommon for those with spinal injuries who have difficulties in regulating body temperature. As time moved on it became obvious that the volunteer who usually joined them to help lift the weights was clearly not going to turn up. As they pushed around, the men noticed a variety of balls and picked up different ones to throw around. With all experiencing hand and arm dysfunction some balls were more challenging to control than others. But the weight and size of a volleyball worked well and it was not long before they were passing the ball between themselves to score points into a garbage can. Soon they had divided into two versus three and, realising they were spending more time trying to pick up the ball that had missed the can, they dispensed with it and introduced the rule that to score a point a player had to cross the line with ball in hand at the end of the basketball court.

During the weekly gym sessions that followed, the five players continued to develop the simple game they had started. They knew immediately they were on to something that could take off because up until this point the only team sport available to those with a spinal injury was wheelchair basketball and this was beyond the physical functionality of the majority of quadriplegics. Over time more individuals joined the sessions, and although all had some loss of function in all four limbs, not all had spinal injuries and even those who did had different levels of function. So it was soon necessary to come up with a system to ensure teams were equally matched. There was already a classification system used for quadriplegic athletes competing in track and field events. This, therefore, became the early basis for the beginnings of a system for wheelchair rugby where individuals were divided into three categories depending on their physical functionality. The greater the function an individual possessed the higher the category assigned.

All that was needed then was to agree the balance of categories in each team so they could be competitively matched. So it was that wheelchair rugby was born, though it would go through many development phases and take 17 years before being recognised as an official international sport for disabled athletes.

MURDERBALL

Over the next couple of years, the game continued to evolve and physical contact became a key feature as players used their chairs to block and hold opponents to stop them crossing the line and to crash their chairs into one another to dislodge the ball from an opponent's grasp. There was no protection and players, mostly paralysed from the chest down, were often knocked out of their chairs and left sprawling on the floor where able-bodied volunteers, often family members or care staff, came to the rescue and lifted them back into action. At this time, the game was being played in ordinary day wheelchairs and these quickly began to get damaged. So, individuals started to think of ways to protect them, resulting in 'do it yourself fixes' such as steel bars welded to the front of chairs, wearing steel-toed construction boots, and modifications to provide protection to the spoked wheels, which suffered the most damage. For safety, players strapped their legs together in the chair, though all other strapping was prohibited. The physicality of the game was soon to became its most distinctive characteristic, giving rise to its original name of 'Murderball'.

Before long, the Winnipeg group started to give demonstrations of the new game in different parts of Canada, usually at other disability sports events. At these gatherings athletes began to get together and form ad hoc teams for a friendly game of Murderball, and an ever-increasing number of people were being introduced to the game. This resulted in the first organised competition in 1978 as part of the Edmonton National Games for the Disabled, with four teams taking part, which in turn laid the foundations for the first national Murderball championships held a year later as part of the Canadian National Wheelchair Games in St John's, Newfoundland.

That same year the game moved across the border into the USA where the Winnipeg team gave an exhibition game at a regional track and field meet at Southwest Minnesota State University. The event was attended by athletes from the universities

THERE WAS NO PROTECTION AND PLAYERS, MOSTLY PARALYSED FROM THE CHEST DOWN, WERE OFTEN KNOCKED OUT OF THEIR CHAIRS AND LEFT SPRAWLING ON THE FLOOR WHERE ABLE-BODIED VOLUNTEERS, OFTEN FAMILY MEMBERS OR CARE STAFF, CAME TO THE RESCUE AND LIFTED THEM BACK INTO ACTION.

Photos courtesy: Megumi Masuda

of North Dakota, Illinois, Michigan and South Dakota. Everyone joined in the games playing in their track chairs, enjoying the opportunity to play in a physically intense and dynamic team game, alongside friends and colleagues with similar impairments. The thrill, excitement and camaraderie became the catalyst for the game's rapid popularity with the quadriplegic community and it was Brad Mikkelsen who led the USA charge.

1979 was also to be a significant year for the future international recognition of the sport. It was the year Pawel Zbieranowski escaped the increasing repression of his native Poland to settle in Canada. Pawel was qualified in physical education and physiotherapy but initially struggled to find employment in his adopted country until 1980 when he got a volunteer position at Lyndhurst Hospital. This was a spinal cord centre in Toronto, home to the Toronto Bulldogs, one of the first wheelchair rugby teams, and it was not long before Pawel was helping out as a volunteer before becoming the team's coach, a position he held for 12 years. Pawel quickly realised the potential of the game but understood that if it was to become a recognised sport it needed structure – rules and referees to manage play on court, a reliable classification system to ensure teams were evenly matched, and a competition framework. He began to work with volunteers across Canada and with those developing the game in the USA, to lay the foundations for the infrastructure and skills needed to grow and administer the sport.

TAKING ROOT IN AMERICA

Paralysed from the chest down following a motor accident aged 20, Brad Mikkelsen was at the lower end of the functionality spectrum and worked as a student volunteer with the Disabled Student Services at the University of North Dakota where he was a keen wheelchair basketball player. Having seen the Winnipeg exhibition game at Minnesota University and taken part in the 'have a go' sessions that followed, he was an immediate convert. In 1981 he formed the first US team, the North Dakota Wallbangers supported by the university. Around the same time Terry Hanson, who had developed polio when he was just 22 months old and worked at the Courage Rehabilitation Centre in Minnesota, assembled a group of players to learn and practise the sport using the centre's facilities. Whilst the centre was supportive, it was concerned about safety and in particular the frequency players fell out of their chairs when they reached forward for the ball or collided with one another, and so introduced safety strapping to be used above the waist. Terry's group eventually formed the second US team, the Minnesota Rolling Gophers, leading in 1982 to the first US match being held between North Dakota and Minnesota as part of the National Wheelchair Games in Marshall, North Dakota. That same year the University of North Dakota hosted the first north American tournament with teams from Manitoba, Saskatchewan, North Dakota and Minnesota competing. At this tournament there was discussion about the name Murderball with some expressing concern that the name often made it difficult to attract publicity for events and fundraising. Whilst there was agreement that it should change, founding member Duncan Campbell wanted it to be renamed Wheelchair Rugby whilst Brad Mikkelsen proposed Quad Rugby, its double meaning of 'quad' being 4 v 4 players, now established as the rule for the number of players on court at any one time, and 'quad' also being a play on quadriplegic. Today the sport is recognised across the world as wheelchair rugby, though in the USA it is still also referred to as quad rugby.

CROSSING THE ATLANTIC

In 1981 the game crossed the Atlantic when Canadian Barbara Montemurro introduced it at the Stoke Mandeville World Wheelchair Games in England. Barbara was on the staff of the Canadian national team attending the games which had been held annually since 1948 and regarded as the origin of the Paralympic Games. She took copies of the early rules to Stoke and distributed them to quadriplegic athletes from the various countries attending, encouraging them to read the rules and inviting them to take part in a demonstration game the following day. There was immediate interest from many of the athletes who returned to their home nations and began playing. Showcasing wheelchair rugby became a regular item at international disability sporting events and at the annual Stoke Mandeville event where ad hoc games were often played in the car park or on the helicopter pad!

BY THE MID-1980S, THE SPORT WAS GAINING REAL INTEREST IN BRITAIN WHERE ALISON STIRLING, A PHYSIOTHERAPIST AT SHEFFIELD SPINAL INJURIES UNIT, LED ITS DEVELOPMENT AND IT SOON BECAME PART OF THE SPORTS OFFERED DURING REHABILITATION AT MOST OF BRITAIN'S SPINAL UNITS.

By the mid-1980s, the sport was gaining real interest in Britain where Alison Stirling, a physiotherapist at Sheffield Spinal Injuries Unit, led its development and it soon became part of the sports offered during rehabilitation at most of Britain's spinal units. In 1987 the Quebec provincial team travelled to England and held a training camp and coaching clinics to support the game's growth and it was not long before teams formed in most of Britain's spinal units and began playing one another in friendly matches. In 1988 Allan Smith took on the role of GB Rugby Secretary and continued the development. Allan had been a Chief Petty Officer in the Royal Navy and the Royal Navy Hang Gliding Champion. In 1984 he hit a tree while gliding in France, suffering a spinal injury, and was introduced to the sport during rehabilitation at the Pinderfields spinal injury unit in Wakefield. As players left the units having completed this stage of their rehabilitation they often returned to play and to introduce the game to those recently injured and starting their own rehabilitation journeys. As interest grew, clubs started in different parts of the country. The first was the Marauders based in Nottingham and drawing players from the spinal injury units at Oswestry, Pinderfields and from Shropshire and the West Midlands. Clubs in Stoke Mandeville and Lodge Moor, Sheffield, Southport, and Cardiff soon followed.

At the same time as the game was taking root in Britain, growth in the USA was accelerating following its arrival in the south of the country with the first demonstration game staged in Dallas in 1987. A year later the USA National Championships were held at the University of North Dakota with teams now represented from around the country – Minnesota, Chicago, Detroit, Dallas, Los Angeles, and North Dakota. At this tournament the US Quad Rugby Association was formed as the sport's national governing body to promote and regulate the sport in the USA. 1988 was also a big year for the sport in Britain as the first national team was selected with Colin Price appointed as coach. Colin was a national wheelchair basketball player and had also coached Britain's women's basketball team. This experience was invaluable because the evolution of wheelchair rugby saw the adoption of many of the elements and chair skills of wheelchair basketball. Colin remained with the squad for a year passing on his basketball knowledge before handing the coaching role to Brian Worrel who was to revolutionise the sport with his tactical skills. Brian, a former paratrooper in the British Army, had injured his spinal cord on duty in the jungles of Belize. He was a keen chess player and brought the idea of the tactical board into his coaching and team preparation. It was Brian who in 1996 took the GB team to its first Paralympic Games in Atlanta.

INTERNATIONAL DEVELOPMENT

Back in Canada, Pawel Zbieranowski continued his mission to develop and promote the sport. By now his vision was clear: he wanted to see the sport included in the Paralympic Games and the first step toward this was to establish an international tournament with teams from outside Canada and the USA. Pawel organised the first Toronto International Wheelchair Rugby tournament in January 1989 which was to become an annual event. It was the first truly international tournament with 10 teams participating including the national teams of Britain and the USA, and teams from Dallas, Boston, British Columbia, Saskatchewan, Quebec, Nova Scotia and Ontario

The 1990s was a period of rich growth for wheelchair rugby. The decade began with the sport introduced as an exhibition event at the World Wheelchair Games at Stoke Mandeville and was to end in 2000 as a Paralympic full medal event. The 1990 Toronto International Tournament attracted Volkswagen Canada as a major sponsor which raised the profile of the tournament and further promoted the sport. An International Organising Committee was established on the back of the tournament with Pawel Zbieranowski as Chair, Allan Smith from Britain and Abu Yilla from the USA. This provided the leadership to drive the sport's global development and in 1991 it was recognised as an official international sport for athletes with a disability by the International Stoke Mandeville Wheelchair Sports Federation (ISMWSF), the governing body for sports which catered for individuals with a physical disability.

In January 1992 at the conclusion of the 3rd Toronto International Tournament, the International Wheelchair Quad Rugby Federation was formed. Pawel Zbieranowski was elected Chair with the USA's Brad Mikkelsen and Britain's Allan Smith as members. Pawel was charged with promoting the game in Eastern Europe and Asia; Brad, Central and South America and Oceania; and Allan, Western Europe. These were to become the three recognised wheelchair rugby zones for international

THE 1990S WAS A PERIOD OF RICH GROWTH FOR WHEELCHAIR RUGBY. THE DECADE BEGAN WITH THE SPORT INTRODUCED AS AN EXHIBITION EVENT AT THE WORLD WHEELCHAIR GAMES AT STOKE MANDEVILLE AND WAS TO END IN 2000 AS A PARALYMPIC FULL MEDAL EVENT.

Photos courtesy: Megumi Masuda

competition and development purposes. By now there were 32 teams established in the USA, 16 across Canada and the game was taking root in northern Europe led by Jan-Owe Mattsson and Peter Andersson in Sweden. Jan-Owe, who had incurred a spinal injury in a diving accident in 1970, was a top international wheelchair racer and took part in some of the exhibition games. At the Barcelona Paralympics in 1992 he and Peter Andersson agreed with their north American racing friends that on their return to Sweden they would get wheelchair rugby started. So it was that in January 1993 they gathered a group of quad friends in their local gym in Stockholm and started playing. Just a year later Sweden had four teams, two in Stockholm, one in Gothenburg and one in the south of the country. Switzerland, the Netherlands, Germany and Belgium also formed teams during this period.

A similar pattern of growth was taking place in the Southern Hemisphere. In 1988 some New Zealand athletes were in Sydney taking part in the Australia all-sports National Championships where they gave a demonstration of wheelchair rugby playing in their day chairs. It was just three years later that Victoria, South Australia, Queensland, New South Wales, the NZ national team and an invitation team, took part in Australia's first national Wheelchair Rugby Championship, held in Melbourne and won by South Australia. A year later the first Australian national team was named with Bruno Morretti as its coach.

By 1993 there were 15 countries actively participating in the game and the same year seven countries met at Stoke Mandeville for the World Wheelchair Games – Australia, Canada, Britain, the Netherlands, Sweden, Switzerland and the USA. The tournament saw the USA defeat Britain in the final 37-30 with Canada taking third place. Away from the court, on August 1, 1993 the first informal meeting was taking place between the International Wheelchair Quad Rugby Federation, representatives from the International Paralympic Committee (IPC), the Atlanta Paralympics Organising Committee and the International Stoke Mandeville Wheelchair Sports Federation to consider the inclusion of wheelchair rugby in the Paralympic Games. A day later it was agreed that wheelchair rugby should be confirmed as the official name of the sport worldwide and that the new global authority for the sport would be named the International Wheelchair Rugby Federation (IWRF). Following the election of its first officers, the IWRF was born on August 6, 1993 with the purpose of establishing an international infrastructure for the sport, providing international championship competition and seeking recognition from the IPC.

The growth in the number of European nations playing the game spawned the first European Championship in Gothenburg, Sweden, in 1995. Seven nations competed, with Britain defeating Sweden in the final to become the winners of the first European gold medal. Bronze went to the Netherlands who pushed Germany into fourth place. The tournament was attended by representatives of the IPC, who were impressed with the sport and saw it as a natural inclusion in the Paralympic Games. In the September 1995 the IPC and the organising committee of the Atlanta Paralympic Games approved wheelchair rugby as a demonstration sport for the 1996 Atlanta Paralympic Games. In the same year, New Zealand staged its first national tournament which included two teams over from Australia. Significantly, making his debut in one of the Australian teams was a fresh-faced 14-year-old boy, Brad Dubberley. Brad was to go on to become one of the world's top high point players before taking up coaching and becoming one of the most successful national coaches. He continues as Australia's head coach today.

PARALYMPIC GAMES

Autumn 1995 was significant with the inaugural World Wheelchair Rugby Championships staged in Nottwill, Switzerland, home of the Swiss Paraplegic

THE GROWTH IN THE NUMBER OF EUROPEAN NATIONS PLAYING THE GAME SPAWNED THE FIRST EUROPEAN CHAMPIONSHIP IN GOTHENBURG, SWEDEN IN 1995. SEVEN NATIONS COMPETED, WITH BRITAIN DEFEATING SWEDEN IN THE FINAL TO BECOME THE WINNERS OF THE FIRST EUROPEAN GOLD MEDAL.

AT THE END OF THE GAMES ON AUGUST 21, 1996, DURING THE IPC PRESS CONFERENCE, HANS LINDSTROM, CHAIRMAN OF THE IPC SPORTS COMMITTEE, ANNOUNCED THAT WHEELCHAIR RUGBY HAD RECEIVED MEDAL SPORT STATUS FOR THE SYDNEY 2000 PARALYMPIC GAMES.

Centre. Eight teams competed with the USA defeating Canada 41-36 in the final to win gold, a prelude to the next seven years of the USA's domination. The tournament was the first international for the New Zealand team, the Wheel Blacks, who took the bronze medal, knocking Britain into fourth place 41-28. The following February, on behalf of the IWRF, Pawel Zbieranowski signed the contract with the organising committee of the Atlanta Paralympics for wheelchair rugby to take part. Its inclusion was a game-changer for the sport and it was appropriate that Pawel Zbieranowski, whose vision, drive and leadership had been instrumental to this achievement, was the person whose signature is recorded on this historic document.

Three years following the establishment of the IWRF, wheelchair rugby players, representing the six countries who had topped the previous year's World Championships, participated in the opening ceremony of the Atlanta Paralympic Games – USA, Canada, New Zealand, Great Britain, Sweden and Australia. The USA dominated the tournament defeating Canada 37-30 in the final to take gold, with the Kiwis beating Great Britain 46-34 to take bronze. Sweden and Australia finished fifth and sixth respectively, both showing strong performances. Australia, despite finishing in bottom position, gained a great deal of experience which would benefit them four years later in Sydney. At the end of the games on August 21, 1996, during the IPC press conference, Hans Lindstrom, Chairman of the IPC Sports Committee, announced that wheelchair rugby had received medal sport status for the Sydney 2000 Paralympic Games.

The first Paralympic Games of the new millennium was also the first where wheelchair rugby was included as a full medal sport. The USA, Australia, New Zealand, Canada, Sweden, Great Britain, Germany and Switzerland all qualified for the tournament which took Sydney by storm and wheelchair rugby became one of the most watched and exciting events. More than 10,000 fans saw the gold medal game between hosts Australia and the USA who went into the final undefeated in their three-game preliminary rounds. The crowd was treated to one of the most exciting and closest finishes with the USA defeating Australia by one point to take gold. The Sydney Games was a turning point for the Paralympic movement and left a legacy of increasing professionalism for Paralympic sport. For the first time, the venues used for the Olympics were the same used for the Paralympics and many of the Olympic event staff and volunteers stayed on to manage the Paralympics. This all made for the same high-quality sports presentation and lifted the experience from a disability event to an elite sporting spectacle.

CLASSIFICATION OF ATHLETES

With wheelchair rugby as one of the spectator highlights of the Sydney games, the stage was set for further global expansion and a shift towards a more professional approach to its development at international level. The USA, Canada, Australia, and Britain led the way in creating high-performance systems. In parallel, the IWRF continued to drive the evolution of the world game, building on the early work of individuals like Terry Vinyard from the USA, who had created an early rule book, and Tony Lapolla and Gilles Brière of Canada, who would lead on the creation of an international set of rules. John Bishop from the USA founded Quadrugby.com which enabled athletes and coaches around the world to network and share ideas. John was to go on to become the President of the international federation.

Meanwhile, Dr Anne-Marie Glenn of the USA, Claire Hart and Alison Sterling from Britain, and various physiotherapists from different nations, led the early work to create a functionally based classification system. Its purpose is to provide for a fair and equitable competition at all levels of Paralympic sport, allowing athletes to compete at the highest level, regardless of individual differences in physical function. It enables athletes with different levels of function to compete side by side giving them a pivotal role in the tactical execution of the game, style of play and athlete and spectator experience. Although the origins of the game lay in those with a spinal injury, its growing popularity soon attracted more disabled athletes with impairments such as polio, cerebral palsy, muscular dystrophy, multiple sclerosis, and amputations. Those with spinal injuries had either no, or very limited, trunk function. Other disability athletes, while still having some loss of function in all four limbs, often had full trunk function which provided the power to propel their chair at speed and create big hits to opponents' chairs.

Based on the track and field system, the first wheelchair rugby classification was medically based with three classes, largely determined by medical diagnosis and level of spinal cord injury. This changed in 1991, when a functional system unique to the sport was introduced. Functional classification systems ensure athletes with a combination of impaired or absent upper and lower limb movement have an opportunity to play the sport. And the strategies and skills of competing teams and athletes, rather than the amount of movement of the athletes, are the factors determining success in competition. Today there are seven classes ranging from 0.5 to 3.5 with functional characteristics identified for each athlete class.

HIGH-FUNCTIONING ATHLETES, THOSE WITH A CLASS 3.0 OR 3.5, ARE IN PARTICULAR DEMAND BECAUSE THEIR UPPER BODY STRENGTH AND MOBILITY ALONGSIDE THEIR RELATIVELY GREATER ARM AND HAND FUNCTION ALLOW THEM TO GENERATE CHAIR POWER AND SPEED WHILST MAINTAINING HIGH LEVELS OF BALL CONTROL. THEY CAN TRULY BE GAME CHANGERS.

In general, the 0.5 class includes those athletes with the most impairment and the 3.5 class includes those with the least impairment eligible for the sport. In international wheelchair rugby the total number of points of all four athletes actually playing cannot exceed 8.0. A team may play with a line-up that totals less than 8.0 points, but not more. Performance staff and coaches scour their respective countries seeking out individuals with the functionality at the top end of each of the respective classes to maximise a team's overall court functionality. High-functioning athletes, those with a class 3.0 or 3.5, are in particular demand because their upper body strength and mobility alongside their relatively greater arm and hand function allow them to generate chair power and speed whilst maintaining high levels of ball control. They can truly be game changers.

MURDERBALL, THE FILM

The Sydney spectacle of athletes smashing into one another with chairs flying around the arena was a film-maker's dream. Add to that some incredible human stories of hope, fear, resilience and courage, and you have the making of a great movie! So it was that following the Sydney Paralympics, film directors Henry Alex Rubin and Dana Adam Shapiro, along with producer Jeffrey Mandel, set about following the USA team as it prepared for the 2004 Paralympic Games in Athens. The result was the Academy Award-nominated film documentary *Murderball*, which at one level centred on the rivalry between the Canadian and USA teams but also examined the lives of those who have experienced life-changing injuries. It was a powerful expression of the triumph of the human spirit, shining a spotlight on the personal lives and challenges of quadriplegics, while also showcasing the

THE SYDNEY SPECTACLE OF ATHLETES SMASHING INTO ONE ANOTHER WITH CHAIRS FLYING AROUND THE ARENA WAS A FILM-MAKER'S DREAM. ADD TO THAT SOME INCREDIBLE HUMAN STORIES OF HOPE, FEAR, RESILIENCE AND COURAGE, AND YOU HAVE THE MAKING OF A GREAT MOVIE!

drama and excitement of the sport for athletes and spectators. The film did much to bring wheelchair rugby to a wider audience.

THE SPORT IN GREAT BRITAIN

Throughout the late 1980s and 1990s wheelchair rugby gained popularity in Britain. Initially it was the spinal injury units which provided the development focus, and most early players were able-bodied people who had incurred life-changing spinal injuries. Whilst motor accidents were a common factor, rugby, diving and water sports featured highly among the causes. There was a strong bond between those who found themselves in similar situations. The slow process of rehabilitation and the often painful mental adjustment to the realities of paralysis were something that could only be truly understood by those who had experienced them. Chances to play the game were also opportunities to come together and share experiences of adjusting to life in a chair, to have fun playing the game and enjoy the all-important, after-game socialising. Often those organising events were the families, friends and support workers. Of these, many learned to become officials and referees, while clinicians, particularly physiotherapists from the hospitals and spinal injury units, came forward to provide medical support and the expertise needed to develop classification.

As the popularity of the sport grew it was recognised there was a need to develop an organisation to promote the game, organise competitions between clubs and, better, create a national team. 1987 saw the start of the first domestic league with teams joining from the spinal units at Oswestry, West Midlands and Stoke Mandeville. This was formalised into a national league a year later with the Pirates, a new team from Cardiff joining. Teams from Southport, Birmingham and Sheffield soon joined, playing in a league structure and the national games at Stoke Mandeville which at that time was a multi-sport competition. Throughout the early 1990s teams also travelled to Europe helping to develop the game there and competing with teams from Sweden, Switzerland, Belgium, Denmark, Holland and Germany.

Teams and competitions were all self-funded, including the first national teams. Players and volunteers raised funds from raffles, and collections outside supermarkets. On international rugby weekends, players often came together at motorway service stations where fans going to Twickenham and Cardiff were treated to a demonstration of wheelchair rugby played in the service station car parks and invited to add a donation to the tin. Players like Allan Smith, Brian Worrel, Bob O'Shea, Jon Nutman, Keith Jones, Mike Spence and Rob Tarr were key drivers in creating the organisation necessary for the sport to evolve and by 1990 it was accepted under the governance of the British Wheelchair Sports Federation. By early 1990 the sport was able to operate under its own steam and the Great Britain Wheelchair Rugby Association was formed as a member organisation. Its first Chair was Alison Sterling with Allan Smith as Secretary. This was an important development as it meant the sport was eligible for charity status and, later, government funding to support the British team as it prepared for the Sydney Paralympic Games. It was also the beginning of Britain developing a professional performance system with Jeremy Moody, a sports scientist at Cardiff Metropolitan University, joining as British coach in 1998 and introducing the first systematic training and conditioning programme. Jeremy took the team, captained by Bob O'Shea, to the Sydney Paralympic Games in 2000 where Britain finished sixth.

The sport grew slowly during the first decade of the new millennium. Led by a strong and committed team of volunteers, the Association organised regional and national competitions and attracted Coloplast, a healthcare provider, to sponsor the national league. By the end of the decade there were seven established clubs: Pirates in Cardiff, Storm and Crusaders in London, Bulls in Sunderland, Gaelic Warriors in Glasgow and Crash in Liverpool. These competed in a league system and an annual national championship. Developing the sport was a continuing challenge. The few widely dispersed clubs meant some players travelled 2-3 hours to play, while for others the distance to the nearest club made it impossible. The costs associated with playing was also a barrier for many who existed on disability benefits. The average chair cost £3000-£5000 and consumables such as tyres racked up another £50 a month. Add to this the high costs of travel, and the sport was inaccessible for many.

Photos courtesy: Megumi Masuda

Those fortunate enough to be part of the GB performance programme were in a more privileged position. Following the UK's worst performance in the 1996 Atlanta Olympic Games, winning just one gold medal, UK Sport was established as a government agency to invest exchequer and National Lottery funding to support athletes to maximise their performance in the Olympics and Paralympics. Wheelchair rugby was an early beneficiary and the sport attracted funding to develop a professional performance programme. In addition to Jeremy Moody joining as a full-time professional coach, other performance support services were commissioned. Funding also enabled a full programme of international training and competition and Britain managed fourth at both the 2004 Athens and the 2008 Beijing Paralympics.

In July 2005, International Olympic Committee President Jacques Rogge announced that London was to host the 2012 Olympic and Paralympic Games. This heralded the start of an unprecedented investment of government and Lottery funding into British sport. With it came a commitment to use the opportunity to ensure a sporting legacy, to be measured in the growth in numbers participating in sport, and an investment in an elite sporting system to promote lasting medal success. Those on the committee of the GB Wheelchair Rugby Association realised this was an opportunity to access funding alongside the profile the sport would get on the back of a home Paralympic games which they hoped would attract new players and volunteers. It was to be three years later that James Price grabbed Richard Allcroft and took him to the Leeds offices of Sport England. James, a larger-than-life Devonian, had broken his neck in a freak diving accident in 1999. This left him a quadriplegic after which he immersed himself in wheelchair rugby having been introduced to the game during his rehabilitation at Stoke Mandeville. James' exuberance encouraged others to get involved and he was a natural to become the Association's lead for development. Richard Allcroft, who in 1992 had also incurred a spinal injury in a diving accident whilst a serving submariner in the Royal Navy, was the Association's Secretary. James had become aware of the Sport England strategy headlined 'Grow, Sustain, Excel' and saw this as an opportunity to get funding to develop the game. Following their meeting with Sport England, the two wheeled out of the offices to the pavement outside and looked at one another. Sport England had encouraged them to put together a funding submission but how would they even begin? Yet six weeks later the plan was completed and submitted, and soon after, wheelchair rugby was awarded £480,000 of government and Lottery monies with a clear remit to recruit a chief executive and a development director to begin the process of establishing a national governing body for the sport.

The appointment of David Pond as Chief Executive at the end of 2009 began the process of transforming wheelchair rugby from a volunteer-led and managed

ONE OF HIS FIRST ACTIONS WAS TO NEGOTIATE A PARTNERSHIP SUPPORT PACKAGE WITH THE RUGBY FOOTBALL UNION WHICH MOST IMPORTANTLY ALLOWED GBWR TO ESTABLISH A HEAD OFFICE WITHIN THE RFU MAIN BUILDING.

---

sport to Great Britain Wheelchair Rugby (GBWR), the professional national governing body formally recognised by the Sports' Councils in July 2015. One of his first actions was to negotiate a partnership support package with the Rugby Football Union which most importantly allowed GBWR to establish a head office within the RFU main building. This in turn enabled GBWR to access and share several corporate services which quickly helped to establish professional business processes giving confidence to grant providers and partners that they were investing in a going concern. In parallel, the organisation set about strengthening its board of trustees by recruiting new members with legal, finance and governance skills. At this point, London wheelchair rugby player and former GB international, Justin Frishberg stood down as the board chair and handed over to Kevin Aitchison. Kevin, the CEO of a London-based international investment company, had first seen the GB team in action at the 2004 World Championships in Christchurch, New Zealand. A sports fanatic, he was immediately hooked and served 10 years as volunteer board chair, steering the organisation as it grew and evolved. His service was recognised in 2020 when he was made an MBE. In the same vein, the CEO formed his executive team. In the early days he relied heavily on Richard Allcroft who had been one of the key volunteers behind the sport. Richard, with his easy humour, national and international network of contacts and competent administrative skills, was an effective bridge as the sport emerged from its volunteer management structure. Allcroft was to go on to become the first British President of the IWRF, a position he holds today. Pond recruited a sports development professional to be the national development director, and a corporate secretary to manage the office established in the RFU. Along with successful funding bids to Sport England and UK Sport, this provided the financial and human resource necessary to develop and implement a strategy based on growing membership to build wheelchair rugby communities and creating a sustainable performance system to enable a winning national team.

Raising the profile of the sport became a key early objective to attract more players, volunteers and funders. The sport teamed up with Onshore Media, a rising digital communications and PR agency in Plymouth. Onshore was founded by Dawn Bebe, a communications and media professional. Dawn and her partner Simon Whittam, quickly identified the media attractiveness of the sport and set about creating a GBWR brand and digital and social media profile, alongside the positioning of the sport and its people in a variety of media settings. Results came quickly with Channel 4 recognising that wheelchair rugby could be an exciting element of its London 2012 Paralympic campaign. Channel 4 had been awarded the Paralympics UK TV rights for 2012 Paralympics, over the BBC which had broadcast the games since 1980. The ambitious C4 bid was attractive for its creativity and its aim to use sport as a catalyst for continual change in public attitude towards disability. Rather than just broadcast the 12 days of Paralympic competition, the channel set out on an ambitious two-and-a-half-year programme where the focus of the Paralympic movement was to be at the core of the channel's programming strategy. From the start, wheelchair rugby became a part of this journey and when the broadcaster engaged the award-winning British TV and film director Mike Christie to create a film to launch the channel's campaign, the sport was quick to support it. The result was the acclaimed feature-length documentary Inside Incredible Athletes which was to become a BAFTA award-winning production. Wheelchair rugby was one of five sports represented in the film with the game shot being played on a barge transiting the river Thames against a background of iconic London sights. With Onshore's clever positioning, a range of media opportunities came the sport's way with individual athletes and the team appearing in mainstream media rather than being limited to the disability and sports agenda. Wheelchair rugby's profile was riding high by the time of London 2012 and tickets for all games were sold out in three days.

A key aim of Britain's thinking was to form closer links with rugby union. CEO Pond recognised the strength of the union brand and the potential of attracting the support from the rugby community. Following an introduction from Tony Woodcock, the former Nottingham Forest, Arsenal and England footballer, Pond met with England rugby fullback Mike Brown and invited him to the London games to watch Britain in action. Mike arrived with England captain Chris Robshaw and both were immediately captivated by the sport and in particular relished the big hits. Soon after, Mike was to join GBWR as an ambassador, further increasing the sport's recognition, and also helping to raise significant funds. He was later joined in the role by former Llanelli and Wales international Rupert Moon, while the legendary Jason Leonard became a patron in 2016.

The sport flourished after London 2012. By 2020, the seven clubs in 2010 had grown to 30 and the sport was delivering programmes in spinal injury units, military

RAISING THE PROFILE OF THE SPORT BECAME A KEY EARLY OBJECTIVE TO ATTRACT MORE PLAYERS, VOLUNTEERS AND FUNDERS.

rehabilitation centres, schools, universities and in partnership with a number of premiership and championship rugby clubs and their charitable foundations. Investment from Sport England and the Lottery for the grassroots game allowed a small workforce to be employed to support the delivery of the game and provide health and sporting opportunities for an increasing number of disabled individuals. GBWR also began working with several different partners including the charity Help for Heroes, established in 2007 to support service personnel wounded or injured on duty.

Help for Heroes was supporting many personnel returning from action in Afghanistan with life-changing injuries. Many were amputees keen to regain their fitness and mobility. GBWR started providing wheelchair rugby in the four military recovery centres where the physicality and dynamism of the sport made it hugely popular with those trying to rebuild their lives.

In 2014, GBWR was approached by representatives of Prince Harry and invited to develop a new format of the sport to be part of what was to become the' Invictus Games. Pond and Richard Allcroft worked with the Invictus planning team to create a version which would allow the competition to be played in a day and which was inclusive, enabling those with a broad range of injuries to take part. Mike Spence, a former GB captain and now GBWR board member, and Paul Jenkins, another legendary former player, took on the coaching role for the UK team. When the inaugural Invictus Games opened at the Copper Box in the Olympic Park in September, wheelchair Rugby stole the show. The UK team reached the final with the USA but ahead of the game the crowd was treated to a celebrity match with England Rugby World Cup icons Sir Clive Woodward and Johnny Wilkinson managing teams which included Prince Harry and England international Mike Tindall and his wife, Zara Phillips. In the final, an already excited crowd was brought to its feet when in the last seconds of the game the UK defeated the USA to take the gold medal.

Links with rugby union strengthened further when in 2015 Britain staged the inaugural World Wheelchair Rugby Challenge to sit alongside the Rugby World Cup. Staged in the Copper Box at the Olympic Park in Stratford, it attracted BT as a title sponsor and many of those who had travelled to the UK for the Rugby

IN 2014, GBWR WAS APPROACHED BY REPRESENTATIVES OF PRINCE HARRY AND INVITED TO DEVELOP A NEW FORMAT OF THE SPORT TO BE PART OF WHAT WAS TO BECOME THE INVICTUS GAMES.

Prince Harry watching the final as the UK defeated the USA to take the Gold Medal

World Cup also came to support their national wheelchair team. ITV broadcast live coverage of the event which was presented by former England international Martyn Bayfield. The event's success captured the attention of many in World Rugby and started a conversation about whether there was an opportunity for the Rugby World Cup and its wheelchair rugby equivalent to join together.

UK Sport ceased funding the GB elite programme following the 2016 Rio Paralympics when GB came fifth. There was a public outcry which contributed to a national debate about whether UK Sport's mantra of 'no compromise' and winning medals as the only criteria for success was a true representation of what the general public wanted to see from its public and National Lottery investment. The GBWR board was determined that even without the £3million UK Sport investment it would still find a way to fund training and competition programmes which would enable a competitive team to participate in the 2020 Tokyo Paralympics and it launched a major fundraising campaign. First to the rescue was the Lloyd's of London insurance market led by Roger Alwen, a former Lloyd's broker who had also been part of the London 2012 commercial team. LMAX Exchange, a fintech company, and the Thai retail group Kingpower, also came forward with financial backing along with charities, philanthropists,

THE COVID VIRUS WAS POTENTIALLY LIFE-THREATENING TO MANY OF THE ATHLETES, PARTICULARLY QUADRAPLEGICS WHOSE LUNG FUNCTION WAS ALREADY COMPROMISED.

and a host of individuals. This enabled the British team to maintain training and international competition and improve its world ranking to fourth ahead of the Tokyo Paralympic Games, postponed until 2021 as a consequence of the Covid-19 pandemic.

The Covid virus was potentially life-threatening to many of the athletes, particularly quadriplegics whose lung function was already compromised. This risk, along with government restrictions, prevented any team training and so measures were taken to provide personal training equipment for athletes to use in the safety of their homes. The coaches were also supported by video analysis of previous games and the performances of their Tokyo opponents and held daily virtual technical and tactical clinics with the athletes. The team sport psychologist provided individual and team support at what was an uncertain and unnerving time for everyone. The team remained resolute and focused on Tokyo and in January 2021 team training resumed in a strict Covid 'bubble' at the Lilleshall training centre.

Without spectators and with many restrictions in place the Tokyo Paralympic Games went ahead in August 2021. The games opened with the wheelchair rugby tournament played in the Yoyogi National Stadium with GB winning its first pool game against Canada, ranked fifth in the world. Day two saw GB crush the Kiwis 60-37 before facing the USA , world ranked two, in the final pool match. It was a tight game which GB lost 50-48 to end the pool stage as runners-up and qualify for the semi-finals. All eyes were on this match as GB faced Paralympic hosts Japan, ranked third in the world and favourites for the gold having already defeated Australia in the pool stage. It was a nail-biting encounter which GB won 54-49, defeating Japan for the first time in six years. GB was now sure of its first Paralympic medal, but the team was clear that a silver was not enough with star player Jim Roberts declaring in a BBC interview, 'We didn't come here for second'.

Paralympic broadcaster Channel 4 reported over 1.2million viewers tuning in to watch GB play the USA in the final which the broadcaster had moved to its main channel. They were not to be disappointed. In a thrilling contest, GB led throughout. The score was always tight and it was a brilliant performance in the final quarter – key to achieving gold. The USA seemed to have no answer to the impact of RAF and Afghanistan veteran Stuart Robinson or the speed and skill of Jim Roberts who consistently burst through a tight USA defence. Having learned the lessons of their pool game defeat, GB overpowered the Americans to win 55-49, the first wheelchair rugby medal for any European team and the first gold medal for any GB team sport in the history of the Paralympic Games. It was a remarkable triumph for a remarkable bunch of athletes all of whom had met head on the challenges presented by their disability, by Covid and by a lack of funding. All believed in one another and never doubted that they could create history and return from Tokyo with a gold.

WHAT OF THE FUTURE?

Forty-five years on from that first gym session in Winnipeg and wheelchair rugby is a global sport played in 31 countries. A further 21 are developing the game, from Bangladesh to Ecuador and Ukraine. The challenges are different in all countries, but they share common elements – availability and cost of chairs, travel to train and play, funding to compete, and sufficient volunteers to organise and support players with high-level physical impairment. Yet the sport and those who play have a life and an energy which inspire and capture those who touch it. Increasingly, there are those who want to play but whose impairments do not meet the strict classification criteria because they have too much function. New disciplines of the sport are evolving to offer a form of the game for them. There are also programmes for children and young people, which in Britain are being delivered in partnership with the Lord's Taverners charity and several premiership rugby club charitable foundations. At international level the sport is becoming increasingly professionalised with all the top world-ranking teams employing coaching staffs and a full suite of performance science and medicine professionals. This is enhancing the quality of the game and the spectator experience. With sport making up a large proportion of global media consumption, whether television, the 'red button' podcasts, sports apps, websites or social media, there are opportunities to grow a global audience. As all media outlets seek exciting, creative and different content, wheelchair rugby with its crunch of metal, screech of tyres, and collisions sending chairs and their disabled occupants sprawling across the court, is the ultimate adrenaline experience!

THERE ARE ALSO PROGRAMMES FOR CHILDREN AND YOUNG PEOPLE, WHICH IN BRITAIN ARE BEING DELIVERED IN PARTNERSHIP WITH THE LORD'S TAVERNERS CHARITY AND SEVERAL PREMIERSHIP RUGBY CLUB CHARITABLE FOUNDATIONS.

9
IWRF

Photo courtesy: Megumi Masuda

1936

On January 4, the Prince of Wales watched Russian Prince Alexander Oblensky play for England at Twickenham.

1941

Coventry won the first of 72 consecutive matches over four years.

1941

Vice Admiral and former England 1913 Grand Slam captain Norman Wodehouse was killed when his ship was torpedoed.

1945

A schools rugby match was played in Kyoto on September 23, only a month after Japan's surrender ended the Second World War.

1945

Jacques Chaban-Delmas played for the French national team. He became Prime Minister 24 years later and was awarded the Légion d'honneur to honour his work for the Resistance during the war.

19/52

In August, before a crowd of 42,000, Fiji won their first test match, beating Australia 17-12 at Sydney Cricket Ground.

19/55

Non-white spectators were banned by South Africa's Orange Free State Union from watching matches against the British and Irish Lions in Bloemfontein.

19/55

Tony O' Reilly won his first cap for Ireland. His last came in 1970, after a gap of seven years, before his subsequent business career saw him become President of Heinz.

19/56

National teams from West Germany, Romania and Italy toured Britain.

19/57

The Barbarians went on their first overseas tour, to Canada.

Photos courtesy: Megumi Masuda

STUART ROBINSON

I came into the game whilst I was in rehab following the loss of my limbs in an Afghanistan IED incident whilst serving with the RAF regiment. From the start I always had this goal of being able to play at a Paralympic Games, an opportunity to perform, and a new focus for me. The team environment is important to me and being part of this amazing sport reminds me of the camaraderie and single purpose I thrived on when serving in the military.

PLAYING THE GAME

Born in 1982, 2021 Paralympics gold medallist Stuart Robinson was on his fourth tour of Afghanistan in 2013 when he incurred life-changing injuries following an IED explosion. He was introduced to wheelchair rugby in 2014 during rehabilitation and became part of the first Invictus wheelchair rugby team. From here he was selected for the GB talent squad before making the full GB team for the Tokyo cycle.

"

ENJOY THE JOURNEY, THERE WILL BE SETBACKS, THERE WILL BE CHALLENGES BUT YOU'RE DOING THIS FOR A REASON – BECAUSE YOU LOVE IT, ENJOY IT AND ALL THE MOMENTS AND ACHIEVEMENTS IT BRINGS.

"

Sarah Hunter

THEY TOO RAN WITH THE BALL

A HISTORY OF WOMEN'S RUGBY

By Debbie Skene,
Director of Sport, Rugby School

Evidence of the origins of women's rugby is limited. On June 25, 1881 the *Liverpool Mercury* reported a women's football game played at the Cattle Market Inn, Athletic Grounds, Stanley, Liverpool. It is assumed this game followed Association Football rules, but the report mentions 'touchdowns' so it may have been played to rugby rules.

Following this report, a series of cigarette cards circulated in 1895, also in Liverpool, featuring women wearing rugby kit like that described in the *Liverpool Mercury*. It is unclear if these were an illustration of a sport not actually being played or a portrayal of real exhibition matches.

Otherwise the official record is silent for most of the 19th century. Some girls played rugby unofficially as part of their games time. In 1872 a school named The Laurels was founded in Rugby at the request of Rugby School's Head Master, Dr Temple. Temple was concerned the daughters of his teaching masters did not have an educational establishment to attend in the area. In the beginning, the school accommodated small numbers in premises on Little Church Street, opposite Rugby School. Daughters were seen playing forms of rugby on the school grounds after watching the boys play during games sessions. Official records of this have yet to be found and as the school grew in numbers and moved its site, the girls were encouraged to play hockey and cricket only.

The earliest confirmed record of any woman playing rugby comes from a school in Enniskillen, Northern Ireland. In 1884, Portora Royal School was run by William Valentine who had three children who attended the school, William, John and Emily. The trio wanted to play rugby but despite their father's approval, the school body was opposed and refused them access to the main sports field. In 1887, the three children began to play rugby with several friends. Emily joined in one game, scoring a try in the process as she later recalled in her memoirs:

Portora Royal School football team.

Emily Valentine.

"I loved rugby football, but seldom got a chance to do more than kick a place kick or drop goal, but I could run in spite of petticoats and thick undergarments, I could run. My great ambition was to play in a real rugby game and score a try. I used to stand on the touchline in the cold damp Enniskillen winter, watching every moment of play, furious when my side muffed a ball, or went offside, bitterly disappointed when a goal was missed.

"One day I got a chance. It was just a school scratch match and they were one 'man' short. I was about ten years old. I plagued them to let me play, 'Oh, all right. Come on then.' Off went my overcoat and hat – I always wore boys' boots anyhow, so that was all right.

"I knew the rules. At last my chance came. I got the ball – I can still feel the damp leather and the smell of it and see the tag of lacing at the opening. I grasped it and ran dodging and darting, but I was so keen to score that try that I did not pass it, perhaps when I should; I still raced on, I could see the boy coming toward me; I dodged, yes I could and breathless, with my heart pumping, my knees shaking, I ran. Yes, I had done it; one last spurt and I touched down, right on the line. I lay flat on my face and, for a moment, everything went black. I scrambled up, gave a hasty rubdown to my knees. A ragged cheer went up from the spectators. I grinned at my brothers. It was all I hoped for."

According to the school's records, which also includes correspondence from Valentine in 1951, Emily would continue to participate with the team in practices and intra-school matches. Some sources indicate Emily, a winger, and her two brothers, at times made up the team's three-quarter back line. Emily married Major John Galwey and spent time in India before settling in England. She died in 1967.

The first recorded women's match, Cardiff Ladies against Newport Ladies, was played at Cardiff Arms Park on December 16, 1917 to raise money for soldiers in France and Belgium. Cardiff players were working at city brewery, Wm Hancock Ltd, while the Newport team, who won 6-0, were mainly from iron and steelmakers Lysaghts & Co. The game generated impressive ticket sales and raised £100,000 for charity.

The women's charitable efforts dismissed concerns of unfeminine behaviour. If the games could be trivialised as an exhibition or charity match, women were not seen as a threat to the conventionally male rugby pitch.

Sixteen-year-old Mary Eley played for Cardiff. She went on to live to 106 and is now believed to be the oldest female rugby player. She reported to journalists before her death that her love of rugby is the reason she lived so long.

'We loved it. It was such fun with us all playing together on the pitch, but we had to stop when the men came back from the war, which was a shame. Such great fun we had.'

Throughout the 1920s a game very similar to rugby, called *barette,* was played across France. Traditionally played by men, *barette* largely disappeared before the First World War, being replaced by rugby. It was a bit of a mystery why the sport should suddenly reappear again in the 1920s as a women's sport, in France. Minor differences to the full game of rugby such as 10-a-side and some restrictions on tackling were observed.

New research by Lydia Furse, who is tracing the history of women's rugby as part of a PhD programme for De Montfort University in Leicester, shows these conclusions were wrong. The new *barette* was explicitly a form of women's rugby. Former French rugby international, André Theuriet, and Dr Marie Houdré coached and promoted *barette* and its public debut was on April 2, 1922 at the Stade Elisabeth in Paris. A short film exists of a game being played in 1928 and several newspapers featured cartoons and photographs. The French Rugby Federation (FFR) banned male rugby clubs from hosting *barette* matches in 1923, but the ban did not prevent women playing it at female-only sports clubs with their own pitches. The Fédération des sociétés féminines sportives de France (FFSF) supported the growth of *barette* under the leadership of Alice Milliat, who saw women playing male-identified sports as a feminist statement.

Marie Houdré and her Hirondelles.

Barette developed into a national championship by 1927 but disappeared during the Western economic depression during the 1930s. The French government banned *barette* and other women's sports which it considered 'unwomanly' by 1941.

The history of women's rugby then jumps to the 1960s. In 1962, Edinburgh University first recorded a women's rugby union team. On May 1, 1968, the first fully documented and recorded women's club match took place in France, at Toulouse Fémina Sports in front of spectators. Its success led to the formation of the first national association for women's rugby union—the Association Francaise de Rugby Féminin (AFRF) at Toulouse in 1970. This accelerated the formation of women's rugby unions in universities across Canada (1970), the USA (1972), the Netherlands and Spain (1975) and Italy (1979).

By 1980 there were club championships in the United States and Sweden, and provincial championships in New Zealand. In February 1982 University College London's women's team went on a tour to France playing, amongst other teams, Pontoise – the first recorded overseas tour by a UK team (and possibly the first international tour by any women's team).

Women's international rugby union began in 1982, with a match between France and the Netherlands played in Utrecht. The game resulted from a meeting between Frenchman Henri Fléchon and a delegation led by Leo van Herwijnen from the NRB, the Dutch rugby union. Fléchon was particularly impressed by the way the NRB had recently officially recognised women's rugby. The Dutch enthusiastically put into effect everything they had learned in France and decided to form a national team. They invited France to send a women's team to play the Dutch in the first international women's rugby match. Two months between the invitation and the match date, the Association Française de Rugby Féminin (AFRF) accepted the request. The Dutch organised trials and selected a team by the end of April, although many of their players had little or no experience of full 15-a-side rugby.

On Sunday, June 13, 1982 the two teams arrived at Utrecht Sportpark Strijland, the home of Utrechtse Rugby Club to play the historic game. The Netherlands were led by head coach Jopie Nessels and captained by their prop Lisa Groenedijk, while France were led by head coach Clause Isoard. The match, refereed by Roel Wijnant of Belgium, resulted in a 4-0 victory for France.

Dutch news magazine *Panorama* sent reporter Henk Hansen to cover proceedings:

"We do not have to take this!" Frieke angrily shouts to her team. The game is deep in the second half as quiet blond Dutch wing Odet Zijlstra is felled by a French tackle round her neck. Anything goes at rugby, you can tackle everywhere

"I AM A WOMAN, SIR, THAT YOU HAVE ALREADY SEEN, BUT I'M EVEN MORE THAN YOU MIGHT KNOW."

– except in the neck. And if your opponent does, you get angry! "Don't moan about it," shouts Frieke "JUST GET BACK AT THEM – HARD!!"

The face of Frieke is set in a mask of determination: she is determined to show the men on the touchline that women can play rugby. In her mind echoes the song that later, after the game, will ring around the bar: "I am a woman, sir, that you have already seen, but I'm even more than you might know."

In 1983, a year after this game, the Women's Rugby Football Union (WRFU) was founded, the oldest formally organised national governing body for women's rugby. The English-based organisation was responsible for women's rugby in England, Scotland, Ireland and Wales, with founder member clubs Leicester Polytechnic, Sheffield University, University College London, University of Keele, Warwick University, Imperial College, Leeds University, Magor Maidens, York University and Loughborough University.

This was replaced in 1994 by the Rugby Football Union for Women (RFUW) in England with each of the other Home Nations governing their own countries. The first Women's Rugby World Cup took place in Wales in April 1991. The tournament was attended by 12 teams and organised by just four ladies! Deborah Griffin, Alice Cooper, Sue Dorrington and Mary Forsyth met through Richmond Rugby Club. They worked tirelessly to get the first World Cup up and running even though it would not be officially sanctioned by the IRB. The 12 participating teams paid their own way to get to Cardiff where the tournament was held. Their determined efforts put the international women's game on the map. Dorrington juggled her administrative role with representing England during the tournament and played in the final against the USA. The United States went on to win the tournament, which was held amid huge financial uncertainty, and received a celebratory reception at the White House.

The New Zealand team caused upset to prominent Maoris by performing the haka before their opening match against Canada in Cardiff. In Maori protocol, women are not in the front line of the haka. The black ferns went on to seek permission to perform an alternative haka entitled Ka Panapana.

The second tournament took place in 1994 but could not be named 'World Cup' as the International Rugby Board did not recognise the event and forced the Dutch

WRWC 1991 programme cover.

organisers to cancel just months before the proposed start date. As there had been some public disagreement over the use of the term Rugby World Cup, Scotland's Sue Brodie was determined to represent her country, so she gathered a group of Scottish rugby players, administrators and advocates to organise the Women's Rugby World Championship. Sue Brodie played in the championship in 1994 and saved the whole tournament. The event remained illegitimate in the eyes of the IRB and prevented New Zealand from competing, but the championship has since been officially recognised as the second women's rugby world cup.

In 1996, the IRB created a Women's Advisory Committee which published a development plan for women's rugby. This endorsed a Home Nations competition for England, Scotland, Wales and Ireland, which developed to become a Six Nations competition in 2007 and is run in parallel to the men's competition.

The IRB eventually approved the 1998 Women's Rugby World Cup. The tournament was awarded to Amsterdam in the Netherlands with a record number of 16 teams competing. Teams were invited by the IRB, and New Zealand defeated the United States 44-12 in the final. New Zealand hold the title with the most World Cup wins, currently standing at five (1998, 2002, 2006, 2010, 2017), whilst England have reached the final seven times (twice winners and five times runners up).

By now, women's teams were accepted on the main stage, and in 2002 Scotland played their first women's match at Murrayfield and in 2003 England staged the first women's international at Twickenham.

BY NOW WOMEN'S TEAMS WERE ACCEPTED ON THE MAIN STAGE, AND IN 2002 SCOTLAND PLAYED THEIR FIRST WOMEN'S MATCH AT MURRAYFIELD AND IN 2003 ENGLAND STAGED THE FIRST WOMEN'S INTERNATIONAL AT TWICKENHAM.

Peter Green, Executive Head Master, with members of the 2014 winning England team.

INSPIRATIONAL PLAYERS AND TEAMS

DR MARIE HOUDRÉ

Dr Marie Houdré developed a new sport known as *barette*. The rules were adopted from rugby union and included the same ball shape and method of scoring tries. Some sources state that blocking was introduced instead of tackling. However, videos of the game in 1928 portray a different story and tackling at the waist was permitted Marie Houdré first encountered the game when working at a sanatorium in Polemuer where she created a women's sport section and, on moving to the French capital, quickly joined the Fémina Sports Club of Paris – a noted all-female club offering facilities for all the main sports. Marie Houdré was captain of the Hirondelles (the Swallows) and coached both teams at Fémina Sport. She argued for the health benefits of women playing *barette* and used her medical credentials to help her promote the sport.

In 2019, Marie Houdré was the first name in the new French Rugby women's Hall of Fame. Serge Simon, who unveiled Dr Marie Houdré's name, said: "Throughout the century, Marie Houdré, a pioneer, tried to create gaps, They closed for Marie

Houdré." He added: "It is thanks to these women that women's rugby is now finally on the right track. She perfectly embodies the image of all those women who fought in the shadows for their love of the game."

PATTY JERVEY

Patty Jervey was the first player to play in five Women's Rugby World Cups, winning the inaugural tournament in 1991, when the USA beat England 19-6 in the final, before appearing in the next four competitions in 1994, 1998, 2002 and 2006. Jervey's career lasted over 31 years. It began when she was a student at the University of South Carolina but gathered momentum after she switched to the Florida State University. Jervey made her international debut in 1989 and as a remarkably resilient athlete won 40 caps – a USA record which stood until 2013. She ended her career as the highest point-scorer for her country with 178.

In 2008, she was one of seven athletes to receive Distinguished Service Awards from the American Sports and Arts Museum and Archives (ASAMA). In 2014, Patty Jervey was among the first group of women's players to be inducted into the World Rugby Hall of Fame and she is one of the most highly regarded players of her generation in the American game.

CAROL ISHERWOOD OBE

A hugely influential figure in the development of women's rugby as a player, coach and administrator.

Carol Isherwood became involved in rugby in 1981 when she set up the first women's team at the University of Leeds, which in turn became a founder member of the WRFU and then the RFUW. Isherwood captained the first Great Britain and England women's sides of the mid-1980s and was awarded a combined total of 15 caps before retiring in 1992 due to a serious knee injury. Embarking on a successful career as a coach, assisting England at the Women's Rugby World Cup 1994, as well as being head coach for Emerging England, England U19 and leading club sides Henley and Richmond, Carol was recognised with an OBE in 2003 for her services to rugby.

In 2008, she was voted the IRB Women's Sports Personality of the Year and the following year became the first woman to be appointed to the IRB Rugby Committee. Carol was one of the first six women inducted into the IRB Hall of Fame in November 2014.

NATHALIE AMIEL

Amiel started playing in the Languedoc region of France. When she was 12, her mother registered her at a club which offered a women's rugby section. It was in her own village, Capestang, that the local coach welcomed her to train with the boys.

In 1986 the women's game in France was not governed by the Fédération Française de Rugby (FFR) and that ensured she could win her first cap in Richmond against Great Britain. Another 55 test appearances would follow as Amiel played in three Women's Rugby World Cups in 1991, 1994 and 2002, captaining them in the latter when they finished third. Under Amiel's leadership they took the Five Nations Women's Grand Slam in 2002.

Amiel held the post of assistant of the France women's team for five years from 2009. She assumed the role of head coach in 2014 and in her only year in charge led France to the Six Nations Grand Slam and a third-place finish on home soil at Women's Rugby World Cup 2014.

Amiel reported at her induction to the World Rugby Hall of Fame in 2014 "It was not easy to deal with everything, between family life and my commitments with the team," she said as she remembered how her son would react each time she left for an international tour.

"But a coach should be happy to have mothers in his team because it shows him that if they are on the field instead of staying at home, it's to give everything to the team."

LIZA BURGESS

Liza Burgess was born in Newport, Gwent, South Wales in 1964. Her rugby career started at Loughborough University in 1983 and continued at Wasps after graduating. Burgess made her international debut playing for Great Britain against the Netherlands and France in 1986. She captained Wales 62 times and participated in six

Women's Rugby World Cups. Twenty years later and with 93 caps to her name, including six appearances for Great Britain prior to the development of the Welsh national side, she finished her test career on the concluding day of the Women's Six Nations in 2007.

Nicknamed 'Bird', Burgess played with Saracens for a decade and led the side to the first treble recorded in the women's domestic game (League and Cup in 15s and the National Sevens).

On her induction to the World Rugby Hall of Fame, Burgess said: "I'm lucky to have played a sport I love and to be honoured in this way is unbelievable. It's genuinely difficult to put into words how I feel. All the other players being inducted are all phenomenal."

MARGARET ALPHONSI MBE

Margaret 'Maggie' Alphonsi is arguably one of the most well-known names in women's rugby and even in women's sport.

She represented her country an impressive 74 times, scored 28 tries, won a World Cup in 2014 and helped England win a record-breaking seven consecutive Six Nations crowns – six of them Grand Slams.

In 2010, she was awarded the *Sunday Times* Sportswoman of the Year followed by being the first female recipient of the Rugby Writers' prestigious Pat Marshall Award. A rising star, playing as a flanker for Saracens who went on to win a league and cup double, Alphonsi finally hung up her boots in 2015.

Alphonsi went on to become an ambassador for Rugby World Cup 2015 and embarked on a successful career in the media as a TV pundit. In 2015, Maggie became the first former female player to commentate on men's international rugby when she was signed up by ITV for the Rugby World Cup.

In 2016, she was elected to the RFU Council. She's also an ambassador of several not-for-profits and charities, all with the aim of giving the youth of Africa hope for the future through rugby.

adidas
NEW ZEALAND

PORTIA WOODMAN (left)

Portia Woodman is one of the most recognisable players in women's sevens, as the leading try scorer on the World Series.

Woodman comes from a family with great sporting pedigree. Her father Kawhena and her uncle Fred are both former All Blacks and her aunt Te Aroha is a former netballer with the Silver Ferns. After starting her sporting career as a netball player, Woodman switched to rugby union in 2012.

It did not take long before Woodman made her debut for the Black Ferns in 2013 against England in the 1,000th Test match of women's rugby. From then, she made herself a regular in the international side. She was included in the 2013 New Zealand squad when they won the World Cup Sevens in Russia.

Woodman has gained success in XV and Sevens forms of the game. She has won three Rugby World Cup titles – two in Sevens (2013, 2018) and one in XVs (2017), a Commonwealth gold medal from 2018 as well as an Olympic Sevens silver medal from 2016 and a gold medal from Tokyo in 2021.

In 2015, Woodman was awarded the World Rugby Women's Sevens Player of the Year Award and in 2017 was named World Rugby Women's Player of the Year. In 2020, she was named as the top women's Sevens and 15s player of the decade.

GILLIAN BURNS

Stephen Jones, rugby writer for the *Sunday Times* wrote in 1996: "It is a long time since I was so impressed by someone in sport. It is not so much that she is a fine player and athlete, such a selfless ambassador for women's rugby, or, indeed, some kind of valiant amateur throwback to rugby as it once was. It is that Burns came across, in every respect, as a genuine, 24-carat English sporting heroine."

Burns took up the sport of rugby after receiving an invitation to play for Liverpool Polytechnic, the only women's team in the area at the time. Burns made her England debut against Sweden in 1988 at Waterloo RFC. Not only did Burns play in the match but she also organised it! She went on to play for Waterloo Ladies from 1989, where she established the women's section at the club.

Burns' international career lasted 14 years from 1988 to 2002, she played in four World Cups winning a then record 73 caps for her country. She was long-standing captain of the national side, after succeeding Karen Almond, and a member of

England's Women's Rugby World Cup-winning team of 1994.

Despite retiring from rugby Burns was still influential in the game. She became the first female president of an English rugby club when Waterloo handed her the honour in 2004. Burns also enjoyed a 10-year term as president of the RFUW.

A string of awards has been bestowed on Burns including the *Sunday Times* Sportswomen of the Year Team Award, the *Cosmopolitan* Achievement Award for Sporting Success and the Sports Writers' Association Awards. Her contribution to women's rugby was also recognised at the BBC Sports Personality of the Year Awards and in 2005 she was awarded an MBE.

WOMEN'S RUGBY IN THE MODERN ERA

World Rugby's ambitious strategic 2017 to 2025 global action plan is accelerating the global development of women in rugby. Transformational governance reform introduced in 2017 allowed 17 female members a position on the World Rugby Council, the largest representation of women. Participation levels are at an all-time high with 2.7 million players globally, a 28 per cent increase in since 2017.

World Rugby Chairman Sir Bill Beaumont said: "We firmly believe that the development of women in rugby is the single greatest opportunity for our sport to grow in the next decade, which is why we are proud to share our exciting new brand identity."

The Women's World Cup remains the highest-profile women's rugby tournament. It started in 1991 and is held every four years. In 2019, World Rugby officially removed sex/gender designations from the title of the Women's World Cup so all future tournaments will be officially known as the 'Rugby World Cup'.

In October 2009, the IOC voted at its session in Copenhagen to include the sevens version of the sport in the 2016 Summer Olympics in Rio de Janeiro and this would include a men's and women's tournament. Australia defeated New Zealand in the final to win the gold medal. The inaugural Women's Rugby World Cup Sevens tournament took place in Dubai together with the men's tournament in 2009. Australia defeated New Zealand 15-10 in extra time to become the first to win the Women's Rugby World Cup.

The primary annual global competition for women's rugby sevens is the World Rugby Women's World Series, launched in the 2012-13 season. It features four to six tournaments each year. Women's rugby sevens has also been added to several regional multi-sport tournaments, including the Pan American Games in 2015 and the Commonwealth Games in 2018.

International tournaments, TV rights and record-breaking attendances (17,440 spectators at Stade des Alpes in Grenoble for the France-England fixture in the 2018 Women's Six Nations) has moved the game to a professional era. France reformed the country's elite club structure in 2016, switching from the long-standing 'Top 10' to form a 'Top 8', a controversial move followed by a period of unprecedented success for French teams internationally. France went on to win the Six Nations, come third in the 2017 XVs World Cup, third in the 2017/18 World Series, and finalists at the 2018 Sevens World Cup. Credit was given to the four extra weekends for international training, as well as ensuring the strongest teams played each other.

The English Premiership made moves in a similar direction, with the RFU confirming that 10 clubs would be offered places in the new women's domestic competition to be called the Women's Super League. It began its first season of the professionalised format of the RFU women's domestic competition in September 2017.

The England Women's rugby team made international history by becoming the first women's team to become fully professional. In 2019, every member of the England Women's rugby team received full-time contracts for the new season. The RFU was determined to show its commitment to growing the women's game.

The Australian Super League received one of the first major sponsors for the female sport. This was a massive step to ensure that all members of female teams got paid for their participation in the sport, just like the male teams.

The first Rugby Africa Women's Cup took place in 2020 with all matches taking place in South Africa. The Springboks won the competition, qualifying for the Rugby World Cup 2021. World Rugby Women's general manager, Katie Sadleir, said: "Rugby Africa play a key role in the continued success for developing women in rugby. Off the field the board of Rugby Africa has made fundamental changes which show its commitment in providing equal opportunities for women in rugby. On the field, by aligning the Rugby Africa Cup to host men's and women's matches at the same time this will have a positive impact in raising the profile of the women's 15s game in Africa."

THE RFU CONFIRMING THAT 10 CLUBS WOULD BE OFFERED PLACES IN THE NEW WOMEN'S DOMESTIC COMPETITION TO BE CALLED THE WOMEN'S SUPER LEAGUE. IT BEGAN ITS FIRST SEASON OF THE PROFESSIONALISED FORMAT OF THE RFU WOMEN'S DOMESTIC COMPETITION IN SEPTEMBER 2017.

The Black Ferns who have dominated women's rugby over the past two decades.

The Black Ferns are New Zealand's senior women's rugby team and have dominated women's rugby over the last two decades in both the XV and sevens international tournaments. They hold Women's Rugby World Cup titles in 1998, 2002 2006, 2010 and 2017. The Black Ferns' successful 2017 season was a landmark one for women's rugby as they became the first women's team to be named the World Rugby Team of the Year. The Black Ferns Sevens have dominated the Women's Sevens Series, claiming five series crowns since its launch in 2012 (2012/13, 2013/14, 2014/15, 2016/17 and 2018/19). They have an 87 per cent winning record in test match rugby and are the only women's international side with a winning record against every opponent. Since their international debut in 1991, the Black Ferns have lost to only four of the 16 nations they have played in test matches.

In the 2014/15 series, the team secured convincing wins in Dubai, Brazil, USA and Canada, finishing the series 12 points clear of nearest rival Canada and won automatic qualification to the Olympic Games in Rio de Janeiro in 2016 when sevens debuted on the world's greatest sporting stage. They picked up silver at the Rio Olympics and went one better at Tokyo 2020, claiming gold. The team are the current sevens World Champions after winning the title in 2013 and 2018.

In time for the bicentenary in 2023, World Rugby have now launched the WXV. This is a new three-tier annual global women's international 15s competition within a restructuring of the test calendar.

Tier 1 (known as WXV 1) will consist of six teams. Participating teams will include the top three teams from the Women's Six Nations (Europe) and the top three teams of the cross-regional tournament featuring USA, Canada, New Zealand and Australia (Oceania/Rugby Americas North (RAN). It will be a standalone tournament in one location, which will be determined on a year-by-year basis. There will be no promotion or relegation in the first cycle. Tiers 2 and 3 follow a similar pattern with round robin tournaments and promotions and relegations.

The new WXV is a major development in the women's rugby game and a major step rugby for women's rugby being catapulted on to a world stage with status as the men's game.

GILL BURNS

I was at a hockey tournament when a defender obstructed me. I was running at pace so accidentally knocked her over then ran through to score a goal. I went straight back to help her to her feet and as I hauled her off the ground she said 'The way you play hockey you should be a rugby player'. I was somewhat put out as I had done nothing wrong so I replied 'You obstructed me, I didn't mean to knock you over,' to which she replied 'I'm not being funny, I mean it. I play rugby and you'd be great.' As we jogged back to the halfway line I had started to think that I'd like to try. After the game we chatted in the bar and she told me she played for Liverpool Polytechnic but it wasn't exclusively for students as they invited any women who wanted to try the game to join in. They trained and played at Waterloo FC who at the time had a very senior men's side that I'd seen on the TV. I fancied trying a new sport and at age 23 I was keen to join a new social circle too. I joined the team the following Sunday, just loved the training and I never looked back.

PLAYING THE GAME

Born in 1964, Gill Burns, OBE, represented England between 1988 and 2003, winning the Women's Rugby World Cup in 1994, and was captain from 1994-9. Gill was appointed President of the Rugby Football Union for women after retiring from the game and was inducted into the IRB Hall of Fame on November 17, 2014.

My career highlight has to be the World Cup win in 1994 up in Edinburgh as to win a world title is truly special. We defeated the hot favourites USA 38-23 in the final. It was a very special time and I will always be grateful to the coaches and support staff who did their jobs as unpaid volunteers and helped us achieve our ultimate ambition. However, the highlight that is a very close second place was from my very first game. The first scrummage of the game was set. Having only trained twice and being selected at number eight I knew I was to pick up the ball at the base of the scrum then run as fast as I could. The scrum nudged forward, I picked up the ball and set off. I pushed the opposition blind side out of the way (my first hand off!) I then did it again and another player fell to the floor. I then weaved past a third player. The ball was in my hands and the lack of restrictions felt good. My first big break! Then after about 30 yards I was tackled. I remembered I was to present the ball, so rolled into position and watched the big girls in the front five compete over the ball. My first ruck! They cleared out well and our little nippy scrum-half pick up and sniped. I jumped up to see what was going to happen next. As I ran to support play I watched her pass to our centre, Sue, who weaved past another defender, threw a massive dummy and I watched a huge space open up for her to run through and score under the sticks. Sue who scored, the usual goal kicker, had damaged her toe and couldn't kick the conversion. Nobody else wanted to take it so I said I'd try. I made a mound of earth, teed up the ball and toe-ended it over the bar. My first conversion! What a great game, for so many different types of players, it was such a buzz. I knew then I'd found the sport I was made for.

I think William Webb Ellis would probably be amazed by the sheer athleticism, fitness and skill sets of the professional players, and the structures that the big teams employ. But he'd probably recognise the remnants of the free-running, wonderfully enjoyable game he invented if he watched the community game. In those matches, without too much structured defence, he'd see spaces on the pitch for attackers to exploit. Long may both versions of the old game exist.

1957 England won the Five Nations grand slam, a feat they would not then repeat for 34 years.

1957 Romania narrowly lost to France 18-15 in a match watched by 95,000 people in Bucharest.

FRANCE RUGBY

1961 France won the Five Nations Championship and repeated the feat the following year.

1961 France's tour of New Zealand was the first to be broadcast live by satellite.

1964 The Georgian Rugby Federation was created, 25 years before Georgia played its first international match, against Zimbabwe.

19
65

Rugby union players were banned from accepting awards from commercial firms.

19
65

Rugby was introduced to Norway by oil workers.

19
65

One of the touch judges in the Five Nations fixture between England and Wales in Paris was Denis Thatcher, husband of future prime minister Margaret Thatcher.

19
67

Newport centre Keith Jarrett scored 19 points aged 18 on his debut as full-back for Wales against England, including a 50-yard try which he then successfully converted.

"

RUGBY WILL ALWAYS HOLD
A PLACE OF PRIDE FOR
THE ROLE IT PLAYED....
DURING THOSE FIRST YEARS
OF OUR NEW DEMOCRACY.

"

Nelson Mandela

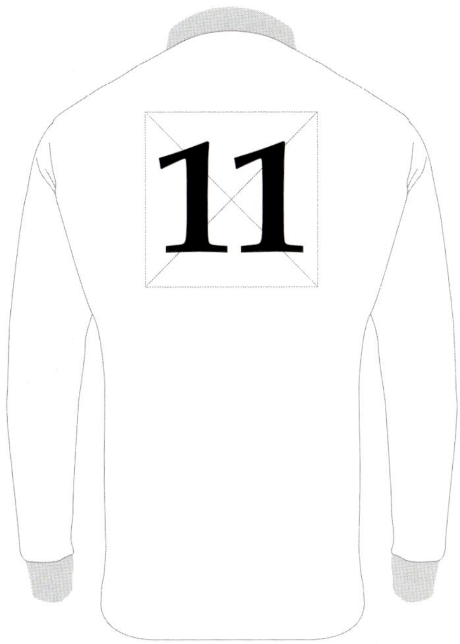

RUGBY AND POLITICS

By David Hempsall,
former Head of History, Rugby School

RUGBY HAS ALWAYS BEEN AMONGST THE MOST OVERTLY POLITICAL OF SPORTS, GENERATING INTERNAL AND EXTERNAL ISSUES. IT IS COMPLEX AND SUBTLE, AND JUDGMENT IS CRUCIAL. THAT ALONE INEVITABLY ATTRACTS CONFLICTING OPINIONS WHICH NECESSITATE DECISION-MAKING.

Rugby has always been amongst the most overtly political of sports, generating internal and external issues. It is complex and subtle, and judgment is crucial. That alone inevitably attracts conflicting opinions which necessitate decision-making.

There are countless references to games involving kicking and carrying a ball. In Great Britain, such games are recorded from the mid-12th century onwards though none can rightly be regarded as the real precursor of rugby. In several countries, there was legislation banning such games, their playing being conducive to public disorder. Whilst football for the common man was being suppressed in Britain, notably by the 1835 Highway Act, which forbade playing on highways and public land, it did find a home in schools around the country.

Until 1885 the laws of rugby were made by England. A disputed try in the international of 1884 between Scotland and England led to a heated exchange over the rules. The English being intransigent, the Scots refused to play the English in the 1885 Home Nations tournament. This prompted Scotland, Ireland and Wales to form an international association to allow its members to decide the rules of the game and in 1897, at a meeting held (ironically) in Manchester, the three unions established the principles of what became the International Rugby Football Board. England refused to join and rejected the IRFB's claim as the game's lawmaker. Internationals against England were boycotted in 1888 and 1889, forcing the English to join in 1890. In that year, the first international laws of rugby were agreed but, by then, a new political crisis was in the making.

In the 1880s, large numbers of industrial workers in the north of England had taken up rugby. Miners, dockers and factory workers had to take unpaid leave from work to play rugby. Rugby being an amateur sport, players could not be compensated for the wages lost playing in matches, so the northern rugby clubs proposed players should receive what were called 'broken time' payments. After receiving a complaint from Cumberland County Union that players were being lured away by promises of money made by another club, the IRFU launched an inquiry.

After it was found that some Yorkshire clubs were making such payments, charges of professionalism were brought against them in 1892. A proposal that players be

The George Hotel, Huddersfield where the Northern Rugby Football Union was established.

paid up to 6 shillings [30p] to compensate them for missing work to play in matches was rejected by the RFU. Despite being warned by clubs in Lancashire and Yorkshire that any sanctions risked a schism, RFU leaders– mainly public school educated and wedded to the amateur principle – refused to countenance the idea.

In 1895, several prominent Lancashire clubs supported a proposal from across the Pennines that a professional organisation be formed. The Northern Rugby Football Union (NU) was established with 22 members. In response, the RFU issued sanctions against clubs, players and officials involved in the offshoot group, including amateurs who played with or against Northern Union sides. In no other sport was Britain's class divide so starkly illustrated. "Why should we hand it over without a struggle to the hordes of working men players who would quickly engulf all others?" asked rugby international Frank Mitchell in 1897. Soon after the schism, the rules of the competing unions diverged, resulting in two distinctly different rugby forms – union and league – each governed by its own code.

The emergence and development of the two codes is redolent of the north-south divide. All stereotypes are prejudicial but information produced in the wake of the 2019 General Election suggests that rugby union is Great Britain's most Conservative and most privileged team sport whilst rugby league is the most Labour and most deprived.

The Reach Data Unit looked at the locations of the home grounds of every cricket, football, rugby league and rugby union club that takes part in a national league.

It then analysed voting patterns in the local parliamentary constituency, and deprivation levels in the local neighbourhood.

Some 40 per cent of the rugby union stadia in England, Scotland and Wales are located in constituencies which voted Conservative in the last election. This was the highest percentage of any of the country's major team sports: it compares with just 3 per cent for rugby league (and 29 per cent for soccer and 33 per cent for cricket).

51 per cent of rugby union stadia being situated in Labour constituencies, electors voted in favour of Labour overall. On the other hand, 97 per cent of those constituencies housing rugby league grounds voted Labour.

The Unit's findings were that whilst rugby league clubs are most likely to be based in the most deprived neighbourhoods, for rugby union the reverse applies. 56 per cent of rugby league stadia are in the top two deciles of social deprivation with only 3 per cent lie in the least deprived. Of rugby union clubs, 18 per cent are in the two top deciles for deprivation whilst 26 per cent are in the two least deprived areas.

Before the 2019 election the Conservative party think-tank Onward identified as one of its targets so-called "Workington man... with his strong rugby league traditions". *Pace* the sexism, making a play for traditional Labour strongholds by promising to 'level up', the Conservatives met with unexpected levels of success, breaching the so-called Red Wall surrounding former Labour strongholds.

A century after the Great Schism in 1995, rugby union joined rugby league and most other forms of football as an openly professional sport, thereby allowing players who wished to participate in both codes. By then, rugby had managed to navigate other political issues, few of its own devising.

The IRFB had originally been constituted with a heavy bias towards England. After the Second World War, its influence was diluted as its four seats – reduced from six in 1911 – were further halved to bring it into line with the other three home nations. In 1948, Australia, New Zealand and South Africa joined the board with one member each, their representation being doubled in 1958. Other countries joined: France in 1978; Argentina, Canada, Italy and Japan in 1991; Georgia, Romania and the USA in 2016. As the game spread, so the governing board was re-styled

A CENTURY AFTER THE GREAT SCHISM IN 1995, RUGBY UNION JOINED RUGBY LEAGUE AND MOST OTHER FORMS OF FOOTBALL AS AN OPENLY PROFESSIONAL SPORT.

The red rose that adorns the shirt of the England rugby team.

A plaque commemorating the 1895 founding of Rugby League.

as first the International Rugby Board in 1998 and then, in 2014, as World Rugby. The name is entirely appropriate with 80 countries joining between 1987 and 1999: at the time of writing, the organisation has some 120 members and associates. There are a further 33 non-affiliated rugby-playing countries.

Political issues have sometimes overshadowed match competition, some better known than others to a western audience. In 2008, for example, relations worsened between Russia and Georgia, former constituent republics of the USSR. Fighting broke out in Transcaucasia between the two and the Russian-backed self-proclaimed republics of South Ossetia and Abkhazia. This led to the 2009 and 2010 international fixtures between the two being cancelled. Matches have resumed: of the 23 games played between the two, Georgia has won 21, Russia one with one match drawn.

Closer to home, there were three decades of The Troubles in Northern Ireland, which saw over 3500 killed and more than 30,000 injured between 1968 and the Good Friday Agreement of 1998.

Rugby provided one outlet for all-Irish, non-sectarian sentiment with players from the province and the republic wearing the same green shirt as one team. How and why? The answer is very largely and simply political. The Irish Rugby Football Union was created in 1879 when the island of Ireland was one, long predating 1921 partition. Instead of creating two separate rugby unions, the IRFU was retained. During The Troubles, however, some tensions were inevitable.

In 2018, former Ireland and British and Irish Lions captain Brian O'Driscoll turned film-maker. In a much-lauded documentary entitled *Shoulder to Shoulder*, he examined how rugby managed to navigate The Troubles. Over such a long period, his documentary highlighted three particularly significant events.

1972 was one of the most savage of years. It had begun on January 30 with Bloody Sunday in the Bogside area of Londonderry when British soldiers shot 26 unarmed civilians during a protest march against internment without trial organised by

Former Ireland and British and Irish Lions captain Brian O'Driscoll.

Willie John McBride, a Protestant from the north.

the Northern Ireland Civil Rights Association. This unleashed further violence in which over 100 British troops were killed during the year. Given the security risks, Scotland and Wales refused to play Ireland in Dublin, thereby throwing the Five Nations Championship into disarray.

One man was determined that violence would not win. Willie John McBride, a Protestant from the north, took it upon himself to contact his friend England international David Duckham, inviting him to come to Ireland to see the situation for himself. The tactic paid off. Defying expectations, England travelled to Lansdowne Road in 1973. On match day, a crowd of over 50,000 gave the team an emotional standing ovation, buoyed no doubt by Ireland's 18-9 victory. This prompted England captain John Pullin to remark at the post-match dinner: "Well, we might not be any good but at least we turned up": cue for laughter and loud applause.

Fifteen years later, on April 25, 1987, Irish rugby itself was in the front line. Three Ulstermen – Nigel Carr, Philip Rainey and David Irwin – were making the journey from Belfast to Dublin to join a training session for the forthcoming inaugural Rugby World Cup. As they were crossing the border at Killean, a 500lb landmine was detonated.

The IRA had targeted one of Northern Ireland's most senior judges, Lord Justice Gibson. Sir Maurice and his wife were killed. The three internationals happened to be on the same stretch of road when the bomb went off. Miraculously, all avoided serious injury but the incident ended Carr's playing career at the age of 27.

The dignity with which the three conducted themselves in the aftermath helped calm the sense of outrage both north and south of the border which the incident had sparked.

The third incident highlighted in *Shoulder to Shoulder* was perhaps the most extraordinary. In 2007, nine years after the Good Friday Agreement, O'Driscoll led the Irish team out to play England in the Six Nations Championship. Whilst the fixture was by now routine, the setting was anything but. The venue was Croke Park, home of the Gaelic Athletic Association.

Croke Park had been at the centre of one of the most violent days in Irish history: the original Bloody Sunday. In the morning of November 21, 1920, the IRA had killed 12 British intelligence agents and two civilians. Retribution was immediate: at Croke Park, British troops opened fire on spectators in the stands, gathered to see the All Ireland Gaelic football final. Fourteen civilians, including one of the players, were killed.

The symbolism of the 2007 match could not have been clearer. Rule 42 of the Gaelic Athletic Association specifically excluded the playing of "foreign sports" on GAA grounds, so for permission to be granted for rugby to be played was hugely significant. The respect spectators showed for the English anthem was as moving as it was dignified: a testament to the power of rugby to unite in even the most controversial of settings.

Rugby was introduced to Argentina in the 19th century by immigrant settlers from the British Isles. Formal tours by overseas teams began in the 1920s, the British and Irish Lions and the Springboks being welcome visitors. At this time, the Argentine XV was made up almost exclusively of expatriates, so names on the team sheet had a familiar ring. The Unión de Rugby de Buenos Aires was the dominant force in Argentine rugby for a generation and after the Second World War, its scions were instrumental in spreading the game throughout South America. Inter-club and international fixtures followed.

In the 1960s, Argentina's rugby credentials were much strengthened by visits from the home nations and by overseas tours. It was during one such tour of southern

RUGBY WAS INTRODUCED TO ARGENTINA'S IN THE 19TH CENTURY BY IMMIGRANT SETTLERS FROM THE BRITISH ISLES. FORMAL TOURS BY OVERSEAS TEAMS BEGAN IN THE 1920S, THE BRITISH AND IRISH LIONS AND THE SPRINGBOKS BEING WELCOME VISITORS.

Argentina continues to be a respected force in world rugby.

Africa that the team, now sporting its distinctive blue and white hooped jerseys, were christened the Pumas by a journalist in Rhodesia (Zimbabwe). The team's prestige was much advanced in the 1970s by Hugo Porta, the first Argentinian to be regarded as a truly world-class player. In the 1980s, Argentina hosted extensive tours by a number of leading rugby-playing countries, including Australia, England, France and New Zealand.

Since 1978, there have been 25 internationals between England and Argentina with England winning 19, Argentina four and two being drawn. In any chronology, however, there is a significant lacuna between 1981 and 1990. This was caused by the Argentinian military junta's invasion and occupation of the British dependent territories of South Georgia and the Falkland Islands, an event which had been preceded by several years of Anglo-Argentine negotiations for joint sovereignty over the islands. Though war was never declared, a British taskforce was despatched and, after 10 weeks of intense fighting, the islands reverted to British rule.

The fall of the ruling junta and Argentina's subsequent political and economic history, meant further military adventurism was unlikely. Whilst nationalist rhetoric – including the constitution adopted in 1989 – continues to lay claim to the Falklands (the Malvinas), behind-the-scenes diplomacy led to a normalisation of relations.

Rugby was one of the immediate beneficiaries though perhaps not in the way the prime movers intended. A charm offensive intended to rebuild trust in the Argentine government was launched by President Carlos Menem in the 1990s.

It initiated contact between Argentinians and Falklanders through telephone calls, presents and videos but was met with puzzlement by the islanders. "Reconciliatory visits" made by groups of Argentinians to the Falklands were greeted with scepticism, none more so than that paid by the Rugby Sin Fronteras (Rugby Without Borders) organisation. Its aim was to organise a fixture between Argentinians and Falklanders, a match clearly intended to involve young people as training sessions were planned on grounds next to the secondary school.

Argentinian claims to the Falklands remain active. In the meantime, fixtures between Argentina and home countries – and England in particular – have resumed. The first to be played, in 1990, was not uneventful: "Armed guards, missiles and brawls – England's 1990 tour to Argentina in the wake of the Falklands'" as the *Daily Telegraph* headlined it. Since then, on the pitch at least, relations have normalised.

The capacity of rugby to transcend national and international divisions is no more clearly demonstrated than in South Africa. For over a century, rugby's relationship with South Africa was ambiguous and often uncomfortable. In 1862, the first official rugby match in the country was played between the Army and the Civil Service. All the players – British and Afrikaners – were white. In 1906-1907, a South African team toured Britain, helping reconciliation after the Anglo-Boer War of 1899-1902. The British press anglicised the tourists' nickname, the Springbokken.

By the late 19th century, some black South Africans had taken up the game. In 1897, the South African Coloured Rugby Football Board was established to oversee matches at a regional level, imitating the whites-only South African Rugby Board which had been set up eight years earlier. Whilst rugby played an important role in reducing inter-tribal and inter-faith tensions between different black communities, the formation of two separate boards was a harbinger of what was to come.

Rugby provided a vehicle for reconciliation between Afrikaner and British on the one hand and for black communities of differing traditions and religions on the other, but the twain could not meet. In the 20th century, any potential for bringing together all South Africans all but evaporated. After the Second World War, segregation was enshrined in law, denying non-whites access to facilities and training which might enable them to represent their country

AFTER THE SECOND WORLD WAR, SEGREGATION WAS ENSHRINED IN LAW, DENYING NON-WHITES ACCESS TO FACILITIES AND TRAINING WHICH MIGHT ENABLE THEM TO REPRESENT THEIR COUNTRY.

Top: The Soweto riots.
Above left: Sharpeville massacre of 1960 in which 67 unarmed black protestors were killed.
Above right: The ugly face of apartheid.

The country joining the International Rugby Football Union in 1948 coincided with the National Party coming to power, which it held until 1994. The new, all-white government began to enact policies of racial segregation. Under the regime of apartheid ("separateness" in Afrikaans), the majority non-white South Africans were compelled to live in their own separate enclaves and had access only to their own designated public facilities, including sports grounds.

South African rugby itself was subject to apartheid. The South African Rugby Board (SARB) was for whites, the South African Rugby Federation (SARF) for people considered to be of mixed race, and the South African Rugby Association (SARA) for blacks. Additionally there was the South African Rugby Union (SARU), a body with a membership which crossed racial boundaries. The national team, however, was solely selected by SARB. In the late 1970s, SARB absorbed SARF and

THE SOUTH AFRICAN RUGBY BOARD (SARB) WAS FOR WHITES, THE SOUTH AFRICAN RUGBY FEDERATION (SARF) FOR PEOPLE CONSIDERED TO BE OF MIXED RACE AND THE SOUTH AFRICAN RUGBY ASSOCIATION (SARA) FOR BLACKS.

SARA but SARU refused to cooperate with the new board, demanding that rugby be integrated at club level and that a number of apartheid laws be rescinded.

Following the Sharpeville massacre of 1960, in which 67 unarmed black protestors were killed and a further 180 wounded, South Africa came under pressure internally and externally to end apartheid. The South African Non-Racial Olympic Committee (SANROC) was formed in 1963 to decry the selection of whites only to represent the country at the Tokyo Olympics of 1964. Whilst SANROC's stance led to the imprisonment and death in custody of several of its leaders, its call for a boycott led to the country's suspension from the games.

In 1970, all blacks had their national identity revoked under the Bantu Homelands Citizens Act which imposed citizenship of the Bantustan assigned to their ethnic group. In 1976, police fired on a peaceful demonstration in the black township of Soweto. The demonstrators were protesting against the obligatory teaching of Afrikaans in schools.

The South African Council on Sport (SACOS), formed three years earlier to press for sporting reform on a non-racial basis, called out the 1976 measures as a ruse to deceive the international community whilst sustaining separate racial development in sport. SACOS's slogan was "No normal sport in an abnormal society".

South Africa remained a member of the international governing body for much – but not all – of the apartheid era. The game could not escape sporting controversy borne of apartheid. In 1965, the Springboks had just returned from a highly successful tour to New Zealand when Prime Minister Hendrik Verwoerd announced that any future New Zealand teams visiting South Africa would not be allowed to include Maori players.

This was a deliberate affront to the IRFB. In response, New Zealand cancelled its tour planned for 1967. In an effort to repair the damage wrought by Verwoerd, the new premier John Vorster declared that, in future, the National Party would no longer prescribe rules about the racial composition of visiting sports teams. The announcement was controversial, not least in South Africa where hard-line conservatives broke away from the National Party in 1969.

Mandela and de Klerk worked collaboratively on a new constitution which came into effect in 1994.

In 1969 too, the Halt All Racist Tours campaign was launched in New Zealand to oppose continued tours to and from South Africa but it was difficult to establish universal compliance. In 1977, heads of Commonwealth governments agreed unanimously to discourage contact and competition with teams and individuals from South Africa at a meeting at Gleneagles in Scotland. Still tours to and by South Africa continued, albeit intermittently and against a background of controversy. South Africa's sporting isolation was at its peak in the 1980s. The continuation of apartheid led to South Africa being excluded from the IRFB from 1984-1992. The 1981 Springbok tour of New Zealand, marred by demonstrations and cancellations, was a disaster. No further internationals were played for 11 years: the country was excluded from the Rugby World Cup competitions in 1987 and 1991.

Under pressure from the international community which now included economic sanctions, the National Party government under premier Piet Botha sought to institute some reforms but, in practice, these fell short of any substantive change. In 1989 Botha was replaced by F.W. de Klerk who, against ferocious opposition, repealed much of the legislative basis for apartheid.

In the meantime, in 1988 the centenary of the SARB loomed. Rugby was still regarded as the preserve of privileged whites but two leaders of Springbok rugby, Danie Craven and Louis Luyt, knew that change was inevitable. They met both

Arguably the most important picture ever taken on a rugby field shows the moment when President Mandela presented the 1995 Rugby World Cup to South Africa captain François Pienaar.

6

the non-racial SARU and the African National Congress (ANC) to consider how rugby might progress in the future. Negotiations over a three-year period led to an agreement to form the South African Rugby Football Union (SARFU) in January 1992. At last, the country had one, non-racial governing body for rugby.

The creation of SRFU could not have been more timely. In 1990, de Klerk had authorised the release of Nelson Mandela who had been incarcerated for 27 years for his leadership of uMkhonto we Sizwe (Spear of the Nation), an armed wing of the ANC. Mandela and de Klerk worked collaboratively on a new constitution which came into effect in 1994. Blacks and other racial groups were enfranchised and elections led to a coalition government with a non-white majority and Mandela as president. Apartheid was at an end.

In the meantime, the IRFB had selected South Africa to host the Rugby World Cup in 1995. Mandela seized the opportunity to work towards reconciliation, describing the new South Africa as the 'rainbow nation'. He worked tirelessly with the Springbok authorities and SARFU on a 'One Team, One Country' campaign. When the tournament got under way, South Africans of all ethnicities painted their faces in the colours of the new national flag and cheered on the team to whom Mandela referred as 'our boys'.

In the final at Ellis Park, South Africa defeated the All Blacks with a drop-goal after seven minutes of extra time. In front of 60,000 ecstatic fans, Mandela appeared wearing a Springbok cap and jersey to present captain François Pienaar with the Webb Ellis Cup. Of the crowd's support for his team, Pienaar observed: "We didn't have 60,000 South Africans; we had 43 million South Africans."

The World Cup victory was cathartic. Mandela led all South Africans in embracing a game which had once seemed to be the very embodiment of apartheid. By donning Springbok garb, Mandela demonstrated to the rest of the world that the meanings attached to what had once been symbols of white supremacy had changed once and for all.

Since then, progress has been made. Of course, there have been bumps in the road such as a taped conversation, aired by the South African Broadcasting Association in 1997, between a Springbok coach and a former player in which the coach used

THE WORLD CUP VICTORY WAS CATHARTIC. MANDELA LED ALL SOUTH AFRICANS IN EMBRACING A GAME WHICH HAD ONCE SEEMED TO BE THE VERY EMBODIMENT OF APARTHEID.

a derogatory racial slur when referring to the vice-president of SARFU. Generally, however, developments have been positive, resulting in increasing numbers of non-white players representing their country: the national squad for the 2019 World Cup consisted of 30 white and 17 non-white players. What Chester Williams began as the only non-white player in the 1995 final, others now continue.

If rugby has rarely avoided being political, what of politics being graced by players? One talent who switched from rugby to politics was Gordon Brown. The former Labour Prime Minister played for Kirkcaldy High School when, aged 16, he suffered a head injury. His retina was damaged, nearly blinding him.

Another rugby-to-politics transfer was former French President, Jacques Chirac. He was a talented player in his youth, playing second row and Number 8 for the youth team at Brive and for the Paris Institute for Political Studies, where he gained a reputation as "le Bulldozer".

The future dictator of Uganda, Idi Amin, learned the game whilst at Sandhurst where coaches turned him into a second row. He continued with the game in Kampala before turning to politics.

All Black Chris Laidlaw was a vociferous critic of apartheid during his playing career. He joined the Civil Service and served briefly as a Labour MP in 1992-1993. In 2007, he embarked on a twelve-year stint as a councillor for the Wellington region. Laidlaw is a vociferous advocate of New Zealand becoming a republic.

Perhaps the oddest aficionado was one Ernesto 'Che' Guevara. Born in Rosario in Argentina, he played at centre for the San Isidro club in Buenos Aires. Whilst he may have lacked ability, his enthusiasm was such that, in 1951, he ran a magazine entitled *Tackle*. It survived for just three months.

If Guevara's interest is understandable, what is baffling is interest in the game shown by citizens of the United States. Amongst the ranks of enthusiasts and practitioners were several who reached the very pinnacle of US political life.

The earliest was Woodrow Wilson, President from 1913-1921. In 1877, a team from Princeton hauled up in Massachusetts to play Harvard at rugby. Amongst the visitors' ranks was one student familiar with 'this English game'. Wilson coached his colleagues: Harvard won.

Three of the Kennedy clan's brothers played the game. The keenest was the eldest, Joe. Groomed by his father – Joe Senior – for the highest office, he died in the Second World War, aged 29. Though rugby was an informal sport at Harvard, friends recall

JFK's younger brother, Teddy Kennedy, played tighthead prop.

his enormous enthusiasm for the game. John – JFK – played alongside his elder brother and proved to be a useful forward.

The star player of the family, however, was JFK's younger brother, Ted. A tighthead prop, the future senator was known as an aggressive competitor, inclined sometimes to lose his composure. In the mid-1950s, in a fixture against the New York Club, he was involved in three bouts of fisticuffs and was sent off.

In 1968, future president Bill Clinton arrived in Oxford as a Rhodes Scholar. Never having touched the oval ball before, he too took an interest in rugby and became a proficient prop forward, playing for University College.

Clinton's successor in the White House, George W. Bush, also played rugby, first at his boarding school and then at Yale. There exists a grainy photograph of Bush grappling with an opponent in the 1968 fixture against Harvard which, in these days of video playback, might well have warranted closer inspection by the video referee. At Yale, the XV was very largely made up of foreign students already well versed in the game. When numbers were short, however, Bush seized his opportunity, playing at fullback. His all-round athleticism – and in particular his ability to run, kick and tackle – made him a useful player. On the campaign trail, Bush made frequent references to his enjoyment of the game.

Whilst all these players-turned-politicians appeared on the world stage, it is perhaps fitting to consider two men whose political contributions may not have been quite so high-profile but, because of the backgrounds from which they emerged – The Troubles and apartheid – were and are hugely significant.

Trevor Ringland was born in 1959 in west Belfast and remembered the time before The Troubles as 'perfectly normal'. Ringland's father was a police officer with the Royal Ulster Constabulary and, when the conflict began, he remembers his father keeping a sub-machine gun in the house and having to check his car each morning to ensure it wasn't booby-trapped. He recalled: "One night my father was being shot at by the IRA in west Belfast. At the same time my mother got a phone call saying that Loyalist paramilitaries were burning policemen out of their homes in my home town…

Actor Samuel L. Jackson (R) presents the Arthur Ashe Courage Award to Dave Cullen (L) and Trevor Ringland (C) for their efforts to bring children in Northern Ireland together through sports.

The police became a third community and threats came in different ways at different times."

Ringland learned his rugby at Larne Grammar School and Queen's University where he read law and played alongside several future Ireland internationals. His own rugby international career ran from 1981-1988. Winning 31 caps for Ireland and scoring nine tries in the process, he was also a British Lion who toured New Zealand in 1983 and played in the 1987 World Cup. After retiring from the game, he continued to practise as a solicitor.

Ringland had a keen appreciation of the possibilities that sport could offer to community reconciliation. In 2002, he became active with Peace Players International, an organisation committed to promoting inter-community unity through sport. In 2007, he was chairman of the One Small Step campaign which lobbied leaders of political parties to reach agreement over the Northern Ireland Assembly and encouraged people to become involved in cross-community projects and to educate their children about other cultures.

By then, Ringland had already embarked on a recognisably political career. In 2003, he courted controversy in a book – *A Long Peace: The Future of Unionism in Northern Ireland* – in which he and his co-authors suggested, amongst other things, that the Orange Order should loosen ties with the Ulster Unionist Party and become more like the Rotary Club. The link, he thought, "works to the detriment of both organisations". Reaction was predictably mixed, much of it hostile.

De Villiers was a leading member of the National Party's delegation attending the Convention for a Democratic South Africa, a multi-racial convention led by F.W. de Klerk and Nelson Mandela in 1991.

In 2006, he was appointed Chairman of the Northern Ireland Police Board. In 2010, he stood unsuccessfully as the Ulster Unionist Party and Conservative Party's joint candidate in East Belfast in the General Election. A conflict with the newly elected leader of the UUP led to Ringland's resignation from the party in the same year and he joined the Northern Ireland Conservatives. By 2013, he was co-chair of the NI Conservatives, holding responsibility for the party's political brief. In 2019, he declined an invitation from the UUP to stand as its candidate in the North Down constituency.

Ringland remains committed to the potential sport has to bring together different communities. He has not been afraid of unpopularity. The Peace Players International initiative was not universally liked: some parents in the Ardoyne had recourse to the law to try to prevent its introduction in the predominantly working-class, Catholic and republican district in Belfast. He has praised the Irish Football Association for eliminating sectarianism at soccer matches hosted at Windsor Park. He has commended the inclusivity of the Gaelic Athletic Association, contributing to the ongoing debate over anthems and the flying of flags. One thing is certain: Ringland's later career will leave an even greater impression on Irish society than any of his triumphs on the rugby pitch.

Dawie de Villiers of South Africa was one of rugby's greatest scrum-halfs. He made his debut for the Springboks in 1962 against England. He made 25 international appearances, 22 as captain between 1965 and 1970.

Dawie's father was an organiser for the National Party and a member of parliament from 1953-1961. Dawie completed degrees in theology and philosophy at Stellenbosch University. Opposed to many of the accepted policies of the National Party, he was regarded as a left-wing radical; this was a source of some consternation to his father who by now was a cabinet minister. After holding a temporary lecturing post at Western Cape University and completing his theology degree, he became a minister in the Dutch Reformed Church, serving from 1967 to 1969. He then lectured at Rand Afrikaans University where the rector persuaded him to take up politics.

In the face of opposition from his father, de Villiers became MP for Johannesburg West, a seat he held from 1972 to 1979. In 1979, de Villiers was appointed the South African ambassador in London. On his return, he became Minister of Trade and Industry from 1980-1994. In 1981, he failed to win the Gardens constituency in Cape Town but subsequently became MP for Piketberg, Cape Town, a seat he held between 1981 and 1996.

De Villiers was a leading member of the National Party's delegation attending the Convention for a Democratic South Africa, a multi-racial convention led by F.W.

DE VILLIERS AND RINGLAND ARE TWO DISTINGUISHED FORMER RUGBY INTERNATIONALS WHO, WITH A PARTICULAR PERSPECTIVE BORN AT LEAST IN PART OF THEIR HAVING PLAYED THE GAME, HAVE SOUGHT AS POSITIVELY AS ANY TO BRING WARRING FACTIONS TOGETHER, TRULY TO CREATE A WORLD IN UNION.

---

de Klerk and Nelson Mandela in 1991. After the transition to majority rule, he was one of three National Party ministers in the government of national unity formed under Mandela's leadership. He was Minister for Environmental Affairs and tourism until the National Party resigned en bloc from government in 1996. He then became a director of the World Tourism Organisation in the establishment of which he had been a leading light.

De Villiers' role in politics and government remains a subject of debate in South Africa. Whilst he opposed many of the traditional views of the National Party, he chose to operate within it rather than joining any of the other more progressive parties. By the same token, hard-liners regard him as having sold out to the ANC, especially over what they regard as his equivocal attitude towards protecting Afrikaans.

In his autobiography, *My Life Journey: Springbok, Politician, Diplomat*, published in 1998, he writes: "My views... were reinforced by many experiences, which was one of the reasons why I was able to find so much satisfaction in my involvement in the transition." In view of how South Africa has been ruled by the ANC, de Villiers has been accused by both left and right wings of being disingenuous and self-serving. Perhaps the last word may lie with Nelson Mandela who reportedly described De Villiers as "a highly capable and experienced South African who has made an excellent contribution to harmony in our nation".

Trying to hold some sort of middle ground is often an uncomfortable position in politics. De Villiers and Ringland are two distinguished former rugby internationals who, with a particular perspective born at least in part of their having played the game, have sought as positively as any to bring warring factions together, truly to create a world in union.

MATTHEW ROBINSON

I remember how I first got involved in the game very well – very clearly indeed. I was seven years old and it was sports day (a Friday). I won a number of races and on my way home a man came out of his house and called me over. He told me who he was: "Hello son, I'm Mr X, boy X's father; do you know him?" I said I did and he continued. He mentioned that he had seen me run that day at sports day and he felt I was talented. He told me to go to the local rugby club the next morning. Mr X told me where it was and who to ask for. He said I should mention his name. The next day I went down to Caerleon Mini RFC at the place he told me to go and asked for the person he told me to ask for. The rest as they say is history. I was hooked from the moment I first touched the ball. I remember being told "When you get the ball, just run and get it over that line and put it down. Don't let anyone grab you!"

The highlights of my career have to be: receiving a phone call from Wales coach Kevin Bowring in 1997 after joining Newport RFC (Kevin invited me to join the Welsh Seven's Squad); winning my first cap in 1999; winning my second cap at Wembley and knowing my parents had flown in from Jamaica and were there to watch me; being the leading try scorer in the European Cup for a number of years; forcing my way back into the Starting XV after being dropped following a blunder against France (I scored four tries on tour in Argentina to stake my claim); winning the Welsh Cup against arch rivals Llanelli during Swansea's rebel season 1998/1999; and winning the Welsh League with Swansea RFC 2000/2001.

I think William Webb Ellis today would recognise the athleticism of the players and the effort they put in to preparing themselves for their 'work'. I believe he would consider it a shame that the 'work' has become so ordered and less creative or imaginative. He would identify the attritional nature of the game today and understand therefore the need for the players to 'bulletproof' themselves. Unfortunately this aspect of the game has made its way into schoolboy rugby as pathways are clearly delineated for those wanting to play at the highest level. I suspect he would want to reinstate some of the free-flowing transitions that he created by picking up the ball and running with it. On a personal level I too would like to see a return to players having freedom to show off skill that can unlock space for others.

PLAYING THE GAME

Matthew Robinson played as centre or wing for Swansea and won four caps for Wales, making his debut on February 6, 1999 against Scotland.

WHEN DID RULE LA

In 1871 the Rugby Football Union was formed. The rules became 'laws', drafted by three members who were lawyers and former Rugby School pupils.

S BECOME

AWS?

19
68

Japan beat the Junior All Blacks 23-19 during their tour of New Zealand.

19
69

Replacements were allowed for the first time in the Five Nations championship.

19
70

Carwyn Jones contested the general election for Welsh nationalist party Plaid Cymru a year before coaching the British and Irish Lions on the winning tour of New Zealand.

19
70

Kicking the ball directly into touch from outside the 25 was stopped.

19
71

Legendary outside half Hugo Porta gained his first cap for Argentina, aged 20.

19
71

The value of a try was raised from three to four points.

19
71

Wales won the first of their three Five Nations Grand Slams over seven years, a feat they repeated in the Six Nations between 2005 and 2012.

19
71

Thirty-two teams took part in a new Rugby Football Union Club Competition, which became the John Player Cup four years later.

19
72

Four universities in California fielded women's rugby teams.

19
72

Rugby was introduced in Tunisia.

"

"I'M STILL AN AMATEUR, OF COURSE, BUT I BECAME RUGBY'S FIRST MILLIONAIRE FIVE YEARS AGO.

"

David Campese

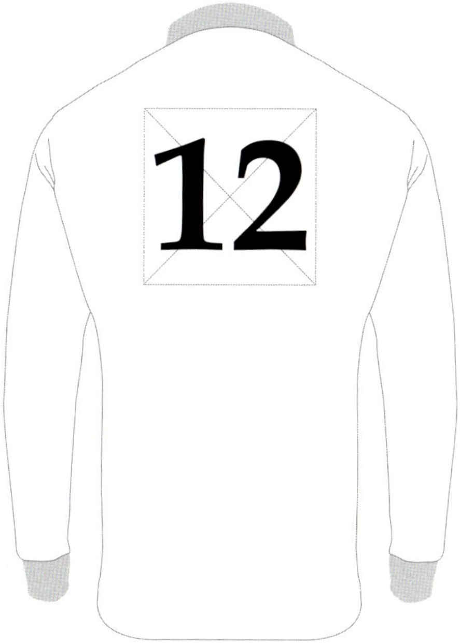

WHAT PRICE THE RUGBY GAME?

By Robin Fletcher,
former touch judge of the XV and former Governor, Rugby School

SO, IT COULD BE ARGUED THAT MONEY HAS ALWAYS BEEN PRESENT, ONE WAY OR ANOTHER, IN THE RUGBY GAME. AFTER ALL, WEBB ELLIS ATTENDED A FEE-PAYING SCHOOL WHICH IN TURN PRESUMABLY PAID FOR ITS PIGS' BLADDERS.

It's likely young William Webb Ellis first ran with a pig's bladder ball supplied by local Rugby family firm, Gilbert's.

Nearly two centuries later on November 2, 2019, his name was engraved on the trophy won by South Africa when they beat England 32-12 in the men's Rugby World Cup final. And Gilbert's again supplied the match ball.

Today, Gilbert is part of a firm which turned over nearly £29m in 2019. Two years later, a limited-edition replica of the ball used in the 2019 final was selling on-line for £250.

This might seem a hefty sum for a ball, but it's modest compared to the £325,000 awarded by World Rugby for winning the Webb Ellis trophy (albeit only £10,000 per player).

So, it could be argued that money has always been present, one way or another, in the rugby game. After all, Webb Ellis attended a fee-paying school which in turn presumably paid for its pigs' bladders.

The bottom-line issue of players and their value in sport was reinforced much more recently in the catchphrase 'Show me the money' chanted by a fictional American football player in the 1996 film *Jerry Maguire*.

In 2020, the value of the America's richest National Football League club, the Dallas Cowboys, was put at $5.7 billion, which might explain why Maguire's client was so insistent.

American Football grew out of rugby union, tracing its roots back to 1869. In doing so however, he could never have imagined running with the ball and money would one day be so closely linked.

In 2021, South Africa's Handré Pollard and former New Zealand winger Charles Piutau were reported to be the world's highest-paid rugby union players, each earning £1m a year.

The British and Irish Lions 2021 tour of South Africa attracted sponsorship revenues of £40-£50m, the largest being around £10m from Sky. Players who completed the whole tour also earned £48,750 for around two months' work, or roughly £800 a day.

Even the Lions pre-tour training camp in Jersey received a helpful cash injection of around £175,000 from the island's marketing budget.

All these six-figure sums link to a test series which home nation rugby fans had waited patiently for four years to watch, only to see the Lions capitulate 2-1, despite coach Warren Gatland agreeing a 'significant cut' to his '£500,000' salary during the Covid-19 pandemic.

For the back-garden purist, therefore, teaching their child how to enjoy oval ball life for free, money may represent a poisonous presence.

The notion of playing games for their own sake, however, and upholding the virtues of amateur sport doesn't help much if every minute you spend on the rugby pitch cuts the food you put on the family dinner table.

The right for all rugby union players to be paid for their efforts has only been in place since 1995. As described earlier in this book, it also required a completely different branch of the sport a century earlier to be created for anyone to find a way to earn a living from the game.

The creation of the 13-player rugby league is undoubtedly one of the great outcomes of the late Victorian schism over whether players should be paid for playing. The oldest original breakaway rugby league clubs were Batley, Bradford, Brighouse, Broughton Rangers, Halifax, Huddersfield, Hull FC, Hunslet, Leeds, Leigh, Liversedge, Manningham, Oldham, Rochdale Hornets, Runcorn, St Helens, Stockport, Tyldesley, Wakefield Trinity, Warrington, Widnes and Wigan.

And of these, Batley, Leeds, Wakefield and Widnes still play on the same grounds as they did in 1895.

More than 120 years on, however, Wigan still lays claim to be the world's most

THE CREATION OF THE 13-PLAYER RUGBY LEAGUE IS UNDOUBTEDLY ONE OF THE GREAT OUTCOMES OF THE LATE VICTORIAN SCHISM OVER WHETHER PLAYERS SHOULD BE PAID FOR PLAYING.

The 1908 touring Kangaroos.

successful rugby league club, winning 22 League Championships, 19 Challenge Cups and four World Club Challenges.

Rugby league's appearance on the world stage took place in 1904 when England were beaten 9-3 in Wigan by a team comprising Other Nationalities. Four years later, Great Britain played their first test match at Headingley, Leeds, on January 18, 1908 against the touring Kangaroos.

During both world wars professional rugby league was suspended, but by 1948 owners of television sets in the Midlands were able to watch the first screened rugby league match when Wigan beat Bradford Northern 8-3 in the presence of King George VI, who presented the trophy.

The game attracted huge crowds in the post-war era, peaking at nearly 70 million watching all matches in the 1949-50 season. As television entered people's homes, crowds began to decline, and when BBC2 Controller David Attenborough introduced the BBC2 Floodlit Trophy in 1965 it gave rugby league an enduring TV presence.

Although league remains primarily a northern game in England, there have been southern success stories too, most notably the London Broncos, established by Fulham FC in June 1980, which play at the top level of the game today.

Rugby League World Cup trophy.

The mid-1990s was marked by the so-called Super League War in Australia and New Zealand in which Rupert Murdoch and Kerry Packer slugged it out in court for control of rugby league and its lucrative broadcasting rights.

For one season, the Australian Rugby League and Australian Super League ran against each other before a new combined National Rugby League was created to replace them both.

Following this development, a new Super League was formed in Britain in 1996 involving elite clubs, a move which also saw the sport move its season from winter to summer, with increased TV revenues and crowds.

Formally known as Super League Europe, the competition features 11 teams from northern England and the Catalans Dragons from southern France.

The Super League season involves each team playing 29 games between February and September (11 home and 11 away), a Magic Weekend and six other matches depending on their league position. At the end of it all, the top six compete in a play-off series with the top two then playing a Grand Final. The eventual champions then play the winners of the Australasia National Rugby League.

Given the financial impetus behind the 1895 creation of rugby league it is interesting to note the financial journey made by the sport over time. In 1901, Salford made history by paying Burnley the princely sum of £100 for James Lomas to join them, a move which they in turn tripled in value when Oldham handed over £300 for the same player 10 years later.

Fast forward a century or so, and the current transfer record in the game is held by Sam Tomkins, whose services cost the New Zealand Warriors £700,000 when they purchased them from Wigan Warriors. This was £350,000 higher than the previous record paid by Wigan to Bradford for Stuart Fielden in 2006.

While the price may be high today for those superstars who play the 13-man game, money also remains integral to the wider sport of rugby league. Witness for example the reaction of the organisers of the 2021 Rugby League World Cup competition when Australia and New Zealand announced they would not be travelling to the UK to take part in the tournament because of Covid fears.

According to Rugby Football League Chairman Simon Johnson, the withdrawal decision was 'selfish, parochial and cowardly' and came after "The World Cup organisers have bent over backwards and turned double somersaults to meet every single requirement that was asked of them, by the Australians particularly."

RUPERT MURDOCH AND FELLOW MEDIA MOGUL KERRY PACKER FLOODED THE SPORT WITH MULTI-MILLION-POUND TELEVISION DEALS PARTICULARLY IN THE SOUTHERN HEMISPHERE. PLAYERS STARTED TAKING SPONSORSHIP PAYMENTS, LEADING TO ACCUSATIONS OF "SHAMATEURISM". UNABLE TO HOLD BACK THE TIDES OF CHANGE, THE INTERNATIONAL RUGBY BOARD (IRB), NOW CALLED WORLD RUGBY, AGREED TO DO AWAY WITH RUGBY UNION'S AMATEUR STATUS ON 27 AUGUST 1995.

The decision, according to the *Daily Mail*, would have 'disastrous financial implications' for a tournament 'projected to generate around £40 million' and that there would be 'significant financial penalties' for any nation that withdrew at 'late notice'.

Despite these words, however, organisers soon announced a delay in the tournament until 2022 to make it financially viable, viability that already included £25m cash support from the UK government to help spotlight the sport of rugby league.

While money has been a clear feature of one part of the sport of rugby for more than 120 years, its presence or absence was hard to ignore in the union game before the International Rugby Board voted for the game to go professional.

The appropriately named *Money Week* recalls the seismic steps taken by the governors of the sport:

"That year in 1995, Rupert Murdoch and fellow media mogul Kerry Packer flooded the sport with multi-million-pound television deals particularly in the southern hemisphere. Players started taking sponsorship payments, leading to accusations of "shamateurism". Unable to hold back the tides of change, the International Rugby Board (IRB), now called World Rugby, agreed to do away with Rugby Union's amateur status on 27 August 1995."

But levelling the playing field between the union and league codes was not a recipe for immediate financial stability, as Paul Rees recalled in the *Guardian* in 2015:

"The three major southern hemisphere sides were immediately able to contract their leading players, having signed a $555m television deal with Rupert Murdoch's News Corporation. No such deal was in place in Europe: in England, the league sponsorship deal with Courage was worth some £200,000 a year and the Five Nations did not have a backer. The result of the chaos was that by 1998, the Rugby Football Union had lost £10.3m: although revenues had by then increased by 228 per cent, thanks to a television deal with Sky, and costs went up by 309 per cent, largely because of an increase in the number of staff. At the end of the decade, the losses of the leading clubs totalled £20m."

"It was like the Wild West when the game went professional," says Rob Andrew, one-time RFU professional rugby director but who in August 1995 was the Wasps and England fly-half and had, a few months earlier, dropped a late goal against Australia to win the World Cup quarter-final.

"We all knew it would happen, but the actual announcement caught everybody by surprise. No player had a contract and soon everyone was running around trying to sign us up. No one had a clue what we were worth: I was a chartered surveyor then working in London but within a few weeks I was on my way to Newcastle in what was a big leap into the unknown."

However, 'wild west' rugby union became when money was formally introduced into the game, top players were never far from inducements to perform long before 1995.

Wales and Lions stars Barry John and Gareth Edwards were among those who received payments from Adidas for wearing their boots in the 1970s, a practice forbidden under the rules of amateurism. In 1978, the great Sir Gareth Edwards was also briefly banned from the game for seeking commercial gain by publishing his autobiography.

For others, however, the allure for players of joining a version of the rugby game prepared to recognise their contribution financially, was as strong towards the end of the 20th century as it had been when rugby league was born in 1895.

On January 7, 1989, former Wales rugby union star Jonathan Davies, who had captained Wales in a 15-9 defeat to Romania the previous autumn, announced he was joining Widnes for a record fee of £230,000.

Having worked down a coal mine, Davies felt unable to turn down the chance to achieve financial security for his family at a time when the average wage in the UK was less than £15,000 a year. Nor was he alone, with fellow Welsh internationals Allan

DAVIES QUIPPED THAT HE WAS COLDER PLAYING RUGBY UNION THAN LEAGUE, A REFERENCE TO WHAT HE SAW THEN AS THE PEDESTRIAN NATURE OF THE UNION VERSION OF THE GAME.

Having worked down a coal mine, Davies felt unable to turn down the chance to achieve financial security for his family at a time when the average wage in the UK was less than £15,000 a year.

Bateman, Scott Gibbs, Scott Quinnell and Paul Moriarty being among those who followed his example over the next five years.

The exodus of such talent severely dented the form of Wales' rugby union side in the early 1990s, until Davies and his fellow travellers all came back to the 15-man game following the announcement of professionalism.

The return of Davies to rugby union in 1996 created as much media interest as his departure seven years earlier. But he was unable to rekindle the form he had showed before heading north or reach the heights he had scaled playing rugby league, winning the coveted Man of Steel Award in 1993.

Davies quipped that he was colder playing rugby union than league, a reference to what he saw then as the pedestrian nature of the union version of the game. Sitting next to him at a lunch shortly after his return, I was also able to ask him directly what he thought about the game he had returned to.

He answered that it was not physical enough compared to league, an observation which was probably true then but is rarely expressed about the high-contact, high-intensity type of rugby union played today, with regular media stories on the physical and neurological impact of the game.

The 'wild west' nature of money in rugby union since the advent of professionalism has been theoretically controlled by home union administrators through the introduction of a salary cap (£7m a year in 2021) for premiership club players in England.

The high degree of success achieved in recent seasons by Saracens, however, was laid bare in 2019 when it was revealed that owner Nigel Wray had overspent the cap by £1.1m, £98,000 and £906,000 in three consecutive seasons from 2016-17.

With such generous terms available, it is no wonder that Saracens had attracted and retained a stable of England and Lions stars such as Owen Farrell, Maro Itoje and the Vunipola brothers, Mako and Billy.

After an inquiry and a 103-page report led by Lord Dyson, Saracens was publicly humiliated for letting the side down, faced a fine of £5.3m, the loss of 35 points and relegation to the level below premiership.

By the end of the 2020-21 season, Saracens had inevitably won promotion back to the top level, but the lack of quality game time for its stars did not help them in the quest to play for England and the British and Irish Lions in 2021.

PREMIERSHIP RUGBY CLUBS IN ENGLAND SOUGHT LOANS OF £88M FROM THE GOVERNMENT DURING THE 20/21 SEASON TO MAINTAIN OPERATIONS DURING COVID-19 WHILE THE RFU TEMPORARILY SUSPENDED END-OF-SEASON RELEGATION TO PROVIDE SOME SHORT-TERM FINANCIAL SECURITY.

Saracens also chose the wrong time to be relegated given the wider financial implications of Covid-19 on the rugby game.

The stark reality of the damage Covid could do to the bottom-line of the rugby game was shown in the finances of World Rugby, whose revenues fell from £381.4m in 2019 to just £10.8m a year later.

Much of this gap can be explained by the high revenues generated by the 2019 Rugby World Cup. But in 2016, after the 2015 tournament, World Rugby revenues fell from £344.9m to £30.8m, a drop of 'only' £314.1m, compared to £370.6m between 2019 and 2020.

CEO Brett Gosper admitted the impact of Covid on rugby revenues had been 'devastating', adding: "The more reliant you are on game hospitality and ticketing particularly, the more devastating it will be.

"In the near future we are going to be getting some good broadcast revenues, but the rest of the picture is pretty weak."

In August 2021, Scottish Rugby's annual report detailed an £18.5m loss in revenue from the national and regional teams in the country, and a further £2m from other income streams.

SRU President Ian Barr said the 20/21 season in Scotland "was one that challenged our sport and our people as never before", a sentiment echoed by Grand Slam winning former flanker John Jeffrey who said it had "tested our tenacity and resolve as never before".

Premiership Rugby Clubs in England sought loans of £88m from the government during the 20/21 season to maintain operations during Covid-19 while the RFU temporarily suspended end-of-season relegation to provide some short-term financial security.

Illustrating the impact, Bath Rugby Club's annual report in April 2021 reported a 16 per cent income drop over the season, an overall loss of £3.5m and government support of £700,000.

Whatever the reason for financial hardship, there is no immunity from the fiscal reality of having enough funds in the bank to run the game – even for the world's best.

Despite winning more rugby world championships than any other national side, and an incredible 77 per cent of all their international matches, New Zealand's All Blacks have spent more money than they generated in most of the past few years.

To help tackle this, New Zealand Rugby proposed in 2021 selling a 12.5 per cent stake in the All Blacks for $387.5m NZ dollars (£197m in August 2021) to US private equity firm Silver Lake, a decision that at first sight seems as smart a boardroom decision as the team's training ground moves.

But securing the financial future of a treasured national and global brand comes at a price, in this case opposition from no other than the legendary David Kirk, who skippered the All Blacks 1987 side that lifted the Webb Ellis trophy for the first time.

Now President of the New Zealand Rugby Players' Association, Kirk alluded to the famous All Blacks 'players creed' which states that stars wearing the silver fern and representing their country are mere custodians of the shirt.

The return of fans post Covid-19 will give national unions, clubs and stadiums the chance to generate money again through standard ticket prices – or enhanced hospitality packages such as a decent seat, fine food and drink to watch England v world champions South Africa in November 2021 at Twickenham costing a mere £749 per person + VAT.

Another well-trodden financial path for rugby venues is the sale of debenture seats. In 2010, the Wales Rugby Union held £37.32m of repayable debentures and hoped to raise £12m from the sale of 2000 new debentures in the south stand of the now Principality Stadium.

In stark contrast, a report on the financial state of rugby in the Pacific islands of Fiji, Tonga and Samoa highlighted a huge disparity between the revenues they generate compared to rugby countries with larger fan bases.

DESPITE WINNING MORE RUGBY WORLD CHAMPIONSHIPS THAN ANY OTHER NATIONAL SIDE, AND AN INCREDIBLE 77 PER CENT OF ALL THEIR INTERNATIONAL MATCHES, NEW ZEALAND'S ALL BLACKS HAVE SPENT MORE MONEY THAN THEY GENERATED IN MOST OF THE PAST FEW YEARS.

Focusing on the issue, the *Guardian* wrote: "When New Zealand did finally play in Samoa in 2016, the game made a loss of NZ$1m once all the expenses had been taken out. The average price of a ticket at the 10,000-capacity Apia Park is £4.

"Not everything in life of course, and sport, can always be equal. Then again, Fiji, Tonga and Samoa – combined population of 1.5 million, fewer than live in West Yorkshire – supply over a quarter of the world's professional players."

And while ocean islands continue to struggle, it was interesting to note in August 2021 that 16,000 kms away, French rugby club Toulon was reportedly on the brink of signing South Africa's Cheslin Kolbe from rivals Toulouse for a mere £1.5m.

Kolbe's big-money move was a consequence of rugby union turning professional, giving players, like their rugby league counterparts, the chance to earn a living for their families from the game.

Newsboy Parfett was 15 at the time of the *Titanic* disaster and just three years later was fighting in the Great War, where, on October 29, 1918, just 12 days before the Armistice, he was killed by a shell.

This 1995 decision in turn can be traced back to the first meeting of the RFU in London, the first official step to organise and regulate the game.

The London meeting took place on the site of what is now the splendidly named Oceanic House at Number 1 Cockspur Street in the heart of London, a few yards from Trafalgar Square, which once housed the offices of the White Star Line, operators of RMS *Titanic*, the luxury liner which sank on May 31, 1911.

Though not at the helm on the night of the tragedy, the first captain of the Titanic while under construction in Belfast was Herbert Haddock (1861-1946), who coincidentally was born in Rugby.

Designed by Henry Tanner Junior, Oceanic House was built between 1903 and 1906. After the *Titanic* sank, crowds gathered by the building, as depicted in the famous photograph showing teenage newsboy Ned Parfett standing outside with a poster for the *Evening News* declaring 'Titanic Disaster Great Loss of Life'.

Parfett was 15 at the time and just three years later was fighting in the Great War, where, on October 29, 1918, just 12 days before the Armistice, he was killed by a shell. His body was buried at Verchain-Maugré in France, a 10-hour drive from Cimetière du Vieux Château in Menton, where William Webb Ellis lies.

The loss of Parfett in the worst human conflict of all time reminds us that the same war also claimed the lives of around 120 international rugby union players from Australia, England, France, Ireland, New Zealand, Scotland, South Africa, France and the USA.

In the current rugby world, where the financial state of clubs and countries is often discussed more than the game itself, there is a sombre poignancy in the memory of those who, like Webb Ellis, picked up the ball and ran, only to pay the ultimate price.

Two hundred years on from Webb Ellis and his antics with a pig's bladder, it is too late for money to be removed from the oval ball game in its many and varied forms.

For those who believe the sport is perhaps sullied for being so financially dependent,

TWO HUNDRED YEARS ON FROM WEBB ELLIS AND HIS ANTICS WITH A PIG'S BLADDER, IT IS TOO LATE FOR MONEY TO BE REMOVED FROM THE OVAL BALL GAME IN ITS MANY AND VARIED FORMS.

however, might reflect on the job advert in October 2021 for a backs coach at Southampton University Rugby Football Club.

With a salary 'to be confirmed' plus a £20 fee for training sessions and £40 for game days, the advert declared the club was looking for "A hard-working and committed coach…A lot of girls that join the team in October may be new to rugby so experience with teaching the basics well is desired. To work well with our forwards coach we will base training around forwards and backs, taking an integrated team approach of the 1st XV and 2nd XV team, rather than segregating."

If professionalism and the money supply that flows with it has helped to make this happen, then one can only hope that William Webb Ellis would approve of the progress made in his name.

PAUL GUSTARD

I grew up in Newcastle where dreams of scoring a goal at the Gallowgate End in front of the local fans far superseded the desire to 'pick up a ball and run' for most. However, my dad was a player in his day and much to the consternation of the wider family I followed his footsteps into rugby at the age of six at Gosforth Rugby Club.

I have been fortunate to win lots of trophies, play for some huge clubs, play for England and coach England. However, I think the memories you make, and the friendships that are created in your journey, far outlive the accolades, trophies and medals. As much as I remember the medals won at Leicester, the premierships at Saracens or the Grand Slam with England, I remember the weddings I was best man at, the trips away and of course the many nights out!

Webb Ellis would look at the game he created with pride, I think. The game is more than the just the game for most. Of course, the internationals and the elite game is one thing, but for the majority of people that is not what it is about. The essence of the game, the spirit of the game, the camaraderie, the brotherhood, the mateship up and down the country and indeed around the world is still there to be cherished and treasured. He gave us that! He can be proud of seeing so many people share in his love for the game and see it grow, expand and explode across countries, across race, across gender and across disability. Rugby is a sport for all!

Paul Gustard played for Leicester Tigers, Saracens and London Irish, England U21s and the Barbarians. He has since been defence and forwards coach for Saracens, defence coach for England, head of rugby for Harlequins and in 2021 became assistant coach at Italian side Benetton.

Cotton
TRADERS
VAUXHALL

adidas

SIMON HALLIDAY

I started playing rugby when I went to boarding school when I was seven. I then moved to a prep school where the headmaster was a very strong rugby supporter, so the game was a feature of school life. I then played for Downside School where sometimes 600 boys would watch and for years we did not lose a game. But I was a better cricketer then and cricket was my first love.

At Oxford, cricket was professional, rugby was amateur, but we started to do well against some top teams. I remember one time, however, Nick Mallett taking me to one side and telling me to take rugby seriously.

There are moments when you realise things are starting to happen. My first representation was for England Students to Japan. Then I went to Bath and we went 25 games unbeaten.

In Canada in October 1983 I dislocated my ankle and was out for two years, so I made my belated full England debut against Wales in 1986 when Rob Andrew left-footed a drop-goal.

I then went on to play in two Grand Slam winning sides and take part in the Rugby World Cup.

Today I am not sure William Webb Ellis would like the amount of kicking in the game (I couldn't kick so I ran with the ball most of the time) but he would also find the game alive and well.

Simon Halliday appeared in three Varsity matches for Oxford University, played 170 times for Bath and won 23 England caps. He played in the 1991 Rugby World Cup Final against Australia and was part of England's Grand Slam winning side in 1992.

WHY DO ENG

ENGLAND RUGBY

PLAY IN W

As many of the first Rugby Football Union were from Rugby School's XV, England's white strip was inherited from the School's original unbleached cotton kit. The founder of Rugby School, Lawrence Sheriff, was presented with a coat of arms by Queen Elizabeth I allowing him to use her red Lancaster rose; thus England's red rose emblem was most likely to have originated from the School's crest.

LAND HITE?

PAUL WALLACE

I started playing rugby when my dad took me to Cork County and threw me in. It was maybe under-12s and I had not really played before. I played back row then moved school to Limerick Under 16s then into the senior team. It was sink or swim in the front row. Then finally I got into the Irish Schools team.

A highlight for me was playing for Saracens when we won the Tetley's Cup. We had a great squad including Philippe Sella, Michael Lynagh and Richard Hall. Then there was our first Celtic League championship with Leinster.

But the biggest highlight was winning with the British and Irish Lions in 1997. That tour had a coach (Sir Ian McGeechan) and Manager (Fran Cotton) who really understood. The players enjoyed themselves, there was equal opportunity, so that made for a very happy camp.

It was the first professional tour but all the players had come from the amateur era. It was serious but a lot of enjoyment off the park.

There were lots of friendships made. I still meet a lot of the guys and we all get on great. I was very close with Dodie Weir on that tour. One of the great characters of rugby.

The game has moved incredibly since William Webb Ellis ran with the ball. It is a little bit static which is the rugby league influence on defence. But in rugby everyone still plays for their team-mates, which shows a lot of character.

PLAYING THE GAME

Paul Wallace played tighthead prop for Munster, Leinster, Saracens, Ireland and the British and Irish Lions, winning 49 caps.

RUGBY
1999
AUSTRALIA

Ellgren
HICSON

MIKE FORD

When I was nine, I went along to the school rugby trials. I remember the teacher giving me one more chance to run the ball 'hard' to get selected…thankfully I did. I played rugby league for 20 years, but my highlight as a rugby union coach would be the 2007 RWC final (defence coach for England) v South Africa…the controversial moment when Mark Cueto scored or not in the corner. To this day I believe his foot was in touch simultaneously as he grounded the ball…therefore benefit of the doubt should be with the attacking team! Massive decision. Today, I think William Webb Ellis would be delighted the way the game has grown around the world and is being played by men, women, girls and boys of all shapes and sizes.

PLAYING THE GAME

Mike Ford was born in 1965 and played rugby league for ten clubs, including more than 200 appearances for Oldham and Castleford, one for England and two for Great Britain. He has been head coach of Saracens and Bath and was England's defence coach for the 2007 Rugby World Cup.

PLAYING THE GAME

JPR WILLIAMS

My father played rugby as a medical student with Jack Matthews. After my christening Jack gave me a small rugby ball and became known to me as 'Uncle Jack'. My father was very keen on sport and was a good rugby player. I went to primary school and the PE teacher was a fullback called Billy Morgan who played for Bridgend. I started off playing outside half, as everyone did in Wales, but Billy moved me to fullback. I was a bit cheesed off to be honest, I thought it was a demotion, but it was the best move I ever made. I could have played for England or Wales, but I got into the Bridgend Under-11 side and the Wales Under-15s, along with Phil Bennett. It was a pretty strong side. I remember playing at Twickenham against England and we beat them. At that time Phil Bennett was taller than me. In total I played against England 14 times, 11 times as a senior, three times as a junior, and I never lost!

I was good at tennis and won the 1966 British Junior Championship, but when tennis turned professional in 1968 I had to choose between the two sports. I was selected to go on the Wales tour of Argentina in 1968 and my father said that would allow me to still play as an amateur. I followed my father's footsteps into medicine, but I was pretty determined not to be a GP like my parents who were on call at the time with very little time off.

There were no caps in those days for tours. I played in two tests but we were not very successful. A lot of Wales players were on the 1968 Lions tour to South Africa so we were a weakened side. I managed to play quite well and had won my place on the tour playing for Bridgend. But then I went to London and John Dawes, who captained the side in Argentina, drafted me into the London Welsh side. It was easy to get to so I ended up playing for both London Welsh and St Mary's Hospital. One of the highlights of my international career was dropping the goal in New Zealand in the fourth test in 1971. The 1971 and 1974 Lions tours were both incredibly successful teams but the fact that we had not won in New Zealand before 1971 it was much harder. We only had about 40 per cent possession of the ball so we had to move it.

On the 1974 Lions tour to South Africa with Willie John McBride as captain, apartheid was rife at the time so we were very keen to make sure we beat them. The greatest thing in the test matches was that all the black spectators cheered for us. It brought us together as a team so we did more.

Another highlight was Wales against Scotland in 1971 when we came from behind to secure a win at the end. John Taylor managed the winning kick which we called the greatest conversion since St Paul.

The older I get the more I am happy about when I played the game. I am not sure William Webb Ellis would be happy with the game today. The problem is that most of the time the ball is kicked in the air, not passed, like aerial ping pong. It is boring to watch and it is safety first.

John Peter Rhys Williams MBE, FRCS is a former rugby union footballer who represented Wales in international rugby during their Golden Era in the 1970s. He became known universally as J.P.R. Williams (or sometimes just as JPR) after 1973 when JJ Williams (also John) joined the Welsh team.

GILBER

19 / 73 A world sevens tournament was held at Murrayfield with Ireland losing 22-18 to England in the final.

19 / 74 The British and Irish Lions achieved their first series win in South Africa for 76 years.

19 / 74 The Rugby Football League gave permission for clubs to allow advertising on players' shirts.

19 / 75 The USA RFU was founded and a year later national team the Eagles played Australia in Los Angeles.

19 / 76 The Hong Kong Rugby Sevens tournament was launched with teams from Indonesia, South Korea, Australia, New Zealand, Tonga, Japan, Sir Lanka, Malaysia and Fiji.

19
77

The Five Nations Grand Slam was won by France, who did not concede a single try throughout the championship.

19
77

At just 5ft 4 inches French scrum-half Jacques Fouroux captained his side to the Five Nations grand slam title. Regarded as the shortest ever international, Fouroux won 27 caps, 23 as captain and was also manager of the French national team when they won the grand slam in 1981 and 1987.

19
78

France was admitted to the International Rugby Board, 65 years after their first request to join.

19
78

In October, Irish club side Munster defeated the touring All Blacks 12-0 before a crowd of 12,000 at Thomond Park in Limerick.

VIENNA CELTIC RUGBY FOOTBALL CLUB

19
78

Vienna Celtic, the first rugby club in Austria, was founded by John Skinner and Will Crisp.

"THE PUB IS AS MUCH
A PART OF RUGBY
AS IS THE PLAYING FIELD."

John Dickinson

CINDER TRACKS AND CITADELS

By Robin Fletcher,
former touch judge of the XV and former Governor, Rugby School

In a 2014 TV advert, British and Irish Lions stars Owen Farrell, Greig Laidlaw, Cian Healy and Sam Warburton recited an adapted version of *If* by Rudyard Kipling.

The 1895's poem's 'triumph and disaster' lines are widely quoted in sport unlike those from Kipling's *I Keep Six Honest Serving-men*, which appeared in 1902 in *The Elephant's Child*:

"I keep six honest serving-men, (They taught me all I knew); Their names are What and Why and When, And How and Where and Who."

Most commentators and fans focus, understandably, on the 'who, when and what' of the game, reinforcing the classic *'I was there'* emotion expressed so passionately by legendary Welsh singer Max Boyce.

But what about 'where'? Is that a sideshow compared to the other components, or can it be equally interesting?

On July 7, 2001, with a small radio clamped to my ear, I boarded a plane at Heathrow Airport bound for Tobago. The second Lions test match against Australia in Melbourne was underway but as I sat down in my seat the radio lost reception.

My hotel in the Caribbean was deeply luxurious, but it did not have public internet access. And as no mobile phones in those days were 'smart', weirdly I only discovered several days later, when chatting to some fellow rugby fans on the beach, that the Lions had lost the match 35-14.

Holiday or no holiday, the implication of the loss was immediate. The third test the following weekend would decide the series and I knew I needed to watch or listen to it, somehow. Yet this seemed an unlikely prospect perched on a tiny island 11,000 miles away from the action.

After a little planning, however, on the day of the match I joined a small group of fans and set off in the half light for a mile walk along a beach road. Our destination was a small café where the owner had an equally small, wall-mounted TV tuned to Fox Sport.

The broadcaster's commentators clearly knew no more about the rules of rugby than I do about the finer points of international tiddlywinks. The picture was also too far away to capture the detail of the match and the reception was a far cry from watching events live.

None of this mattered, however. Because although the Lions lost that match, the

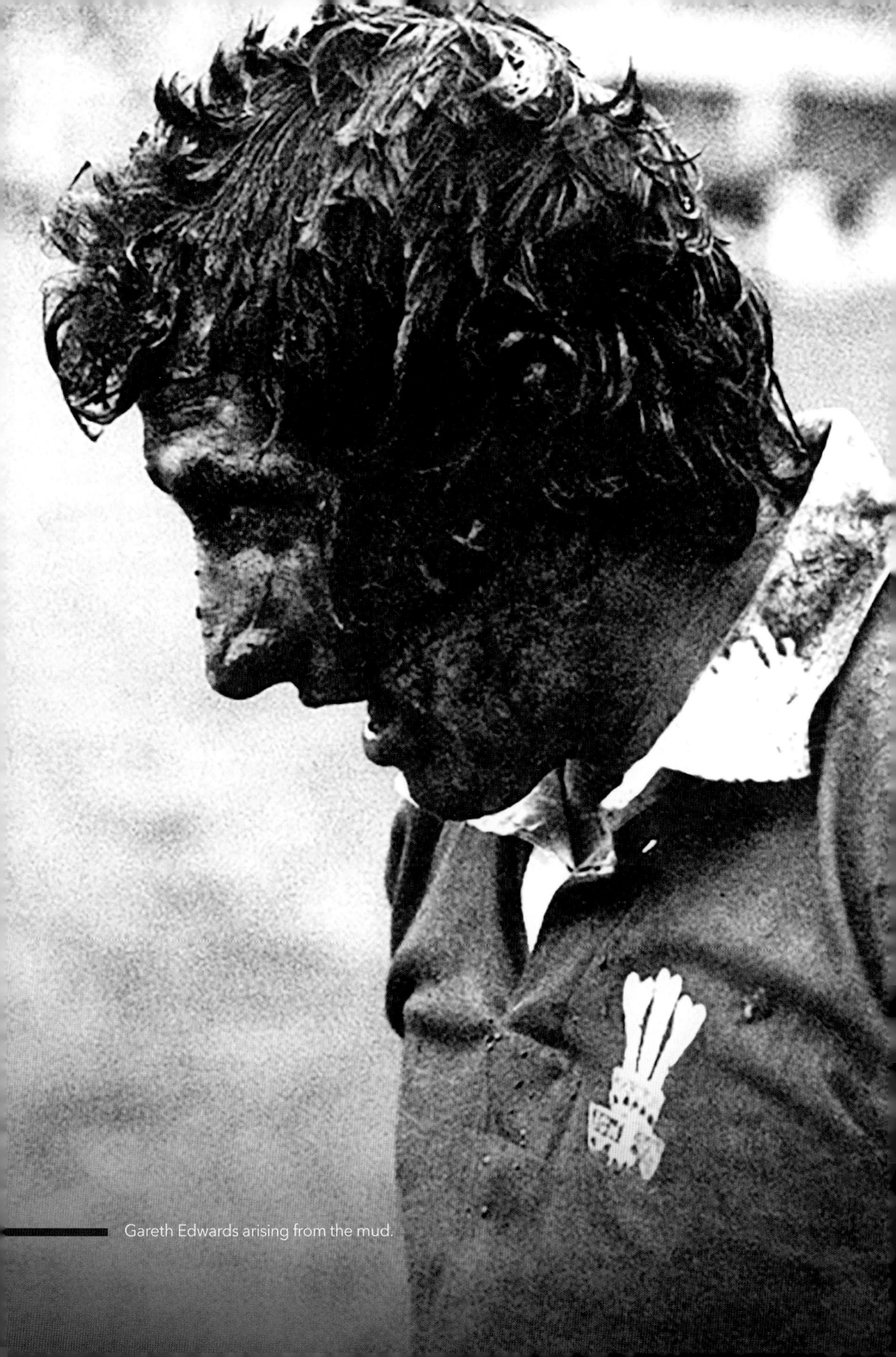

Gareth Edwards arising from the mud.

IT MATTERS NOT IF THAT PLACE IS A FORLORN, WINDSWEPT, HACKED-UP SLAB OF GLORIFIED FARMLAND, OR THE ENVELOPED WARMTH OF A MODERN, PURPOSE-BUILT, INTERNATIONAL STADIUM. RUGBY IS TRULY PORTABLE.

occasion ended with the sun rising over an idyllic Caribbean beach, while the café owner very decently produced a round of perfectly cooked bacon sandwiches.

The recollection of this moment reminds me that for every star-studded player whose skills drive us to delight and despair, the 'place' where rugby takes place can be just as important.

It matters not if that place is a forlorn, windswept, hacked-up slab of glorified farmland, or the enveloped warmth of a modern, purpose-built, international stadium. Rugby is truly portable.

A Five Nations match against Scotland in Cardiff in 1972 illustrates the importance of location well, when Wales scrum-half Gareth Edwards (now Sir Gareth) chipped and chased the ball more than 20 metres and dived for a try in the top right corner of the national stadium.

The enduring image of that heroic moment is Edwards rising covered from head to foot in what at first sight appears to be blood.

Closer inspection revealed that the substance daubed over him was dark red cinder, a change from the regular mud and grass. In those days, the perimeter of Cardiff's national stadium and rugby shrine was a slightly more prosaic dog racing track.

Back to Cardiff, the demolition of the national stadium (erroneously called by many Cardiff Arms Park, the home of Cardiff Rugby Club next door to it) and several surrounding buildings in 1997 to make way for the Millennium Stadium (now called Principality), had some profound location effects.

Before the new stadium opened, Cardiffians sampling a pint outside the City Arms in Westgate Street on a summer evening in 1998 could enjoy something almost as rare as Halley's Comet – a clear view across the River Taff to the Victorian homes standing on the far bank.

While this vista was short-lived as the new stadium rose, the absence of a new ground meant Wales needed a new location to play their home matches for two seasons, with the now demolished 'old' Wembley Stadium in north-west London chosen to perform the role.

Like children evacuated to avoid enemy bombs in wartime, it is no simple task recreating a 'home ground' feel in temporary accommodation 120 miles away, as Wales discovered to their cost when they spent a long afternoon in 1998 watching visiting Frenchmen score 54 unanswered points.

But perhaps with a little luck, an army of supporters, and Sir Tom Jones chipping in an enthusiastic rendition of *Delilah* before an appreciative crowd, the men in red proved it is possible to turn dislocation to your advantage when Wales beat England 33-32 a year later. This narrowest of victories was thanks to a last-gasp, bullocking try from centre Scott Gibbs and a cool-as-cucumber conversion from kicking stalwart Neil Jenkins. Fittingly, it was the last game of the old Five Nations tournament, Wales' last home game away from Cardiff, and a feat which denied England their first Grand Slam under coach Clive (now Sir) Woodward.

The British and Irish Lions have proved that you do not need to play your rugby in the same place to taste success. In their most famous of all tours, led by Irish rugby folk hero Willie John McBride, the Lions played 26 matches in 15 locations across South Africa in 1974. Between May 15 and July 23, they never lost, including three tests in which the Lions racked up 66 points and conceded only 32. A clean sweep, however, was sadly unachievable, with the final match and test ending in a 13-13 draw in Johannesburg.

But such records go against the rugby grain, with location and the success of major rugby international and club teams linked umbilically.

The notion of major teams turning their home ground location into impenetrable fortresses is well illustrated by Eden Park in Auckland, New Zealand, host arena for the All Blacks. A sports ground since 1900, Eden Park hosted its first international rugby match on August 27, 1921, when the All Blacks beat South Africa 5-0 before a crowd of 40,000.

Since then, the legendary rugby citadel has maintained its reputation as a fearsome location for visiting teams.

BUT THE INTIMIDATING NATURE OF A RUGBY LOCATION EXISTS NOT JUST AT INTERNATIONAL STADIA BUT ALSO AT CLUB GROUNDS, AS VISITORS TO KINGSHOLM IN THE HEART OF GLOUCESTER IN SOUTH-WEST ENGLAND WILL TESTIFY.

The world-famous Eden Park stadium in Auckland, New Zealand.

But the intimidating nature of a rugby location exists not just at international stadia but also at club grounds, as visitors to Kingsholm in the heart of Gloucester in south-west England will testify.

On one side of the ground is a non descript covered terrace known to everyone as 'The Shed', which, when brim full of one-eyed, partisan supporters of the Cherry and Whites, transforms into a fire pit of public opinion.

In April 2006, Peter Wilby wrote in the *Guardian*: "In rugby union folklore, the Shed at Gloucester is the equivalent – the only equivalent in the game – of the Kop at Liverpool or the Stretford End at Manchester United.

"It is to be treated with a mixture of fear and grudging respect, admired for its wit and knowledge of the sport, but also admonished for excess."

In a 2018 interview, Wales and Lions centre Jamie Roberts, a qualified doctor, added: "The Shed are ruthless. They'll speak their mind."

Larger-than-life former Bath and England prop Gareth Chilcott recalled the nature of his club's local derby visits to Gloucester, which sometimes involved riling the occupants of The Shed.

"I still love going to Kingsholm because they appreciate rugby in all its fineries, and all its dark sides and its lovely beautiful sides."

If the location of a rugby ground is significant some places feature either because of where they are, their physical appearance or a mixture of both.

On So Kon Po island, the Hong Kong Stadium strikes the visitor by its resemblance to a giant blinking eye. Four and half thousand miles away to the south-east stands the 85,000-seater ANZ Stadium in Sydney, resembling a giant upturned silver Pringle crisp. Built originally for the Sydney Olympics, it has already proved a happy hunting ground for the British and Irish Lions who dispatched Australia 41-16 in the third and final test of their 2013 tour.

The size and scale of the ANZ Stadium and its position in Australia's largest, busiest and best-known city, contrasts sharply with the continent's Ailsa Fitzsimmons Memorial Oval, 700 km away in Cobar in north-western New South Wales.

Cobar has a population of fewer than 4000 people and the region is best known for its zinc, lead and silver mines located 47 miles to the north.

Yet it is the Ailsa Fitzsimmons Memorial Oval that stands out, home to local club the Cobar Camels, and positioned effectively in the middle of the desert.

The sheer remoteness of the ground presents the Camels with an interesting recruitment challenge when it comes to finding new players.

"The Shed are ruthless. They'll speak their mind."

The Cobar Camels at their home ground, the Ailsa Fitzsimmons Memorial Oval.

For some however, Cobar is a godsend destination, as Netava Tagi, former Fijian international, recalled:

"There was an opportunity to play for the Camels and they provided me with work," says Tagi, who took a call from the club before taking up the role of player-coach.

"I asked what sort of work and they said, 'In the mine'. I was over the moon."

The chance to play rugby in a place so far away from just about anywhere was also appreciated by English prop John Hammond.

"I saw a photo of the pitch. It was bang in the middle of the desert. So I thought, yeah, that's for me."

While the Ailsa Fitzsimmons Memorial Oval might win the prize for remoteness, the accolade for altitude goes to a ground nearly 11,000kms west.

"I SAW A PHOTO OF THE PITCH. IT WAS BANG IN THE MIDDLE OF THE DESERT. SO I THOUGHT, YEAH, THAT'S FOR ME."

Johannesburg's Ellis Park has little to commend it architecturally, but plays its location trump card by being the highest international test arena at 5940 ft above sea level.

What South Africa can boast in height however, Ireland can beat with the weight of history as its national ground at Lansdowne Road hosted the first representative rugby match (Leinster v Ulster) in December 1876.

It took another 105 years for a club to be formed in Ushuaia in Terra del Fuego, Argentina, but what it loses in history it makes up for by being based in the world's most southern city.

The city's motto translates into English as the 'end of the world, beginning of everything' and what this means for rugby enthusiasts is enjoying your sport surrounded by the mountain range of the Martial Glacier and only 680 miles from the coast of Antarctica.

The theme of rugby located in the far south of the world was expanded on December 13, 2009 when 34 players from Argentina, including some former internationals, played what is claimed as the first official game of rugby in the Falkland Islands. Organised by Rugby Sin Fronteras, the occasion also included a fixture four days later against British military stationed there 'who knew how to play'.

There is something rather romantic about the notion of rugby played in island locations, especially those not automatically associated with the games, like the UK, New Zealand, Fiji, Samoa or Japan.

To illustrate the heart and soul of the game, and the notion that its vehicles could cope with any terrain, however remote, Land Rover featured the Isle of Mull Rugby Club as part of its global advertising and sponsorship of the 2015 Rugby World Cup.

The club was founded shortly after the first game of rugby was played on the island off the west coast of Scotland on July 30, 1978. Ruggedness and simplicity

TO ILLUSTRATE THE HEART AND SOUL OF THE GAME, AND THE NOTION THAT ITS VEHICLES COULD COPE WITH ANY TERRAIN, HOWEVER REMOTE, LAND ROVER FEATURED THE ISLE OF MULL RUGBY CLUB AS PART OF ITS GLOBAL ADVERTISING AND SPONSORSHIP OF THE 2015 RUGBY WORLD CUP.

were themes of the club's pioneer days, with games played for several years on 'the airstrip and various farming fields' according to its website.

More than 40 decades later, after determined work by a club pulling together, it now has a permanent home at Garmony, near Craignure. And it has also boasted a women's side too since 1992.

If rugby in Mull represents the spirit of the game in the north of the UK, then the first-ever sevens rugby tournament 450 miles to the south in the Isles of Scilly, 28 miles from Land's End, in May 2014, shows that islands and rugby ideally mix together.

Travellers then heading 226 miles east from Scilly will discover an Isle of Wight rugby club founded in 1924 which boasts men's 1st and 2nd XVs and a women's XV. While 169 miles further south, Jersey became Warren Gatland's Covid-bubble training camp for the 2021 British and Irish Lions squad, 76 years after the island's liberation from its wartime German occupiers.

A replica of The Siam Cup at the World Rugby Museum in Twickenham, England.

Jersey is the largest of the Channel Islands and claims a rugby heritage dating back to the mid 19th century. Moreover, the annual contest between the Jersey Reds and Guernsey RFC 'next door' for the Siam Cup, dates to 1920 making it, apparently, the second oldest rugby trophy competition after the Calcutta Cup. The cup is really a circular rose-bowl manufactured from Siam coins (called, wonderfully, ticals) by King Rama VI's royal silversmith.

The King's son intriguingly once served in the Durham Light Infantry and when he succeeded to the throne he gave the cup to a fellow officer based in Siam, who eventually brought it to the Channel Islands. Plans by the occupying Germans to melt it down during the war were thwarted when it apparently 'disappeared', only to magically reappear after they had left.

Today's cup is a replica of the original, which now resides in the World Rugby Museum at Twickenham.

The Siam Cup story is a 'what' and 'how' tale, which, however entertaining, deflects from the 'where' theme of this chapter. So where then should the nomadic reader of the game head next to appreciate the great geography of the game.

Lovers of Rugby 5s Beach Rugby, an official branch of the sport with its own set of rules, could in summer 2021 take in tournament matches in Balaton Lake (Hungary), The Hague (Netherlands), Porto (Portugal), Alba Adriatica (Italy), Barcelona (Spain), Marseille (France) before heading back for the grand final at Italy's Lignano Sabbiadoro beach (where other nearby landmarks include a Unicef Adventure Park and a 'doggy beach').

If this wonderful European tour is not enough, a world wanderer could head for the Alaska Mountain Rugby Grounds, impressively created through a great deal of sweat and hard labour by Justin Green, who according to the venue's website, learned 'good manners and the Queen's English' at St Lawrence College in England. Growing up in Alaska, Green made it his mission to create and build the 'state's first and only rugby facility…and host international sides from around the world.'

MOREOVER, THE ANNUAL CONTEST BETWEEN THE JERSEY REDS AND GUERNSEY RFC 'NEXT DOOR' FOR THE SIAM CUP, DATES TO 1920 MAKING IT, APPARENTLY, THE SECOND OLDEST RUGBY TROPHY COMPETITION AFTER THE CALCUTTA CUP.

In the same cold vein, fans liking their rugby in fresh conditions would have enjoyed the most northerly game ever played at 78 degrees latitude, in Nanavut, Canada on April 28, 2015. Supporting the The Wooden Spoon Society rugby charity, the two teams involved covered 95km to the Certified magnetic North Pole, proving beyond doubt that players will go to the ends of the earth to get a game.

This impressive one-off match can be compared to the more regular world's most northerly rugby tournament (sevens, not 15-a-side) played in the snow at Saariselkä, about 250kms north of the Arctic circle.

Those for whom frozen rugby is a tad extreme, could journey instead to Suva in Fiji to the 4000-seat ANZ Stadium, or the Teufaiva Sport Stadium in Nuku'alofa, Tonga, which, as well as football, also hosts home matches for the national football team.

More nomadic fans of the game, anxious at the notion of watching their rugby in the same place, might have enjoyed 'The Global Pass', an idea coined by former Rugby School students Toby Marsh and Matthew Hodder-Williams to help the School celebrate its 450th birthday in 2017.

Their dream was to see a Gilbert rugby ball (original supplier to the School of footballs made from pigs' bladders) pass 450 times around the world between other 'old Rugbeians'. The journey started on January 9, 2017 when a pupil dressed as William Webb Ellis received the first pass, at the School, from fellow OR the late Micky Steele-Bodger (former Harlequins, Barbarians and England flanker).

Passing around various parts of the School (including my own hands in one of the boarding houses), the ball, equipped with a GPS tracker, then went global, with visits to England, Scotland, Wales, Ireland, Italy, France, UAE, Hong Kong, Singapore, India, Australia, New Zealand, South Africa, Canada and the USA, before returning to the School on September 27, 2017.

Lying at the heart of this last story is the realisation that while a game that started in a relatively plain Midlands town 200 years ago may have expanded its reaches to all corners of the world, when it comes to where it is played, the original location is the only one that really counts.

Welsh bard Dylan Thomas enjoyed his rugby too, watching London Welsh play at Herne Hill Velodrome before retiring after matches to the Half Moon pub, which stands opposite Milkwood Road.

Whether his love of the game inspired in some way the name of Thomas' best-known work (later famously voiced by fellow rugby-mad Welshman Richard

Burton, who played the game in his home village of Pontrhydyfen) is speculation.

We can thank Thomas, however, for giving us those opening words 'To begin at the beginning', which again neatly takes our rugby back to Rugby, the true home of the game's beginning.

The Close is the heart of Rugby School, developed as a playing field in 1810-1815, just a decade or so before Webb Ellis performed his on-field rule breaking.

Like scores of former students at the School, I have passed it thousands of times. But passing is not the same as daring to step on such hallowed ground. As a young boarder in the early 1980s, I quickly the learned the rules about even thinking about touching a single blade of grass on the pitch belonging to the First XV in the top corner of The Close.

If you were a member of XV you could, of course, wander as freely as a sheep across it and likewise if you belonged to the Levée, the given name to the School's prefects. Beyond that, it was out of bounds.

Given my talent at the game rose no higher than narrowly losing out for selection for the Under 15s Third XV, and I was never elevated to the Levée, that pitch on The Close then represented somewhere I did not tread. I had not earned the right and to this day I feel a sense of impostor syndrome if I ever touch its surface.

The nearest I ever came to accessing The Close legitimately was in 1983, my final year at the school, when economics teacher David Ray (author of two chapters in this book), who was also chief rugby coach, asked me to be touch judge for the XV. At the time my father, legitimately concerned about his son's many extra-curricular distractions, banned me from taking on any more non-academic activities. In a call home from my boarding house payphone, however, he relented to David's request, but only if I ran the line for just the XV's home matches (a rule I agreed to and only broke twice during the season).

So it was that, despite not having the talent to represent the School playing the game, I joined a member of staff to help cut half-time oranges before each match, consulted with the referee before he blew his whistle, and concentrated hard in

THE CLOSE IS THE HEART OF RUGBY SCHOOL, DEVELOPED AS A PLAYING FIELD IN 1810-1815, JUST A DECADE OR SO BEFORE WEBB ELLIS PERFORMED HIS ON-FIELD RULE BREAKING.

The famous Close on a frosty morning.

sunshine, wind and rain to work out exactly where the ball had gone in to touch or whether a conversion or penalty had sailed between the uprights.

The privilege was enormous, even if my home-made outfit of House rugby top and tracksuit bottoms looked ragged compared to the School-branded apparel sported by my opposite number from Harrow when their teams journeyed up from north London.

Like most schools, Rugby's oval ball season started in September and ended when the Advent term closed in December. My experience of sharing the same blades of grass as young William Webb Ellis therefore probably only extended to half a dozen matches over three months.

However fleeting this association with The Close, I realise, looking back, if you are not good enough to be selected among the 30 athletes on the field, then being a referee or touch judge is perhaps the next best thing.

The simple task I carried out also appeared to be appreciated by others, to my complete surprise, when I started to be asked to join after-match drinks (a single bottle of beer) with real members of the XV, followed by attending their end-of-term black-tie Christmas dinner.

This last honour proved a social challenge, as the School's second XV, who had also prevailed upon my line-running services one Saturday on The Close (but only at the pitch next door to the 'proper' one), also invited me to their Christmas drinks on the same night as the XV dinner.

With a lower Sixth Form boy's inability to turn down any free drink or food that might come his way, I somehow managed to attend both events in the same evening, although the details of how this was accomplished are obscured by the thick mists of time.

During my time at the School, I was not the only one who regarded that corner of The Close with reverence. In 1982, a touring international team visited so they too could 'touch the pitch'. A year later the School hosted an international sevens tournament and some of the very All Blacks themselves visited during their tour of England.

On that occasion, I pinched myself when David Ray asked me to host two All Blacks players to lunch in my boarding house. My awe at the enormity of their visit was offset by my amusement when they asked if I played fly-half for the School XV. Some promotion for a mere touch judge.

The following day, on November 8, the All Blacks lost 13-19 against a Midlands Division side and a week later went down 9-15 to England at Twickenham. So, however inspired the players were to visit The Close, either the journey, or the boarding house food they shared with me, certainly did nothing to help their game.

All sports start somewhere, and rugby is unusual in being one where historians can point to the very patch of grass where the game began. The fact that it is still played on the spot where it began and in thousands of other locations around the world, speaks of continuity, tradition, change and evolution in the same breath.

There is no best location for rugby. Every player, official and enthusiast has their own favourite place where they have kicked or caught a ball or watched their heroes do so with greater skill than their own. Place is personal and with rugby it ultimately does not matter if that place is your back garden or the largest stadium in the world. All that matters is the game.

England forward John Scott breaks with the ball during the international against the All Blacks at Twickenham which England won 15-9.

WHY IS A TRY

The original rules, written at Rugby School, stated that grounding the ball only gave the opportunity to 'try' to score with a kick at goal. No points were given for grounding the ball behind the opponent's goal line.

CALLED A TRY?

PLAYING THE GAME

MAGGIE ALPHONSI

I first became involved because of a PE teacher called Liza Burgess. She was the one who suggested I take up the sport because my behaviour at school was so bad! Rugby then definitely did the job, it gave me all the values, respect, attitude and discipline I needed. I was 12 or 13 at the time and as rugby was non-existent at school Liza suggested I join my local rugby club, Saracens. That was how I found rugby because in north London at that time it was not a sport you played, as everything was very much about football or athletics. For me to find rugby was very unusual.

My first best highlight was playing junior rugby, playing for my club at festivals, sevens tournaments and at regional 10s festival for my region, London and South East. That was a real high because back then you just played for the fun of it, no pressure, it was all about being social with your friends. When I started playing for England there were two big highlights. First, the Women's Rugby World Cup Final hosted in England in 2010 for the first time. We lost the game but what made it a highlight was that we were the host country and women's rugby was being acknowledged. The stadium was packed as were all the roads leading to it for the final. 2010 was a change in momentum for women's rugby. Second, was winning the Women's Rugby World Cup in 2014 in France when we beat Canada. It was not just winning but the fact that for me and many others in the team it was the peak of a 12-year journey, a very significant experience. England had won it in 1994 but to win again 20 years later was an incredible journey.

I think William Webb Ellis would be happy he left a legacy and that the game is still being played today. He would be very proud that the game has evolved and become a sport for all, regardless of your gender, race, sexuality, religion or background. So thank you, William, for creating the sport that saved my life.

Saracens flanker Maggie Alphonsi MBE was born in 1983 and played 74 times for England before retiring in 2014. She was *Sunday Times* Sportswoman of the Year in 2010 and was inducted in the World Rugby Hall of Fame in November 2016. Maggie was named in the 2014 World Cup Dream Team and was a Rugby World Cup 2015 Ambassador.

ENGLAND
WOMEN

PLAYING THE GAME

DAVID PICKERING

My father Frank played for the Royal Navy post-war so his love for the sport transcended down the generation. As a 10-year-old boy at Ynysmaerdy Primary School, after much maligning of the headmaster, we had the school's first rugby team.

The following year as a Neath schoolboy winger, I scored the only try to beat Llanelli during a curtain raiser at Stradey Park in front of 15,000 Scarlets fans, who were about to witness the 9-3 victory over the All Blacks. By the age of 15 I was cemented to the game, scoring two tries again at Stradey Park in my Welsh Schools debut – the first-ever rugby schoolboy cap from Cwrt Sart School in Briton Ferry.

Two years later I was playing as a flanker for Wales under-18 Schools. I was spotted by Llanelli RFC which led to Derek Quinnell calling at my home and encouraging me to sign with Llanelli instead of my home town, Neath. At 18, I played against New Zealand and against the legendary Graham Mourie. At 21 I was selected to play for Wales against England at Cardiff Arms Park. A dream come true during a rugby career that has lasted over four decades.

Reverend William Webb Ellis would have been delighted with his rugby legacy. His grave in Menton, France, was renovated by the French Rugby Federation and this epitaph is a lasting testimony to his part in the world rugby story.

Webb Ellis was born in 1806 and I am sure he would be amazed to see the emergence of a sport that encourages diversity and inclusivity. Rugby boasts millions of participants of both sexes and allows able-bodied and disabled athletes to enjoy the sport around the globe.

He would see a sport that promotes wellbeing, fitness, fair play and passion, and which encourages respect for officials and fellow players alike. He would witness an honourable activity that crosses political and social divides and which unites people of different classes, colour and creed.

The game is a positive addition to society and education, and if Webb Ellis were judging Welsh rugby today, he would inevitably see it as a force for the good of the nation, uniting and spreading the gospel of harmony and team spirit.

He would see how the game's success in recent years has inspired young people to be as bold and ambitious as the legendary Webb Ellis himself.

David Pickering played club rugby for Llanelli and Neath, won 23 caps for Wales between 1983 and 1987, and captained his country eight times. He has also been coach of Neath, manager of Wales, Chairman of the Welsh Rugby Union, a member of the International Rugby Board Council and a Director of the Rugby World Cup.

19/82 The first women's international match took place in Utrecht with the Netherlands losing 4-0 to France.

19/83 The home unions rugby children's charity Wooden Spoon was founded in this year. It has since funded more than 1000 projects, across the UK and Ireland, totalling over £28 million.

19/84 Tourists Australia beat all four home nations for the first time.

19/84 Scotland won their first Grand Slam for 59 years beating France 21-12 at Murrayfield.

19 86 A trophy to be awarded to the winner of the following year's inaugural Rugby World Cup was named after William Webb Ellis.

19 87 Brewers Courage paid £1.65m to be the three-year sponsors of a new league comprising 1200 clubs.

19 90 In May, Romania beat France 14-6 at Auch in the Midi-Pyrenees.

19 91 Wales hosted the first women's rugby union world cup, which featured 12 competing nations.

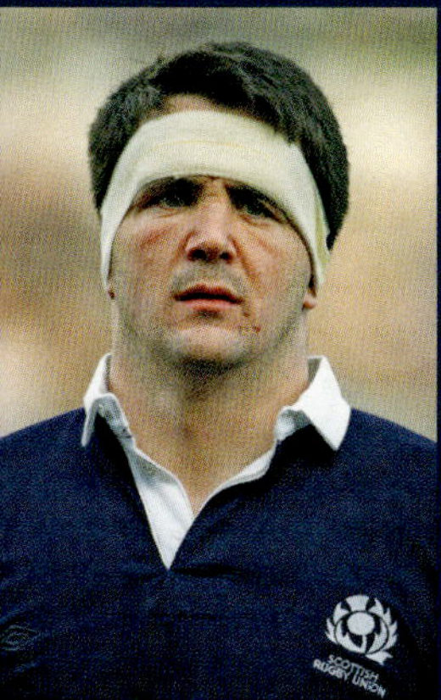

19 92 Scotland captain David Sole scored the last four-point try in international rugby on June 21, in Brisbane, Australia. The value of tries was subsequently raised to five points.

"

ALL SPORTS ARE TEAMWORK, BUT RUGBY PARTICULARLY IS ABOUT TEAMWORK AND I THINK TEAMWORK IS THE ESSENCE.

"

Gordon Brown

FOOTBALL AT RUGBY – A FUTURE VISION

By Mike Bayly,
Director of Football, Rugby School

FIRMLY HOLDING ON TO OUR HERITAGE AND INSPIRED BY WILLIAM WEBB ELLIS (IN SHOWING A FINE DISREGARD FOR THE RULES OF FOOTBALL), WE ARE RESTLESS TO CHALLENGE RUGBY WITH INNOVATION AND VIGOUR, PLAYING A FAST-PACED, HIGHLY SKILLED, SUPPORT-BASED ATTACKING GAME WITH UNCOMPROMISING DEFENCE.

As a young rugby player in South Africa in the 1980s the prospect of helping students at the very school where the game started was so remote it never crossed my mind.

Everyone has responsibilities and I am very aware that leading the game of rugby at Rugby School in the town of Rugby is not one to be taken lightly.

This sense of responsibility forced me to think in a way that was beyond my next game as a player or later as a coach in South Africa and Italy.

It has helped me to distil and refine the essence of my job into a simple question: "what's our vision for rugby at Rugby?"

After much discussion with my fellow coaches, colleagues, and young players, we have now expressed this as:

"Firmly holding on to our heritage and inspired by William Webb Ellis (in showing a fine disregard for the rules of Football), we are restless to challenge Rugby with innovation and vigour, playing a fast-paced, highly skilled, support-based attacking game with uncompromising defence."

There's a lot to unpick in these 45 words. Not least those about not abandoning our history and tipping our school caps to William Webb Ellis, the world's original rugby union player.

The rugby union game is still evolving and needs many things to continue to grow and be a successful, thriving sport. It also needs William Webb Ellis, or what he represents: the clear sense of how, why and when it all began.

Rather like growing up not knowing where you where born, most sports cannot be certain of their origins. But rugby can, and we are all blessed by this knowledge. Our vision also speaks of being 'restless', something we encourage among all students. Rugby School has never been about being passive or simply achieving

academic excellence by rote learning, but rather about exploring new things and becoming involved in the life of the School. We specifically encourage that restlessness in all students who play rugby.

Finally, our vision references the style of game we'd like to play. Like William Webb Ellis, we strive for innovation, not simply aping what others do. Yet we also recognise that to be innovative and succeed we will need speed, skill and a commitment to attack and defend.

Knowing our vision and our playing style is one thing, but as important is our motivation and approach before we even run out on to the pitch. We call these our seven core values, with 'love for the game through enjoyment and responsible involvement' being top of the list.

KNOWING OUR VISION AND OUR PLAYING STYLE IS ONE THING, BUT AS IMPORTANT IS OUR MOTIVATION AND APPROACH BEFORE WE EVEN RUN OUT ON TO THE PITCH. WE CALL THESE OUR SEVEN CORE VALUES, WITH 'LOVE FOR THE GAME THROUGH ENJOYMENT AND RESPONSIBLE INVOLVEMENT' BEING TOP OF THE LIST.

The next three challenge us to be 'exceptional characters on and off the field', demonstrate 'sportsmanship, showing integrity and self-discipline' and show 'compassion and team before self'.

Our final three values call on every player at the School to show 'respect for our heritage, opposition, officials, staff and fellow pupils', to be 'warriors, no matter the opposition or situation' and strive for 'excellence, to always be the best we can be'.

With a strong vision and granite-hard values agreed, the final jigsaw piece is all about what we would like players to do when, like William Webb Ellis, the game comes their way.

Unlike William, who clearly coached himself, we have established five 'rules of play' for all players at Rugby, regardless of their level of ability.

These are:
If you can pass before contact, PASS
If you can't pass, use your feet and ATTACK SPACE
In contact, keep driving forward and look for OFF-LOAD
Fall forward in tackle and look for POP PASS off ground
Last resort, work on ground to facilitate QUICK RUCK.

You will see all these rules involve keeping and using the ball, with no overt mention of kicking. We do, of course, coach players how to kick from hand or

execute penalties, conversions and drop-goals – but these should be secondary or the result of pursuing a ball-in-hand running game.

Raised on the hard, sun-baked grounds in southern Africa, for me it is still a privilege to walk out at Rugby School on to The Close and touch the grass where the first game began.

That sense of history energises the School's First XV to take to the pitch, remembering that the first caps awarded for any sport were done so at the School.

From all this history however, we have a responsibility to consider the future too. To be part of the celebration of two centuries of the rugby game is amazing, but how will others be marking the tri-centenary in 2123?

When that celebration happens, I hope the game will have changed in some ways but also stayed the same. I hope, for instance, that it will have evolved to become even faster and more skilled, with all players participating in moving the ball, and there being less of a distinction between the traditional roles of forwards and backs.

I hope, too, that more care will have been taken over player welfare, particularly head injuries, so their rugby remains a physical game but not one which threatens players health.

Finally, I hope that by 2123 the world thinks of rugby as a sport that transcends background, gender, race, religion, and other strands of diversity. It is already a global sport, but if it could also be one that embraces, encourages, and supports everyone who wants to play, coach or watch, that would, I believe, be a 300th birthday worth celebrating.

Before we get there, however, let us concentrate on a mere two centuries of this wonderful game and say thank you again to a young man for having the restless courage to disregard the rules.

FINALLY, I HOPE THAT BY 2123 THE WORLD THINKS OF RUGBY AS A SPORT THAT TRANSCENDS BACKGROUND, GENDER, RACE, RELIGION, AND OTHER STRANDS OF DIVERSITY. IT IS ALREADY A GLOBAL SPORT, BUT IF IT COULD ALSO BE ONE THAT EMBRACES, ENCOURAGES, AND SUPPORTS EVERYONE WHO WANTS TO PLAY, COACH OR WATCH, THAT WOULD, I BELIEVE, BE A 300th BIRTHDAY WORTH CELEBRATING.

'PASS THE PIG'

William Gilbert, in the early 1800s, made the first Rugby School football, a round leather ball inflated by a pig's bladder which, after being carried and kicked, started to change shape.

S

BLADDER'

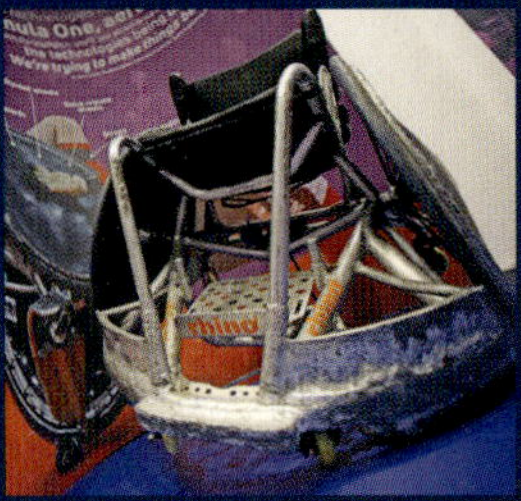

19
93

The International Wheelchair Rugby Federation was founded.

19
94

Philippe Sella of France became the first player to win 100 caps.

19
95

On June 24, hosts South Africa beat New Zealand 15-12 to win the Rugby World Cup and on August 26, the International Rugby Board agreed the game could become professional.

19
95

Italy beat Ireland, a feat they repeated twice more over the next three years.

19
95

The Kings Cross Steelers in London, the world's first openly gay rugby team, was founded. Nine years later, the Sydney Convicts became the first gay Southern Hemisphere club.

19
95

Rupert Murdoch paid professional rugby league clubs in England £87m to switch their games to the summer as part of the launch of a new Super League. On August 27, the International Rugby Board also legalised professionalism in rugby union.

19
97

The first game was played by an Indian national rugby team.

19
99

Argentina qualified for the Rugby World Cup for the first time, playing in the opening match against Wales at the newly built Millennium Stadium in Cardiff. Four years later they secured third place in the competition.

PLAYING THE GAME

SARAH HUNTER

I was nine years old, getting ready for my weekly PE lesson when our teacher told us that we would have a special coach coming in to teach us a new sport. Little did I know that that day would change my life for ever! That new sport was rugby league and the coach was Mick Hogan (who has since gone on to have senior management roles at Sale, England 2015 and Newcastle Falcons). I was a very sporty child growing up in North Tyneside but, with no connection to rugby, I had no idea what I was doing running around with this funny shaped ball, but what I did know was that I had just had the best PE lesson ever. I went home and told my parents how I had played rugby that day and loved it! In the early 1990s, rugby (either code) was not a sport girls played but they never told me that, they encouraged me and told me to enjoy it. Little did I know until later down the line that if it weren't for my head teacher, Sheelagh Tickell, I may never have had the opportunity to pick up a rugby ball! The coach coming into our school wanted to work with a group of boys but she said "If you're coming into our school you have to coach all pupils as they must all have the same opportunities." Without her forward and equal approach I may never have picked up a rugby ball. After eight weeks of coaching I was lucky enough to be selected to a north-east team which was (mainly) made up of boys apart from four girls. We were to play in a curtain raiser at Wembley before the Great Britain rugby league team played Australia. It was the most amazing experience for a nine year old who had only been playing this sport for a few weeks. Following this, I went on to join Gateshead Panthers rugby league team, who many of the team I was with at Wembley already played for. They welcomed me and treated me like everyone else, despite my being only one of two girls! This was just the very beginning of a journey I never even knew was possible. Having played rugby league I made the move to rugby union when league struggled to provide opportunities for girls after the age of 13. Then at the age of 16 I went to watch an England rugby union game and that's where my dreams began....I wanted to play for England women. Fast forward five years and I gained my first cap... my dreams had come true! However, my dreams were about to magnified when in 2014, after heartbreak in 2010, I was part of the England team that went on to become World Champions! Never in my wildest dreams did I ever think as a nine year old on my school's playing field, that I would become a world champion! Having gone on to become World Player of The Year, being honoured with an MBE for services to rugby, having the honour and privilege of captaining the Red Roses and becoming a professional rugby player, has gone beyond what I even thought was possible! Rugby has changed my life for ever. I hope William Webb Ellis would be proud to know that the day he picked up a ball and created rugby, has led to a little girl from North Tyneside having the most amazing life, creating the most incredible memories and being part of something that is so special in what is happening in the women's game right now! That, just like him, who inspired people a hundred years ago, the Red Roses are now doing the same thing for a new generation and a new gender.

Sarah Hunter, MBE, was born in 1985 and has represented England 130 times since the 2010 Women's Rugby World Cup. Sarah has played for Loughborough Lightning since 2017 and was named World Rugby Women's Player of the Year in 2016.

PLAYING THE GAME

MICHAEL LYNAGH

The family moved to Brisbane in 1974 and the new school I went to played rugby. So that is what I played in the winter while I was waiting for the cricket season to start. My career highlights were the 1984 Wallaby Grand Slam tour of the UK, the 1986 Bledisloe Cup series win in New Zealand, the 1991 Rugby World Cup win and watching my son Louis win the Premiership Final with Harlequins at Twickenham in 2021. I think today William Webb Ellis would say: "You can have the ball, I am not picking it up – those guys are so big I don't want to run with it."

Fly-half and centre Michael Lynagh, AM was born in 1963, was capped 72 times for Australia from 1984 to 1995 and was captain from 1993-95. He was the world points-scoring record holder when he retired, with 911 points.

BOB NORSTER

PLAYING THE GAME

From my understanding, the bedrock of Rugby School from where our beloved game emerged 200 years ago was built on key elements that include discipline, moral and religious principles (not forgetting academic abilities, of course!) and all undertaken with a liberal dose of gentlemanly conduct prevailing throughout. It's encouraging to note that, after all these years, many of those qualities remain key values to those playing the game successfully today.

Lock Robert Leonard 'Bob' Norster was born in June 1957. He played club rugby for Abertillery, Cardiff and the Barbarians, gained 34 caps for Wales and three for the British and Irish Lions. He was captain of Cardiff RFC for two seasons and for Wales in New Zealand in 1988. He was Honorary Team Manager for Wales in 1994, the year they won the Five Nations Championship.

RUNNING THE BO

Herbert Hayton Castens, 1864-1929, an Old Rugbeian, was a South African rugby union footballer and cricketer. He was South Africa's first rugby and cricket captain. Castens played an important role in the development of rugby and cricket in South Africa, both on and off the pitch.

OKS

1999

Uruguay's debut Rugby World Cup team featured captain Diego Ormaechea, aged 40, the oldest player to play in the tournament. Diego, who won 73 caps for his country, scored a try in Uruguay's 27-15 win over Spain.

1999

Australia won their second consecutive Rugby World Cup final on British soil, beating France 35-12 at the newly built Millennium Stadium in Cardiff, eight years after defeating England 12-6 at Twickenham.

2000

A record 109,874 spectators watched the All Blacks beat Australia 39-35 at the Olympic Stadium, Sydney, in July.

2001

Ireland's Keith Wood became the first winner of the then IRB World Player of the Year. His fellow nominees that year were Australia's George Gregan and George Smith, team-mate Brian O'Driscoll and England's Jonny Wilkinson. Wilkinson won the accolade two years later as part of England's World Cup winning side.

2002

The RFU made a £7m profit and England beat Romania 134-0 at Twickenham.

20
03

Research on rugby fans in the UK showed that 61 per cent were professional/managerial, 57 per cent earned more than £30,000 a year and 21 per cent were women.

20
03

Ninety-two teams entered the Rugby World Cup, up by 24 on the previous tournament.

THE 'AULD' ENE

MY

George Henry Reeves Hart, an Old Rugbeian, was a founder of the Calcutta Club which joined the Rugby Football Union in 1874. The Club prospered during that first year. However when the free bar had to be discontinued, the membership took an appreciable drop. The members decided to disband, but keen to perpetuate the name of the Club, they withdrew its funds (which were in silver rupees) from the bank, had them melted down and made into a cup which they presented to the RFU in 1878, with the provision that it should be competed for annually.

Illustration of the Scotland v England match at Raeburn Place in 1892.

vs SCOTLAND

PLACE, EDINBURGH — ALDERSON RELIEVES THE ENGLISH LINE

PLAYING THE GAME

TOM SMITH

My best friend's dad was a Welshman and a big rugby fan. My dad died when I was six. I had a lot of energy and my mum needed something for me to do, so, he took me to London Welsh mini rugby for eight and nine year olds. I had never played before. Things have changed now but I went straight into a game. It was a lot of fun and the club is still going strong today. It was a nice place to go to on a Sunday and I made some friends for life. When you got into the school system it became a lot more serious. I went to a small Scottish boarding school in the middle of nowhere and there was a very enthusiastic rugby coach who was happy to drive a couple of us to Perth and Edinburgh to play some representative rugby. I was then selected for the Scottish Schools trials. I had one game at number eight and then moved to prop because I was quite quick. I could either be a fast prop or a slow number eight. By then I got into the age-grade system and at university in Dundee I pretty much languished in the second XV for four years. Then I went to Watsonians and a year or so later I was on a Lions tour.

After the announcement of professionalism following the 1995 Rugby World Cup I went down to Edinburgh and I got offered a contract. I was not 100kg but just enjoyed playing and the opportunity came along, so the timing was good. In those days we would play against the Scotland team just before a Five Nations game. We were cannon fodder and they would smash us but then I got invited to play with Scotland on their 1996 tour to New Zealand.

Winning the Scottish district championship for the first time for the North/ Midlands district was a big moment for me as a younger player. We were an unfashionable team and it was about the border between amateurism and professionalism, working hard and playing hard.

My first Scottish cap was a highlight although we had a tough day at the office at Twickenham and were very well beaten. Later in 1999, the last Five Nations, I was injured and visiting relatives in Surrey, when England lost to Wales at Wembley and we found we had won the championship.

On the 1997 Lions tour I was quite a naïve guy but coming into it without any great preconceptions was not necessarily a bad thing. There were low expectations before we went and people wondered whether the Lions would have a place in the professional game. But then you get to the hotel and the first game and realise how many supporters are there and how big that tour was. It was 70 per cent red shirts and was like playing at home. That only seems to exist with the Lions.

That tour in itself was special for me for a variety of reasons. All the rivalry disappears. There was a very steep learning process with such a high quality group of players and coaches. There were so many of the amateur values because they loved rugby and mixing with supporters, probably a lot harder to do now. It was a different era and I occasionally get messages from people who were on the tour. Very nice memories.

I guess one of the things rugby has managed to retain is the family values and togetherness. It could be the fiercest contest on the pitch but supporters and players after the game will go off and enjoy each other's company.

But I am not sure there were many 130-140 kg players knocking around when William Webb Ellis created he game. He would probably be a little bit shocked by the physicality and the size of the players, but could relate to the values and friendship.

The late Tom Smith (1971-2022) played as loosehead prop for Glasgow Warriors, Caledonian Reds and Northampton and won 61 caps for Scotland and 6 caps for the British and Irish Lions between 1997 and 2001.

PLAYING THE GAME

KYLIE GRIMES

British para-athlete Kylie Grimes was born in 1987 and is one of two women, along with Bieke Ketelbuters, who competed on wheelchair rugby teams at the 2012 Summer Paralympics. She was part of the GB team to win their first gold in the event, at the 2020 Summer Paralympics in Tokyo, Japan, beating the USA 54-49. In doing so she became the first woman of any country to win a Paralympic gold medal in the sport.

I became paralysed after an accident in a swimming pool and during rehabilitation I knew I had to get straight back into sports, not only for the health benefits and to get physically strong again, but because of the social aspect and being around people. It really helped me to focus on something and work towards a goal. I was hooked on wheelchair rugby, especially the fast pace and extreme full contact between the rugby chairs. I had to play this sport – it's the best feeling in the world.' Winning the gold medal in Tokyo has been the highlight of my life to date and I am now looking forward to Paris 2024 and a repeat performance.

2012
IWRF
Wheelchair Rugby

SCOTLAND
canterbury
RBS
TESTS
RBS

RUARIDH JACKSON

My parents got me into rugby although I was more into football when younger and only moved to a rugby-playing school when I was a bit older. I was taken along to a local rugby club, Aberdeen Grammar, when I was nine or 10 and fell in love with it straightaway.

I would say the highlight of my career was kicking the winning penalty in my second test against Samoa. It was special to do anyway but the game was up in Aberdeen where I grew up so I had so many friends and family watching.

Professionally, I think the game is at a pretty interesting point. I think it very close to focusing too much on the kicking game and set pieces but there are some brilliant teams that are breaking the mould very successfully and are more focused on finding clever ways to break down these incredible defences. I think William Webb Ellis would still enjoy the game but, more importantly, I think he would be pretty proud to see how big the sport has become globally and the positive effects it can have at all levels of the game.

PLAYING THE GAME

Ruaridh Jackson played full-back for Glasgow Warriors. He was called up for Scotland in 2010 and gained 33 caps.

20
05

Mexico took part in the Los Angeles Sevens tournament for the first time.

20
07

Kenya beat England in the semi-finals of the Adelaide Sevens, but later lost to Samoa in the final.

20
09

The first Women's Sevens World Cup was held in Dubai, featuring 16 teams. On October 9, the International Olympic Committee also agreed to include Rugby Sevens as an Olympic sport from 2016.

20
09

Ireland won their first Six Nations Grand Slam for 61 years.

2010

France won their ninth Grand Slam when they beat England 12-10 before a crowd of 80,066 spectators.

2015

Japan played their first senior-level test match against the Springboks, beating them 34-32 at the Brighton Community Stadium on September 19.

2017

On September 11, the New Zealand All Blacks became the first test side to score 2000 international tries in a 38-18 victory over France. Back Ryan Crotty, who played 48 tests for New Zealand between 2013-19, achieved the landmark.

2020

New Zealand's Dan Carter and Australia's Matt Giteau were reported to be on contracts worth 1.1m a year as players for Kobelco Kobe Steelers and Suntory Sungoliath.

A FINE EXAMPLE OF FAIR

PLAY

Old Rugbeian Ronald Poulton Palmer was a rugby superstar. Joint captain of the School's XV from 1905 to 1907, he captained England from 1909 to 1914 and was capped 17 times.

Regarding his time playing for England, sporting journalist Arthur Croome, wrote: 'Not in all those years had any opponent caused him to lose his temper, or any referee had him question the correctness even of an obviously wrong decision.'

A fine example, then, of fair play.

JAMES SIMPSON-DANIEL

I was one of four boys and we all played in the garden. I went to Sedbergh School where I was mediocre and because I was small I had to try to keep up with everyone else. In my final year I suddenly found a level where I could excel.

When I became a senior player I was on the bench for Gloucester for 15 games in a row. With my first touch somebody nearly took my head off and I looked up to the see the Gloucester pack piling in. I was really the coffee and tea boy who kept my head down and respected my elders. I respected them and they had my back. When I got my first score at Gloucester I looked at The Shed and they were going wild.

I was lucky to play against Jonah Lomu for the Barbarians when I was 19. I was full of terror and fear but managed to get a try against him.

Then I got my first full cap for England playing against New Zealand at Twickenham on Remembrance Day 2002, which we won.

Today, William Webb Ellis would think he was watching a different sport. He would be fascinated by the size of the players now.

PLAYING THE GAME

James Simpson-Daniel appeared 276 times for Gloucester and played 10 times for England. He represented England at the 2002 Hong Kong Sevens and scored a hat trick in the final.

O2

ROB HOWLEY

PLAYING THE GAME

Following my rugby career in both the amateur and professional game, I am delighted to raise a glass to William Webb Ellis. When he decided to run with the ball during a game, he had no idea through his actions that the game of rugby enabled me to live out my childhood dream of playing for my country.

It has allowed me to travel the world, make some incredible friends and, without doubt, has given me some of the happiest days of my life.

Srum-half Robert Howley was born in Bridgend in 1970. He played club rugby for Bridgend, Cardiff, and Wasps, gained two caps for the British and Irish Lions and appeared 59 times for Wales, 22 as captain. Since retiring as a player he has been a coach for Wales, the British and Irish Lions and Canada.

IMAGE CREDITS

Principal image sources used for this book are shown below. The publisher apologises for any sources which have been inadvertently omitted.

Rugby School Archives
Webb Ellis Museum
World Rugby Museum
Alamy
Getty Images
Magdalena Konik
Marlborough College
Portora Royal School
Tim Mercer
Megumi Masuda
Balliol College Oxford – Photographs by kind permission of the Master and Fellows of Balliol College, Oxford.
OURFC – Team photographs for 1910 and 1911 by kind permission of Gillman and Soane, Oxford.
Rugby Football Union – Photograph of 1914 England team provided by kind permission of World Rugby Museum, Twickenham.
Scottish Rugby Union – Photographs by Scottish team for 1913 and 1914.
Trinity College Oxford – Photograph of the Trinity College rugby XV 1908 by kind permission of the President and Fellows of Trinity College, Oxford.
Anthony Stileman – For his assistance in providing various images of Poulton from James Corden's book *For Poulton and England*.

SOURCES

Principal sources used for this book are shown below. Where possible print sources are listed alphabetically by author's name, title, publisher and year of publication. The surname and first name of people who have contributed directly to a chapter or section, and online sources, are also listed alphabetically. The editor apologises for any sources which have been inadvertently omitted.

Acton.org/research/lord-acton-quote-archive
Alaskarugby.org/facility/the-dream/
Allblacks.com/news/eden-park-winning-streak-on-the-line-2/
Allcroft, Richard
Anon, *Meteor*, rugbyschoolarchives.co.uk, 2015
Anon, *News from Rugby School*, (NFRS), Rugby School Archives
Anon, *Rugby is the secret of 106-year-old's longevity*, Penarth Times, www.penarthtimes.co.uk/news/6658453.rugby-is-the-secret-of-106-year-olds-longevity, 23 January 2006
Anon, *Old Rugbeian Society Football Records of Rugby School 1823-1929*, George Over, 1930
Anon, *'The Centenary Match'*, in *The Rugbeian* November 23, 1923
Anon, *The Rugbeian* (Rugby School student publication), Rugby School Archives
Anon, *The Rugby Football Annual 1929-30*, Sporting Handbooks, 1930
Anon, *A timeline for women's rugby*, www.angelfire.com/pa3/esurugby/rugbyhistory.html, retrieved 2021
Balaam, L, *125 years of Manchester Football Club*, 1985
Bathrugby.com
Bathrugby.com/club-news/bath-rugbys-201920-financial-results/
Bbc.co.uk/news/uk-england-33239560
Bbc.co.uk/sport/rugby-union/45342130
Bbc.co.uk/sport/rugby-union/46736372
Beach-rugby.eu/
Beachrugby.nl
Birch, J, Letchworth *Girls' Rugby: Women's rugby in 1928*. http://letchworthgirls.blogspot.com/2008/03/womens-rugby-in-1928.html, retrieved 2021
Birch, J, *New Zealand women's rugby 100 years ago*, www.scrumqueens.com/news/new-zealand-womens-rugby-100-years-ago, 2018
Birch, J, www.rugbyrelics.com/Museum/topics/womens-rugby-history.htm, 2021
Bloomberg.com/news/articles/2021-06-01/all-blacks-players-fret-over-team-s-fate-if-silver-lake-buys-in
Bourke, B, *The Laurels 1872-1972*, 1972
Bowker, Barry, *England Rugby*, Cassell and Co. Ltd, 1976
Bradby, H.C., *Rugby*, George Bell and Sons, 1900
Brennan, P, Donmouth.co.uk *England v Scotland – 1881*, 2016
Brown, Mike
Burns, Gill
Campbell, Duncan
Campbell, Joseph, *The Hero with a Thousand Faces*, Fontana, 1993
Campese, David
Cbssports.com/soccer/news/lionel-messi-tops-forbes-list-of-worlds-highest-paid-soccer-players/
Chubilleau, B, *The great history of women's rugby*, 2007
Clearwater, Ken
Cliftoncollege.com/the-schools/upper-school/co-curricular/rugby/
Cobarweekly.com.au/cobar-rugby-owes-a-lot-to-foundress-ailsa-fitzsimmons/
Collins, Tony, *The Oval World – A global history of rugby*, Bloomsbury, 2015
Collins, T, *Hidden history of women's rugby to be revealed for first time by DMU researchers*, https://www.dmu.ac.uk/research/research-news/2017/june/hidden-history-of-womens-rugby-to-be-revealed-by-dmu-researchers.aspx, 2017

Cooper, Ian, *Immortal Harlequin*, Tempus Publishing, 2004
Corden, James, *For Poulton and England*, Matador, 2009
Cortie, J and Pinilla, Y, *Girls in ovalie: 40 years of history*, 2005
Crewdson, K, *BBC Sport – Rugby Union – Valentine was first lady of rugby*, 2016
Dailymail.co.uk/home/you/article-492708/Maxine-Peake-From-rugby-league-starring-actress.html
Dailymail.co.uk/sport/rugbyunion/article-3231983/MARTIN-JOHNSON-Sacrifice-Shut-it.htmlHolt, Oliver, Mail on Sunday, 2015
Dailymail.co.uk/tvshowbiz/article-7056553/Rugby-star-George-Burgess-shows-new-headshots-prepares-pursue-career-actor.html
Dailymail.co.uk/sport/rugbyleague/article-9813367/Australia-New-Zealand-WITHDRAW-Rugby-League-World-Cup-England-amid-coronavirus-fears.html
Dailymail.co.uk/sport/rugbyunion/article-6951995/SIR-CLIVE-WOODWARD-Jonny-Wilkinson-set-benchmark-No-10.html
Dallaglio, Lawrence
Davies, D.E, *Cardiff Rugby Club, History and Statistics 1876–1975*, 1975
Dcl.co.uk/property/oceanic-house-1-cockspur-street-london-sw1y-5dl/
Deserter.co.uk/2019/05/drinking-with-dylan/
Dmu.ac.uk/research/research-news/2017/june/hidden-history-of-womens-rugby-to-be-revealed-by-dmu-researchers
Discover.agl.com.au/community/grassroots-rugby-remote/
Dubberley, Brad
Dwyer, T, *History of Women's Rugby*, https://rugbyreader.com/womens-rugby/, 2020
Edwards, Gareth
Englandrugby.com/news/article/rfu-to-mark-150th-anniversary
Englandrugby.com/news/article/rfu-council-vote-in-favour-of-covid-recovery-plan
Enquoted.com/jonny-wilkinson-quotes.html
Espn.co.uk/newzealand/rugby/player/10091.html
Espn.co.uk/scrum/rugby/player/7225.html
Expedia.co.uk/Lignano-Sabbiadoro.dx6046836
Facebook.com/27958657562/posts/richard-burton-from-planet-rugbycom-rugby-is-a-wonderful-show-dance-opera-and-su
Fitzpatrick, Sean
Frost, Albert, *Meteor Magazines*, 1895-1900
Ft.com/content/c8cb003d-e81f-422c-b410-8797a9d700eb
Furse, L, Barette: Le Rugby Féminin in 1920s France, The International Journal of the History of Sport, 2019
Furse, L, Women in Rugby Union: A Social and Cultural History, c. 1880-2016, 2021
gbwr.org.uk/team_member/stuart-robinson/
Gallagher, B, *The history of women's rugby: Growth in wartime years*
www.therugbypaper.co.uk/features/329408/history-of-womens-rugby-growth-in-wartime, 2021
Gloucestershirelive.co.uk/sport/rugby/rugby-news/the-shed-ruthless-bath-wales-2054526
Goodreads.com/quotes/756045-money-equals-power-power-makes-the-law-and-law-makes
Goulburn, Edward, *The Book of Rugby School (1856)*, Kessenger, 2010
Grimes, Kylie
Griffiths, John, The Book of English International Rugby 1871-1982, Willow Books, 1982
Griffiths, John, *The Phoenix Book of International Rugby Records*, J.M. Dent and Sons, 1987
Griffiths, John, *Rugby's Strangest Matches*, Portico, 2020
Guinnessworldrecords.com/world-records/79729-most-northerly-rugby-match
Guinnessworldrecords.com/world-records/largest-rugby-ball
Gutenberg.net.au/ebooks06/0608221h
Hartmann-Tews,I & Pfister, G, *Sport and Women: Social Issues in International Perspective*, 2003
Hope Simpson J.B, *Rugby Since Arnold*, Macmillan, 1967
Howley, Rob
Hughes, Thomas, *Tom Brown's School Days*, Macmillan, 1894
Humbert, F, www.dailymotion.com/embed/video/x2l6os, retrieved 2021
Imdb.com/list/ls008221494/
Independent.co.uk/sport/sport-book-of-the-week-gareth-edwards-the-autobiography
Insidethegames.biz/articles/1110815/world-rugby-revenues-crash
Irishexaminer.com/sport/rugby/arid-40343342.html
Irishmirror.ie/sport/rugby-union/men-you-never-knew-played-5564488

Irishtimes.com/life-and-style/motors/arctic-circling
Irishtimes.com/sport/rugby/international/rwc-moments
Japantimes.co.jp/sports/2020/11/03/rugby/world-rugby-finances-coronavirus/
Jones, Keith
Keithprowse.co.uk/twickenham-stadium/
Lionsrugby.com/2022/03/08/feature-martin-johnsons-rise-to-lions-captain/
Linkedin.com/jobs/search/rugbyunion
Liveabout.com/top-celebrities-who-played-rugby
Lynagh, Michael
Macrory, Jenny, *Running With The Ball*, Collins Willow, 1991
Majorcabeachrugby.co.uk/
Marshall, F and Tosswill, LR, Football, *The Rugby Union Game*, Cassell, 1925
Marshall, Howard, *Oxford versus Cambridge: The Story of the University Rugby Match*, Clerke and Cockeran, 1951
Mattsson, Jan-Owe
Mikkelsen, Brad
Meteor (Rugby School record) in: rugbyschoolarchives.co.uk
Mirror.co.uk/sport/rugby-union/toulon-toulouse-france-rugby-kolbe
Myactivesg.com/read/2018/3/8-famous-people-that-you-didnt-know-played-rugby
Moneyweek.com/405912/27-august-1995-rugby-union-turns-professional
Mullrugby.co.uk/
Nation.africa/kenya/sports/rugby/crotty-scores-all-blacks-2-000th-try-in-france-romp
Nationalarchives.gov.uk/titanic/stories/ned-parfett.htm
News from Rugby School (NFRS), Rugby School Archives
Norster, Bob
Nutman, Jon
Nzherald.co.nz/sport/introducing-the-top-celebrity-rugby-fans/
Ourwarwickshire.org.uk/content/catalogue_her/rugby-school-the-close-rugby
Owen, O.L, *The History of the RFU*, Playfair Books Ltd, 1955
Parliament.nz
Peerdeman , P, The real issues facing Women's Rugby, https://lastwordonsports.com/rugby/2020/08/30/issues-facing-womens-rugby/, 2020
Pickering, David
Pinterest.co.uk/pin/541346817708708033/
Poetryloverspage.com/poets/kipling/i_keep_six_honest.html
Portora Royal School/Robert Northridge/Emily Valentine
Michael Raw, *Thread of Gold*, Stramongate, 2012
Rea, Chris, Rugby, *A history of Rugby Union football*, Hamlyn, 1977
Reason J and James C, *The World of Rugby*, BBC, 1979
Richards, Huw, *A game for hooligans, The history of rugby union*, Mainstream Publishing, 2007
Robertson, Stuart
Ruddock, Mike
Ruck.co.uk/he-really-was-the-complete-player-sir-ian-mcgeechan-ranks-his-top-5-rugby-players-of-all-time/3/
Ruck.co.uk/ranked-10-highest-paid-people-in-rugby-union-2021/3/
Ruck.co.uk/rugby-players-turned-actors-including-a-game-of-thrones-star/
Ruck.co.uk/the-five-smallest-international-rugby-players-ever
Rugbyfootballhistory.com
Rugbyfootballhistory.com/referee
Rugbysinfronteras.org/en/Rugby
Rugbypass.com/news/rugbys-rich-list-the-worlds-highest-paid-players-in-2020
Rugbyspeakersuk.com/
Rugbyspeakersuk.com/news/evolution-womens-rugby
Rugbyworld.com/in-the-mag/is-this-the-most-beautiful-rugby-ground-in-the-world-102167
Rugbyworld.com/news/matt-damon-talks-learning-rugby-ivictus-105913
Rugbyworld.com/rugby-positions/second-rows/martin-johnson-66332
Rugbyworld.com/tournaments/rugby-world-cup-2019/highest-ever-score-rugby-world-cup
Sarugbymag.co.za/lions-coach-players-take-pay-cut-sa-series/
Scales,I, Portora – *The School on the Hill – A Quartercentenary History: 1608-2008*, 2008
Scottishfield.co.uk/news/isle-of-mull-rfc-to-feature-in-land-rovers-wedealinreal-global-campaign-

for-rugby-world-cup/
Scottishrugby.org/news/scottish-rugbys-annual-report-for-covid-19-affected-2020/21-season-published
Senior women's rugby history, https://www.armyrugbyunion.org.uk/aru-info/history/womens-rugby-history/, 2021
Sewell, E.H.D., *Rugby Football Up To Date*, Hodder and Stoughton, 1923
Simpson-Daniel, James
Skysports.com/rugby-union/news/12380/7526904/against-the-enemy
Smith, Allan
Smith, Tom
Spence, Mike
Sportingnews.com/au/rugby/news/bledisloe-cup-why-playing-the-all-blacks-at-eden-park-is-so-intimidating/
Statista.com/statistics/193534/franchise-value-of-national-football-league-teams-in-2010/
Tarr, Rob
Theculturetrip.com/europe/united-kingdom/articles/the-oldest-rugby-clubs-in-the-world/
Theguardian.com/sport/2005/may/15/rugbyunion.comment
Theguardian.com/sport/2006/apr/02/rugbyunion.features
Theguardian.com/sport/2020/jan/22/saracens-keen-publication-salary-cap-report-rugby-union
Theguardian.com/sport/2015/aug/25/rob-andrew-wild-west-rugby-union-professional
Theguardian.com/sport/2020/nov/17/exploitation-pacific-islands-rugby-gone-on-long-enough
Thetelegraphandargus.co.uk/news/17868742.hollyoaks-actor-owes-remarkable-bradford-teacher/
Thetimes.co.uk/article/from-vibrant-clermont-to-the-southern-tip-of-new-zealand-rugbys-greatest-stadiums-ranked
Thetimes.co.uk/article/money-not-morality-will-ensure-that-british-amp-irish-lions-tour-reaches-the-tests-against-south-africa-fm
Thetimes.co.uk/article/my-career-high-watching-jonny-wilkinson-conquer-his-demons-at-the-world-cup-dq9nj02tz
Thevarsitymatch.com/history
The Rugbeian (Rugby School student publication), Rugby School Archives
Thomas, C and Thomas, G, *The History of the British Lions*, Mainstream Publishing, 1998
Thorburn, Paul
Totalrl.com/forums/index.php?/topic/329828-celebritiesfamous-people-that-like-rl/
Turley, Alan, *Rugby: The Pioneer Years*, Harper Collins, 2008
Venables, Cedric, *Instructions to Young Rugger Players*, Museum Press Ltd, 1960
Vinyard, Terry
Walesonline.co.uk/business/business-news/wru-aiming-raise-12m-tranche
Walesonline.co.uk/news/wales-news/adidas-used-pay-bungs-welsh-1820555
Walesonline.co.uk/sport/rugby/rugby-news/23-best-rugby-stadiums-world-11366548
Walston, Catherine, *with a fine disregard: a portrait of Rugby School*, Third Millennium Publishing Limited, 2006
Williams, JPR
with a fine disregard..., Third Millennium Publishing Limited, 2006
Women's 6 Nations, https://www.rugbyfootballhistory.com/W6Nations.html, retrieved 2021
Women.rugby/news/672926/world-rugby-ups-the-pace-of-womens-rugby-with-second-phase-of-womens-strategic-plan, 2021
Woodenspoon.org.uk
World.rugby/news/593315/hooper-100-caps-record-youngest
World.rugby/olympics/history
Zbieranowski, Pawel

EDITOR'S NOTE

Legendary coach Sir Ian McGeechan once urged his team to play for all those who had put the famous British and Irish Lions badge on their shirts.

If these people mattered to a player, he said, then they mattered to the whole team, and if they mattered to the whole team the Lions would surely win. Which on that occasion they did.

In the same spirit, therefore, sincere thanks are owed to the many who have helped to get this book, like William Webb Ellis' ball, into the hands of those who love the rugby game.

In particular:
Executive Head Master of Rugby School Group **Peter Green**.

Chapter authors, namely Rugby School alumni **Simon Penniston** and **Guy Steele-Bodger**; former School archivist **Jonathan Smith**; Director of Sport **Debbie Skene**; Director of Rugby **Mike Bayly**; former staff **David Ray** and **David Hempsall**; and former GB Wheelchair Rugby CEO **David Pond**.

Current or former players and coaches who kindly gave up their time to be interviewed or answer questions by email.

Tim Mercer and **Reuben Wakeman** at Mercer Books.

Many dozens of print and on-line sources, but especially Chris Rea's *A History of Rugby Union Football*, Tony Collins' *The Oval World*, John Griffiths' *Rugby's Strangest Matches* and Huw Richards' *A Game for Hooligans*.

For those inadvertently overlooked for their contribution, thanks too and apologies for this omission.

Finally, apologies also to anyone with an interest in the rugby game for any inevitable errors of fact or judgement. Consistent with the values and tradition of rugby, I will not argue with the referee on these and will accept any penalty awarded against me with good grace.

Robin Fletcher, Editor and Co-author, August 2022